To Tony

Happy 70th Birthday

Keith Sham (signature)

Happy Birthday

KENNETH HANSEN

FOURTEEN

by

Hal Ridge

Photography
Tom Banks
Jan Tore Brustad
FIA
Paulo Maria
Toni Ollikainen
Hal Ridge
Tim Whittington
Henk de Winter
World RX

From the Hansen Motorsport archive:
BMW AG
Citroen Sport / Citroen Racing
Johan Daveus
Johan Dingenen
Ulf Fabiansson
Hansen family collection
Soren Lindell (Sachs)
Johnny Loix
Teddy Morellec
Jan Peter
Lennart Pettersson
Peugeot Sport
Red Bull Content Pool
Jaanus Ree
Roger Schederin
Tommy Svensson
Tony Welam
@World

Specific Credits:
Jorgen Ring Andersen (p144-148 crash sequence)
Maria Berglind (p269)
Andrea Ivares Berglind (p370 right)
Luke James (p234)
Andy Lasure (p151)
Jonny Persson (p139, 171, 357 right, 372 second portrait)

Design, layout and editing: RallycrossWorld.com

The author thanks all those who gave freely of their time and knowledge to help and assist in the research and production of this book.

"As a driver I think he was fair but tough.
He knew all the tricks.
Everybody outside of the car thinks he was a gentleman,
but on the track he knew how to play the game.
He was fair and professional, but hard too."

Marko Jokinen

The FIA World Motor Sport Council confirmed the composition of the Drivers' Commission in March 2013. The rights and interests of drivers across the FIA's disciplines are represented by its members. Kenneth Hansen has been a member since its inception.

Danish driver Tom Kristensen has won the 24 Hours of Le Mans a record-breaking nine times in a glittering career. He has also been part of the Drivers' Commission since it was formed and holds the position of President.

Left to right: Marc Duez, Kenneth Hansen, Manuel Reuter, Tom Kristensen, Derek Warwick, Yannick Dalmas.
Front: Emanuelle Piro, Karun Chandhok.
Following pages, Top left: Hansen talks to Hal Ridge.
Bottom: FIA European Rallycross Championship drivers pictured during 2010. Hansen is seated left of centre in the front row. Ridge (in dark overalls) is standing in the second row to the left of Hansen.

My dad was Danish Rallycross Champion in 1980 and won races internationally too. He was actually in negotiation with Volvo to race the 343 for 1982. Volvo Denmark wanted my dad [Carl-Erik Kristensen] to be in one of the cars in the European Championship, but then Volvo Sweden unfortunately decided to pull out. That was around the time when Kenneth started his career, so I have a natural link into rallycross from when I was a kid.

I have never actually been present when Kenneth was racing, but of course I knew of him. He was going incredibly well and I became particularly aware in the years when he was getting close to Martin Schanche's record [of six European Championship titles], because he [Schanche] was the guy, together with Per Inge Walfridsson, Piet Dam and John Welch from those years I was watching when my dad was competing.

I can't say exactly when I first met Kenneth, perhaps at an end of year awards ceremony, but I am a member of motor sport so I was very aware of him and what he had achieved. I remember when we first met properly and he explained that he has (surprisingly to me) a Danish background. His family is from Norre Bork on the west coast of Jutland – not too far from where I was born and live again now.

We started to work together in the FIA Drivers' Commission. Kenneth was there from when I entered as Vice-President, and then later as President. He has been a very important and loyal member, he hasn't missed a meeting. His contributions are more than just from off-road and rallycross because he has a good logical approach to the different things that we look at in the Commission.

It wasn't until Jean Todt was elected [as FIA President, in 2009] that the Drivers' Commission was created, which I think was something that was sadly missing for many years. Nowadays you have drivers contributing back to the sport, in many different roles such as advisors and driver stewards. But the Drivers' Commission, which is a group of selected drivers from the many categories we have under the FIA, is key to many aspects. The human element in the FIA is the most important and we are there to make progress with many different things from the drivers' point of view. The experience that different people bring to the table is pretty unique and even though we spend an entire day four times a year together, there never seems to be enough time.

It's very important to have clear logic and experienced feedback from drivers from the different disciplines, like karting, single-seaters from Formula 4 to Formula 1, GT, Le Mans, American racing, rally and of course, rallycross.

Genuinely, everyone absolutely appreciates what Kenneth has done for the sport, but he has also integrated his whole family into a passion and a business. That's something you can only do with the right tools, commitment and hard work.

What he, Susann and his boys have achieved is something that is very admirable and I absolutely respect the way he has done what he has.

Kenneth is a hard working, low key guy who you can look straight in the eye and have 100% trust in what he has done. That is really something I and the Drivers' Commission appreciate. He's very loyal to the sport and a great ambassador for rallycross.

FOREWORD

Hal Ridge

For someone usually so quick and concise with responses to questions, there's a telling pause: 'You know, sometimes I still don't believe it' muses Kenneth Hansen, acknowledging my reference to the 14 FIA European Championship trophies on display in the foyer of his team's workshops in Gotene.

It's almost 0700 on a cold December morning, it's still dark outside and having spent another couple of days sorting through thousands of images and discussing a near lifetime in a sport, we're into another two hour chat, recording memories from an illustrious career, before I hit the road.

Having visited Hansen's base to collate material on several occasions, I've become accustomed to those most precious pieces from his horde of silverware, but even for the quiet, consummate Swede, who walks by the rewards of over four decades work almost every day, those trophies seem almost a surprise.

I believe him when he says that he did not set out to make it to the big league when he began competing. For me, that's what makes his passion for his sport all the more genuine. He has done it for the love of it.

I don't come from a motor sport family, but discovered rallycross for myself in my teens, during the height of Hansen's success and I'd exchanged pleasantries with him on several occasions over the years prior to meeting him properly.

I began competing myself at an entry-level in the UK in 2005. At the season-closing Superprix event at Croft that year, I was excited to have my name appear on the same entry list as Hansen, more so when we exchanged a handshake in the driver's briefing.

Having also started to cover the sport as a writer a few years later, I spoke with Kenneth many times at events, but a standout encounter of note was as a driver, at the Czech season finale of the European Championship in 2011, what would be his final European start.

As an under-funded amateur running down the field of the second-tier category, I was one of the first to encounter dangerously dusty conditions in the opening qualifier, held in the low sun of a late afternoon in October. Venting my frustrating of the conditions to fellow British drivers led to the leading contenders getting involved with the race officials. Somewhat embarrassed that my relatively inexperienced opinions could be about to affect an entire FIA event,

I rushed to race control and met Hansen on the stairs as he left the race directors' office. I explained my concerns, but in the same kind of calm, warm approach I've subsequently seen so often when he speaks to people, Kenneth explained that they could see it was dangerous, that he and the other leading drivers had taken my word and pressured the race director to postpone running until the following day on safety grounds.

My time competing regularly and working in the paddock as a journalist intertwined for a while, and it was only after I stopped driving that I got to know Hansen much better. For me as a journalist, he has so often been a go-to resource for a considered, concise opinion on any aspect of the sport. As the trust between us has grown, those interactions have extended to detailed discussions both on and off the record.

I'm not afraid to admit that I underestimated the task in creating this book when formulating the concept, several years ago. Viewing raw facts alone, Kenneth's career appears fairly straight forward. The reality though is that there is far more to his story than winning in red Citroens. The more people I spoke to, the more I learned, and the more interesting it became.

The intention was never to produce a chronological account of Hansen's life or career, but to compile a range of separate stories so the book can be started from any point at any time and each chapter or even page is of interest in its own right, while hearing from various members of the rallycross community and beyond.

Included are some brilliant, fascinating insights and some wonderful imagery too.

Getting the opportunity to sit down and discuss Hansen's story, for what turned into countless hours with some 'A-list' motor sport names like Loeb, Ekstrom, Solberg, Todt, Famin, Kristoffersson, Eklund, and Kristensen, along with star rallycross specialists like Gollop, Isachsen, Skogstad, Rustad, Pinomaki, Timerzyanov, Pailler and the list goes on, has been a small boy's dream. I hope you enjoy the range of tales that I have found highly entertaining, sections like Hansen's rivalry with Per Eklund, his friendship with Christer Strand and exclusive anecdotes about how if talks with other manufacturers gone just slightly differently, a whole career could have changed.

A term used by some Swedes within these pages is that Hansen has a 'fox behind the ear.' There's no direct translation for the saying, but it fundamentally means that there is more to a person than meets the eye. That is unquestionably the case here, without having a full hand of cards to play, Hansen couldn't have survived at the highest level of his discipline for so many decades and achieved what he has.

There are so many people to thank for help in creating Fourteen, but my biggest thanks must go to Kenneth for being so willing and helpful, and for his readiness for people to air their opinions within these pages, even if he doesn't necessarily agree with them.

Legend is a term used far too often in sport, but to have got so close to a real bona fide legend has been an absolute pleasure.

CONTENTS

Martin Schanche and Kenneth Hansen exchange points of view after one of their duels.

The success of a career in motor sport, both as a driver and as a team owner, can be judged not only in raw statistics, but by the names competed against and conquered. In Kenneth Hansen's case, he took on and beat some of the best contenders in the history of rallycross, and those that achieved at a top-level elsewhere before switching to the discipline. What's more, that success has been sustained for almost four decades.

The following pages detail memories, both on and off track, of some of Hansen's biggest rivals.

I. RIVALS

Tommy Kristoffersson

While Hansen was claiming Division One European rallycross titles aboard his Ford Sierra in the late 1980s and early 1990s, fellow Swede Tommy Kristoffersson was competing in Division Two (later known as Supercar) with Audi quattros. The duo shared liveries and sponsors in 1992, then competed against each other from 1993 when Hansen graduated to the premier category.

The pair finished second and third overall that first year, but while Hansen went on to score 10 titles at the highest level, Kristoffersson netted just a pair of wins, and having already switched to circuit racing, concluded his rallycross career with a one-off return and victory at his home circuit in Arvika in 1998.

More recently, the experienced Swedes have competed against each other as team owners in World Rallycross and in managerial roles for manufacturer-supported squads, while their sons, Timmy and Kevin Hansen and Johan Kristoffersson have continued the rivalry at the very top of the sport.

Kristoffersson on Hansen

Kenneth has two sides to him. One side is a very friendly, nice guy and a good friend. The other side is the Kenneth who is a very tough competitor.

We all know that Kenneth is very careful when it comes to spending money, and he's very clever at doing nice things that don't use money for no reason. But, when he was sat in the car he didn't care if he only had the steering wheel with him when he got back to the paddock. When he is competing he really doesn't care about anything!

We've seen so many fights, especially like between him and Martin Schanche at Lyngas [in 1994, see chapter two] when he doesn't care what happens.

But, we raised our kids together and he's a very friendly and nice guy. He's very family oriented, he's really been a good friend over the years and still we have a very good connection. I have very big respect for him and I think he also respects our work and professionalism.

In some ways I think he destroyed the sport because he was too good. That's one way to look at it – he dominated for many years, but for sure he's done a lot for the sport too. I know he had a lot of political discussions in the past trying to get good TV for rallycross. We've all known for many years that we have a very good product but we never had the possibility to show it. I think the work that Kenneth has done behind the scenes is a big part of the stuff we can see today.

I don't have many stand-out memories from our time racing, I tried to forget it – most of the time he beat me so I tried to put it behind me.

I do remember one time we were out travelling together though, we were supposed to share a hotel room. We had been at a big party, we got to the hotel very late and we had had a lot of food, so we had a competition who will go first to the toilet. He was really fast into the toilet. Because it was not so nice to visit the toilet after him, in the meantime I took his bed and put it outside on the balcony.

When he came back I said: 'Sorry it's only a single room, but I put the blanket on the floor so you are supposed to stay there Kenneth.' He was quite pissed because I was already in the bed, so he was crying a little bit but then he got down on the floor. He was laying just on the blanket on the floor, but I was too kind for that so I had to tell him that his bed was on the balcony. That was a nice moment for me. That day I beat him.

Hansen on Kristoffersson

We have known each other a long time. We were never one team but many years ago we had the same sponsor so it looked like one team and we had a good time together. Tommy is a fun guy, but he still owes me for what he did with my bed in the hotel in Germany once.

We still have good fun today in the spotters' tower and the paddock, even if we are both working hard like always. I think we have both learned that you can relax on the side a little. Of course, it's hard and the pressure is on, for him from Volkswagen and for us it was from Peugeot, but still you need to enjoy, you need to have fun. We are doing everything to win, and I'm sure Tommy is too, but it's good when you can have some fun at the same time.

Previous page: Hansen leads Kristoffersson at Holjes.
Left and below: The two Swedish drivers had BP and Sachs as a common sponsors but each ran their own team.

Pat Doran

British driver Pat Doran began competing regularly in the European Rallycross Championship with a Group B Ford RS200 in 1990, while Hansen was storming to Division One titles. Doran claimed a single European win in 1992, before the pair properly met on track for the first time in 1993 when Hansen graduated to the top class. Doran made sporadic forays into Europe for the next 15 years of Hansen's career but the pair got to know each other best when Doran bought the Lydden Hill circuit and took international rallycross back to the UK in 2009, before Doran's son Liam signed to drive for Hansen's team for 2010.

Left: When the technical rules changed and demanded a new type of car for the 1993 season, Hansen moved to a Citroen ZX while Pat Doran replaced his RS200 with an Escort Cosworth.

Doran on Hansen

I was in my old Ford RS200 and Kenneth was racing this new super-fast Citroen Supercar that was so much quicker than the Group B cars, so I was determined to beat him in this race at Croft, for the Grand Prix 2002. It was at a right-left corner onto the loose and Kenneth went wide; I went for the gap but he cut across me. Our wheels touched and his car went about six feet up in the air. I never felt it was my fault, even Per Eklund who was behind me commented that he would have done exactly what I did and gone for the gap that Kenneth left open, but Kenneth wasn't happy.

We only really raced together for one full season, but we were both around and racing for a lot of years. At the start he was in Division One, the Group A class and I was in Division Two, which was the top class at the time, but we got to know each other because we both had families in the paddock.

One year after the Grand Prix at Brands Hatch, before the Scandinavians got the boat the next day, I suggested a few of them came and parked outside my place. I lived in a tiny little house on a housing estate and Michael Jernberg, Kenneth, Bjorn Skogstad and Eklund all parked their buses on this bloody road. Kenneth asked me: 'Why do you all live so close together in England in these little tiny houses?' I just laughed and told him it was all that could afford, because my rallycross car was worth more than my house! He thought it was quite funny because there is so much space in Sweden.

His driving ability was incredible and he wouldn't touch anybody. In my day you knew he wouldn't touch you when you were racing him, you'd never have red paint on your car, unless you hit him! Things just didn't often happen around him. He had one big crash, but for the thousands of races he done, really, it's nothing.

I couldn't have thought of anyone better to take Liam into the professional world of rallycross. Liam would never listen to me. Who listens to their father? I thought that because Kenneth was almost the total opposite of Liam, to put them together could work well. Kenneth is a real laid back, nothing really unsettles him kind of Swede. Liam's a very moody, angry person at times, typical Anglo Saxon really.

In one of Liam's first drives with Kenneth in 2010, I was Liam's spotter. I must point out that I didn't do that for long because it all got a bit personal. Anyway, I told Liam it was five laps, because it was a short circuit they ran an extra lap. 'Don't forget', I said.

So, Liam was leading the race, but after the fourth lap, he stopped. The other cars go by and then he remembers, gets going again and comes round to the finish in second. It was a still a good time but he started screaming down the radio: 'Why didn't anyone tell me that it was five laps?' I explained to him in a very quiet way that his father did tell him that it was five laps. When he went quiet I knew he'd remembered.

That was the end of it as far as I was concerned, but then as the car pulled into the awning, Rickard Toftgren, the number one mechanic, opened the door and there's this raging bull behind the wheel, punching the steering wheel. In that very laid back Swedish way, Rickard closed the door again and said to Graham Rodemark: 'We have problem with the driver!'

That night, at about 11 or 12 o'clock, we had played the video for hours and hours looking at how to go faster. Kenneth and Rickard were sitting there looking at it and they let the video play after the race. All they could see on the in-car camera was this nutcase punching the steering wheel, screaming in language that you couldn't believe. There was complete horror on their faces. I tried to play it down by making a joke and telling them it was Martian language, and they wouldn't understand it. I could tell Kenneth was thinking: 'Oh my god, what have we taken-on here.'

Within half an hour, even at that time of night, every Swedish team that was parked nearby was watching this show of Liam driving between the track and the paddock screaming and shouting.

I couldn't do what Kenneth's done for as long as he has. I have come in to rallycross and gone out and come in and gone out but he's been there year after year and there isn't anyone like him in any motor sport I don't think. He's not a wild personality like a Martin Schanche or a Liam and he's not a Petter Solberg but he's a lovely personality and goes out and does the job, day after day, year after year.

Top right: Doran as the 'racing dad' congratulates Hansen.
Below right: Hansen and Doran on the podium together at Lydden Hill in 1991.

Hansen on Doran

I didn't actually race Pat that much, but that fight we had at Croft was quite bad. In my opinion he pushed me off. He didn't apologise either, or at least I didn't feel he did so it took a long time before I spoke to him again. I was very upset with what he had done.

We became closer when we ran Liam in our team for two years, but my big memory of Pat at that time is not from a race. We went with Liam to the Autosport Show in Birmingham in the UK. It was the biggest motor sport show in Europe and Liam was going to drive the C4 in the Live Action Arena. We went there with the car, and Liam had built a jump, an open gap jump.

I straight away said: 'I don't want you to do that, because it's quite dangerous and we have a season coming soon.' He did some practising and so on in a buggy and it went okay, even on the jump, then I went around the exhibition and Liam did some practising in the C4, but I didn't know.

When I went back to the paddock of the Live Action area Pat came straight to me. 'Sorry' he said. 'Sorry?' I replied. 'Ah, you were not here, okay let's get a coffee.' Liam had tried the jump and it didn't finish well.

I saw a video afterwards and Liam didn't fly far enough, he clipped the edge of the jump and it threw the car in the air. It landed on its side. I don't think anyone has ever been so keen to offer me a coffee as Pat was that day.

Bjorn Skogstad

Norwegian Bjorn Skogstad won his home round and season finale of the European Rallycross Championship's second-tier category in 1984 at Lyngas, on his way to third overall in the points with an Opel Ascona.

He repeated the result the following year, before switching to a Ford Escort RS Turbo in 1986 and then the newly introduced Ford Sierra RS Cosworth in 1987. After a year of development with the new Ford, and its evolution to RS500 specification, Skogstad won the European Championship in 1988. Then, for the next four years, he finished second to Hansen as the Swede started to accumulate European titles.

Skogstad joined Hansen in graduating to the headline category in 1993, the Norwegian with a Ford Escort, but while he would not fight for another title, he did beat Hansen in a straight fight to victory at Lousada in Portugal during his final campaign in 1995.

Skogstad on Hansen

Kenneth is a very professional bloke and he was a hard one to win over. Sometimes he was a little bit hard and I was the same, so I think we were equal in the end.

He was a hard man on the track but nothing special. He was just a racing driver, there was nothing special around him.

We did not always agree about everything and we had some arguments about the regulations of the cars sometimes, but it was in a professional way I think.

I remember one time at Lydden Hill [in 1990] when he took Ludvig Hunsbedt off the track, and that cost me the championship.

Coming down the Hill onto the gravel he pushed Ludvig out over the bump onto the start line. He had to have that place otherwise he would have lost the championship. I think he was a bit hard to Ludvig that day, but I was the most angry man because I lost the championship.

I lost the championship by four points to Kenneth. I didn't agree with the regulations, they had got a fine about something wrong in the regulations, but didn't lose points. It wasn't Kenneth that I was unhappy with, but the judges.

If you've done something wrong and get a fine, then you should lose some points. But because they didn't lose the points I missed out.

The problem was around the turbo pressure; the turbo pressure should have been standard and there was some anti lag; there were small things on the electronics. No big things, but important things.

In the races Kenneth and I did not always get on so well, but afterwards it was okay. Both of us wanted to win. I think [Juan Pablo] Montoya and [Michael] Schumacher were not good friends, nor Schumacher and [Damon] Hill either, but that's life as a racing driver.

Kenneth was one of the best, for sure. I think he was a very technical guy, to set up the car, he was good.

I was the man to have good sponsors to start with, then Kenneth got BP and got some good sponsors and had good money, then he was number one for a lot of years.

I tried to be very professional for all my sponsors and very aware of what the car and team and bus should look like, but still I was not the nicest man on the track all the time, I want to win, and Kenneth was the same.

We had some hard races at Lyngas, my home track, because that's the one I wanted to win the most, but Holland [Valkenswaard] was my favourite, that was also good for Kenneth so we had some hard races there too.

I enjoyed it very much, all the arguments, all the happiness we had together with Kenneth, Eivind [Opland] and Ludvig.

Previous page: Bjorn Skogstad leads Hansen at Lyngas in 1989.
Above: The Swede and Norwegian battled hard for several years, this is at Suonenjoki in Finland in 1992.

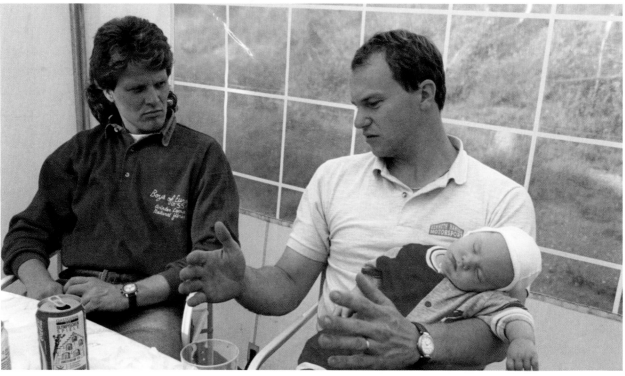

Hansen on Skogstad

We were big rivals. He was the star in Norway with a very professional team, he did it very well and we were the ones who battled against him. We were really competitors and we didn't have coffee with each other. We spoke, but very, very briefly. I've met him sometimes [since] and it's nice to see him. I think he misses motor sport.

We were professional at the time because we knew we needed to be the two competitors, we needed to fight, we need to have the media on us, so we had this thing like me and Martin [Schanche] had later. I think it was very good for me, for him, and the sport.

He was very professional, the team looked beautiful and we learnt from that. It was very good for us that he was there and showed us this way. We became more professional then.

Racing against him in Norway many times was special, and we had something happen in Holland too. One time we went to some appeal court after the race, where I won.

He had been very rough to me before and at some point you need to put the level there, you need to put your foot down and say 'enough'. That was the one time where that had ended and he was quite right [to appeal] but I won the incident.

Perhaps everything was not fair, because perhaps I was a little guilty there. It was give and take and I think in the total picture it was fair. But in that situation, I think it was not fair. Perhaps I should have been disqualified from the race.

He won the [European] championship in 1988, then I came with the Cosworth the next year. It was hard because he knew the car, he knew everything, but we managed take the battle to him. I think it was very hard for him that we won four years in a row, I feel a little sorry sometimes, because he also deserved to win. He won races, but I won the championship.

Then when we went to Supercars, him with the Cosworth and me with Citroen. In Fuglau [Austria] I took the first win and I think he was surprised, like me, that I did it and I think he got more bored by me.

Top left: The Hansen versus Skogstad duel, this time at Arendonk in Belgium.
Below left: Timmy Hansen sleeps in his father's arms while Hansen and Skogstad talk racing.

Michael Jernberg

Widely regarded as the best driver never to win a European Championship, Swedish driver and engineer Michael Jernberg was the nearly man for most of Hansen's top-flight career in the European Rallycross Championship.

Jernberg joined Hansen in graduating to the sport's highest category for the 1993 season, the pair having raced a similar Ford Sierra RS500s for the previous two seasons.

While the subsequent 18 years resulted in 10 titles for Hansen, Jernberg won events and came close to the crown a number of times, but never claimed the biggest prize.

Both drivers ended their full-time European careers at the end of 2010 and while Jernberg continued to race in America for another term, their rivalry continued later as Jernberg worked with young driver Robin Larsson, in direct competition to Hansen's sons in the World Rallycross Championship.

Michael Jernberg joined the European Championship in 1991 and was one of Hansen's closest rivals for the next 20 years.

Jernberg on Hansen

The closest I came to winning the championship was in 2005. It was between me and Kenneth, and whoever was first in the final at the last race in Germany was going to be European Champion. I was ahead of Kenneth in the final. That would have been enough, but I hit a barrier with two laps to go.

Kenneth had already been driving in Division One for a few years when I started in 1991. Every year I tried very hard to beat him but he did everything right, to get the sponsors and to make the money to have a good car and good team around him. He had the best opportunity when he got Citroen in 1993 because he had a lot of help from Citroen I think.

Every time he was behind me in a race I trusted that he wouldn't do anything wrong or stupid. He was a fair driver, not a rough guy and we both knew if we drove as fast as we could then we would be near the front and we just had to race each other.

I did my best, in the last three or four years it was very good for me, I had a good car and very good sponsors, but it was very hard to win the championship and in the end it was [Sverre] Isachsen who was my biggest rival. But most of the time it was the same as Formula 1 when Michael Schumacher was there; Schumacher was very good and very hard to beat, just like Kenneth.

I had more luck in the Swedish championship against Kenneth which was good for me and my Swedish sponsors. We did the best we could in the Europe but sometimes we had a little bad luck and sometimes were not good enough to win.

It doesn't matter now that I didn't win it. Of course it would be very nice to have won it, but we won some races and it was close. When Lars Larsson won the championship I had more wins, but I had too many races where it didn't go well and that was the difference. Our team was not strong enough to have the consistency.

For the last years Kenneth was driving, maybe after his 14th championship, I don't think he was so hungry any more. He tried to beat us but he was second in 2010. He was not there to be driving for third, and of course he had his sons coming too.

At that time we used to go to each other to get some parts if we needed them at a race, but that is not possible now in the World Championship; it has changed a lot. Then we shared everything, even if we thought the other might beat us if we helped them. We did everything on the track, not in the paddock. It's good fun now, but it was very, very good fun then.

Everybody lived in the paddock, not in hotels and we often took a coffee with each other between the races, then in the evening after the race we had a party.

I got some help from Stig Blomqvist when I bought the first RS500 from him and I always said when I stop I should try to help a younger driver more than the help I got from our old drivers from Sweden then.

Me and Kenneth are doing that now, and we do our own racing in the spotters tower.

Hansen on Jernberg

I feel sorry for Michael that he never won the championship. That time in Germany when he went off, he felt like I stole the championship because he had it in his hands. I don't know why it was like that for him. I think it could have been that there was a lot of positive pressure around him, and that was too much for Michael. People want the best, with that is pressure and I think it became too much for him and at least at that moment he couldn't take it.

Michael is one of the genuine good guys and I think we have always been the same that we want to give something back, because the sport has given so much to us. It's good that we have both been able to continue in the sport too, and it's easy to see that the young guys, like Robin, give Michael motivation back even after all the years. That's very similar to me with Timmy and Kevin.

Petter Solberg

Most famous for beating Sebastien Loeb to the World Rally Championship in 2003, Norwegian star Petter Solberg begun his career in bilcross [the Norwegian version of folkrace] and then rallycross, before switching to rallying. Drawing a line under his full-time rally career at the end of 2012, and with the promotion of rallycross having been taken over by IMG, Solberg decided to return to the discipline.

He held discussions with Hansen about buying a Citroen DS3 Supercar, but Hansen decided that it was in his team's best interest not to sell to Solberg and the Norwegian built his own version of Citroen's machine. Hansen's squad won the first title of the new era with Timur Timerzyanov, but Solberg went on to claim the first two World Rallycross Championship Drivers' titles, beating Timmy Hansen to the biggest prize in 2015 when Team Peugeot Hansen took the Teams' crown. The 2015 season wasn't without its controversy however, most notably in the Canadian round when Solberg and Timmy Hansen came together at the first corner of the semi-final, forcing both to retire.

Canada 2015, Timmy Hansen and Petter Solberg clash at the start of their semi-final.

Solberg on Hansen

I already had a lot of Citroen experience from rallying and also had support from Citroen Norway, so to buy a car was the easiest way to come back to rallycross. Hansen was in Sweden and I needed to get a car because it was a very short time before the season, we had three months.

I didn't look at the car, we met in Torsby around Christmas and I agreed with Kenneth to buy a car, then he changed his mind over the new year.

I was really not happy because a word is a word. He was afraid that I would develop the car. He didn't want me to use my own dampers and do different things, but that doesn't work. If he can decide what I can do with the car I bought then it's not right, you know.

I wanted to come into the sport, I thought they were maybe happy to get me in, I think that would have been a positive thing, I got many other drivers in after that. Of course I was disappointed that I couldn't get the help to do that in the short term. He was thinking the best for his team and his drivers. If I developed the car and it got faster than his team then it would have been a problem in his team. Things changed quite a lot over new year and it was a big surprise when I got that phone call and I was pissed off.

But at the end of the day that was the decision he made and I found another solution.

That's when we built up a car, it was a big rush and a big stress. That first year [2013] my car was

fast, reliability was the small issue, we made everything very high performance, but the year after – after the learning year – everything worked well and we won the World Championship. Of course it was a much better kick [to beat them] then.

Kenneth is a legend in rallycross, he has done incredible things, winning a lot and having the stability for many years. That's been very, very impressive. He's a calm guy and together with guys like Martin Schanche he has been a part of getting rallycross to where it is.

This is rallycross, you always have some disputes. Sometimes you win and sometimes you lose. This is part of the game. I think Kenneth has always been very good at communication and

discussion, he has been a good guy in those situations.

Kenneth is always thinking about the best for the sport, to keep it good and get it to lift. You have to help each other and help other teams and go in the right direction and I think he has got better and better at that over the years. He's always calm and controlled and knows what he is doing. He has a lot of experience, the Peugeot team was lucky to have him to help with all the details. He's not the guy who is jumping around, he's very controlled.

I like the whole family, it's fantastic that they have the possibility to work together. They are very professional and I love their passion, there's nothing better than that.

Left: Timmy Hansen leads teammate Timur Timerzyanov and Solberg in Hungary in 2013.
Above: Their relationship was rocky in 2013, but Hansen and Solberg have a mutual respect for each other.

*Above: Solberg, Jeanney and Timmy Hansen
in Norway 2015.
Right: Germany 2015, winner Jeanney
flanked by Solberg and Timmy Hansen.*

Hansen on Solberg

Petter contacted us about a car. Of course, Petter and Henning [Solberg, Petter's brother] are guys you look up to because they have been very positive for motor sport, especially rallying in Scandinavia.

I had met them sometimes, Petter visited us once in Gotene too. Then he wanted to come into rallycross. He contacted us and Susann and I went to a meeting in Torsby. He wanted to buy a Citroen from us.

This was before Christmas [2012]. It was interesting for us, but he didn't want to take our concept, he wanted to buy a car and then be free with whatever he wanted to do with it. We discussed and talked a little to people in the team, and then we decided. I called him around new year, or just before I don't remember exactly when, and said we could run him in a car as part of the team, but we couldn't sell him a car. That was about two weeks after the meeting.

He was completely furious! For me it was a shock because I never thought he could be like that, what he called me and what he said, you know, saying it was me that was totally a fool. It was a shock that a guy like him could behave like that.

We said we didn't want to go that way because we felt that if we sell a car and he took what he wanted and changed the engine with another engine manufacturer, it goes completely against our concept and it would be very strange. We had created our concept together in the team with our partners and obviously we wanted that to continue, but he didn't respect that at all.

Then it took quite a long time to get past that because every time I spoke to him during the year he more or less said that I didn't dare to sell him a car and I was stupid.

Of course he was not happy, but sometimes he is living in his own bubble and believes what he says is exactly what will happen, and when someone goes against him and doesn't follow the route, he can't take that.

We had a similar thing in Canada in 2015, after he and Timmy had crashed in the semi-final. We discussed driving behaviour, and it was how he reacted. I said: 'Okay, this is the incident, I've seen what you did and I've seen the onboard, but we can let it go. If you say you made a mistake it's fine.'

But he couldn't shake my hand, everything was Timmy's fault and then he was back again, I was stupid and he should go back to rallying because it's just stupid people that want to hit him in rallycross.

He let it go quicker the second time, and after that I think he respected more that I will say what I feel. Driver-to-driver is one thing, but sometimes as the Team Manager I need also to say what I believe is right. Things happen on a rallycross circuit. But I think it's a side of Petter that not many people really see.

It's not all like that of course, he is a fantastic driver and a brilliant character for the sport. He gives a lot for the fans and the media and he has done a lot for rallycross since he came back.

Now we are really good friends. Petter's a great guy and I hope we see him in rallycross again.

Marko Jokinen

Finn Marko Jokinen made his international rallycross debut with an MG Metro 6R4 in a Swedish Rallycross Championship round at Hedemora in 1994, and for his first race lined up against Hansen, Per Eklund and Tommy Kristoffersson in their European Championship-specification machines.

For the 1997 season, Jokinen built a Citroen ZX that while aesthetically similar to Hansen's own car, bore few similarities under the skin. While competing in the European series in the Citroen and subsequently with Peugeots; a 306 followed by a 206 and then 207, Jokinen met Linda Bergvall [Susann Hansen's sister] at Holjes in 1999. The following spring Jokinen emigrated to Sweden and married Linda, in the process becoming Hansen's brother in-law.

More recently, Jokinen developed the Speedcar Crosscart class in Sweden. The Hansen family's Yellow Squad young driver programme used a Speedcar machine in its first season [2019], with testing undertaken by Kenneth, Timmy and Kevin.

Jokinen on Hansen

Kenneth and his father Svend knew my father Mauno when he was racing in the European Championship. It was Kenneth's first season, in 1987, we arrived at the Austrian border on the way to the first round and they were in front of us. I stopped our bus just one metre away from theirs, then suddenly the reverse lights came on and bang. There was a line on the road and Svend had gone too far. You know they are quite strict in Austria, so he wanted to reverse quickly, he panicked with it being their first trip and not wanting to make a mistake, and he reversed into us. When Svend was alive I would often remind him of that.

When I built my Citroen in 1994 I asked Kenneth for some advice, then I met Linda at a race in 1999 and we became relatives as well that way.

Kenneth was the professional of his time. There were not many professionals, maybe Martin Schanche, Kenneth and Per Eklund, but he was a true pro with the testing and everything. The rest of us were just hoping to be the best, he was testing so he would be the best.

When I started with the Citroen it was our own build back in Finland. Then I built a Peugeot when I moved to Sweden. They were not the same components as Kenneth's cars though.

As a driver I think he was fair but tough. He knew all the tricks. Everybody outside of the car thinks he was a gentleman, but on the track he knew how to play the game. He was fair and professional, but hard too.

We had some incidents. I remember one time at when he was behind me at Gotene, his home track. Just as he got beside me I had some failure on my car in the steering, something came loose and I was steering towards him and took him out.

Then he pushed me a lot. Yes, I was slower, but I was in the front and he was not happy with that. I told him that if he thought I was going to use the indicator to let him past just because he was the European champion then he was wrong.

Otherwise Kenneth was always faster so we didn't have many duels, but I gave him a free ride at Lyngas in 1999 when Per Eklund won the championship. I got the start into the first corner, Kenneth was behind and he needed to try and catch Per in the time sheets, so I gave him an open door to pass me. I never got that favour back. But like I said, I was usually behind him.

Hansen on Jokinen

I got called to the stewards at Essay in 1999 to get a warning because they said I had shown the finger to another driver after a race. I know you can get quite into things, but normally I do don't that, that's not my thing. I asked who I was supposed to have shown the finger to. It was a French guy that I hadn't driven against. I explained that and they checked the start list from the heat. I saw Marko was there. Red car, Citroen. It was him!

I also tested Marko's Peugeot a few years later at Kinnekulle, but we didn't mention it to anyone because at the time I was racing a Citroen.

I told him: 'I will go out, make a few laps and when I come in, I will just talk, so don't interrupt and I will tell you everything I feel.' Because the second time you're in a car, you're already a little familiar. I also told him not to get upset if I said anything bad, and that I would just be completely honest.

I did the run, then afterwards everything flowed out, I gave my thoughts on seat position, gear lever, the noises, how the car turned-in, everything. That was interesting for me, it's not often I drove other cars like that and I hope it helped him to get a little further in the development of the car.

We didn't do the test on the rallycross track though because if you rent the track at Kinnekulle you needed to pay for cleaning it. Over the years we had many opportunities to borrow the track up there, but it was often when they were having lunch at the driving school, or they were just using one part of the circuit. Many times we didn't use the rallycross track. Every time we were racing there, people believed that we had tested and tested there, it was not true.

To race Marko when he was family was a little different, but not so much. Of course, if you are a relation with someone you try to be fair, because you don't want to have discussions after the race. That's the same with everyone though. If they treat you well on track, you treat them well. If you have someone who is quite rough then of course you are rough back. It's an easy equation.

Previous page: By his own admission, Jokinen
was not often close to Hansen on the track,
here Finn chases Swede in Austria.
Top right: Messing around.
Below right: The brothers-in-law discussing
car characteristics.

Jean-Luc Pailler

As France's most successful rallycross driver, 11-time French Champion Jean-Luc Pailler stepped up to race his Citroen BX in the FIA European Rallycross Championship's top category from 1991.

When Hansen graduated to the top category in 1993 as a new breed of Group A-based cars replaced Group B, it was also with a Citroen.

Pailler won that first title, beating Hansen to the crown by a single point. While Pailler was only full-time for a handful of years, he was a regular on the international scene for much of Hansen's driving career and won on his final one-off appearance in 2008 at Kerlabo.

Along with Hansen Motorsport, Pailler Competition was consulted over running the Peugeot World RX programme in 2014, but the French marque went the way of the Swedish team.

Left: Jean-Luc Pailler has been a marque-colleague, friend and rival. At Kerlabo in 2008 Hansen led the chase as the Frenchman took his last major win. Following page: Hansen joins Pailler during a parade lap at Loheac in 1993.

Pailler on Hansen

I first met Kenneth at the first European Championship race with my four-wheel drive Citroen BX in Portugal in 1991. I think it was then that he saw there was some potential to build a Citroen for the regulations that would come in for 1993 and after he had contact with Citroen and built a car, we both ended up with cars that were capable of winning.

Kenneth was a much cleaner driver than Martin Schanche or Per Eklund and because we drove for the same brand we had a good relationship. He was very lucky though, always lucky; when it was raining it would always rain just after his heat race, it was like that.

Our cars were not so similar. Citroen was giving us the same engine with intercooler, injectors and everything, then I had a good deal with Citroen for the car, the Xantia [built to replace the BX for the 1994 season], and Kenneth built his ZX himself with a different concept of suspension.

It was Citroen's choice to have a hydraulic suspension on the Xantia, and with this suspension choice it was much harder to drive the car. That was the most frustrating thing, that I was not able to fight on the same level as Kenneth was.

The best memory I have of racing Kenneth was winning at Gotene, Kenneth's home track, in 1996. I was really sick, with 40 degrees of fever, but to win there in those conditions, at Kenneth's home is a very nice memory.

Also when we switched to Peugeot in 2001, Guy Frequelin [Citroen Racing boss] told Kenneth to come and get the French title, but I won the championship for Peugeot and that was a good!

When Peugeot was looking to come into the World Championship, they checked both of our teams, but Hansen had more personnel and a better team to be able to have an official programme. I'm not bitter that they went with Hansen, we didn't have the structure to do it and Kenneth was able to take the opportunity, it's good he could do that and work with Peugeot.

We kept doing things at our level and we are still able to run our own car and to be independent, that's good enough for us.

Hansen on Pailler

We wanted to go into Division Two for 1993 and we had some meetings with Ford but it didn't feel like they were really interested, so we had made contact with Citroen Sweden. They were surprised that somebody wanted to do rallycross with a Citroen but they contacted Guy Frequelin in France and we were invited to go down and present our idea.

Jean-Luc was there also because he was already a Citroen driver. I think he had spoken quite well about us and we had a meeting with Guy and the engineers. I don't know how long it took, perhaps just one hour and then it was settled. When we walked out of the meeting, Guy stopped me and Jean-Luc and said: 'I don't care who wins, but I want one of you to win the European Championship.'

So, that was it. We competed over it through the year in 1993 and in the end, at the last race in Buxtehude, it was down to the one who beat the other.

Many people told me that I would not be allowed to win because Jean-Luc is French and I would have to let him win. When that starts to happen you begin to think that perhaps there will be some team orders, but there were never any.

We had a close fight in the race, I got a puncture, and Jean-Luc beat me. I was really happy with that at the time, it was a good result for our first year and also because Jean-Luc had helped me quite a lot to be with Citroen, so it felt fair, but it was good that I was able win it the next year.

Jean-Luc was big in the French Championship. One year I did three races there, and in 2001, I did six rounds. We were going for the Swedish, French and European Championships and we did 21 races. That was very hard.

I finished behind Jean-Luc in the French Championship because we couldn't be in every place at the same time. But Jean-Luc was also stronger, he won more races than me so that was fair. I won the European title and was third in Sweden that year.

It was then that I realised it's easy to just compete, but for two weekends we had a race in Sweden on Saturday and a race in France on Sunday. So we had two teams, two buses and two different cars. It was hard to be motivated, to do the traveling and to be able to focus again. I learned then that there is a limit to how much you can do.

I remember Jean-Luc came back to the European championship for some races before I stopped driving and he was still fast. He won in France in 2008 at his home track. It's always nice to have him in the paddock.

Tommy Rustad

Moving from rallycross and enjoying a successful career in circuit racing makes Tommy Rustad a member of the rallycross elite.

Having graduated from karting into the Norwegian Rallycross Championship, where he claimed six consecutive Supernational titles, Rustad made his top-flight rallycross debut in a Martin Schanche-run Ford RS200 and won the Irish round of the European Championship at Mondello Park in 1992, the year before Hansen made the step up to the top category.

While Rustad switched to circuit racing in 1993, winning titles in single-seaters and touring cars, both in Scandinavia and throughout Europe, he returned for a full rallycross season in 2006 with a Ford Focus and finished one place behind Hansen in the standings, in third. He also raced an ex-Hansen Citroen Xsara with Morten Bermingrud's team at his home round in 2007 and battled for victory until the race was stopped following Hansen's infamous roll [see chapter two].

Having drawn a close to his touring car chapter, Rustad refocused on rallycross from 2013, claimed an emotional European Championship title in 2015 and then battled Hansen's youngest son Kevin in the defence of his crown the following season, with Hansen coming out on top. Rustad continued to compete regularly until 2018, when he stopped racing to focus on his daughter's karting career.

Left: Hansen celebrates victory in Norway 2004 with Tommy Rustad the runner-up on the road before being disqualified from the final.

Rustad on Hansen

When I started driving in rallycross everyone was older than me. But in the end, everyone was younger. I had a long career, I drove with Martin Schanche in the beginning and he could have been my father, and in the end, when I was racing Kevin [Hansen], I could have been his dad.

I drove in some races with Schanche in the early 1990s in a Ford RS200 and Kenneth was racing in what was called Division One then with his Volvo and then a Ford Sierra.

I think the war between the Swedes and Norwegians was more in the media. For sure there was a big fight on track, but I think the media also loved to make a story about it. But of course, in Norway we are always joking that it's not so important to win, but it's very important to beat the Swedes!

I have been very impressed with Kenneth's skills in racing, which is shown by his results, but I've also been impressed by the way he has been able to make a business out of it. That is not very easy in motor sport.

There are a lot of good drivers, but there's not so many that can make good results on the track and also make good business out of it. I think Kenneth and Petter Solberg are very similar how they have

the passion for motor sport, for Kenneth especially for rallycross. But they have a very different mentality. Petter is the kind of person who loves to be in the media and loves to make a show, with much focus about his fans. Kenneth is a bit more neutral in this way, more focused on the team and the business, how to run it right and make it correct.

But Kenneth is also sometimes like a wet soap. If you try and take your hands around a piece of wet soap it slides out of your fingers. He can be a little bit like that but in the end he has a very big heart for rallycross and I think that is why he has had so much success.

He drove hard but fair; that's my opinion. For sure he's a winner, but he knows it's not important to win every battle, he wants to win the war. He was a clever driver like that.

I had some good fights with him. In Norway in 2004 when I rented a car from Isachsen Motorsport he won and I finished second [before being disqualified for a parc ferme rule infringement]. For sure dropping in for a one-off outing and being able to race with and sometimes beat the big guys, it's a good feeling.

Hansen on Rustad

Tommy is a very professional and disciplined guy. He's very fast, also I think hard on the circuit, but not rough, just a very good driver who could use a car to the maximum.

He's done a lot of different kinds of racing and continued a long time. We had a good relationship, we helped him when he was racing the Xsara in Norway [in 2007] and he had good speed.

I was impressed that he was really determined that he wanted to have the European Rallycross title. He came back with a good effort, a professional team behind him and he did it the right way. He really deserved that championship [in 2015].

The main race I remember driving against him was at Momarken when I rolled so heavily [see chapter two]. I remember he was fighting for the lead when the red flag came out.

He has always conducted himself in good a way. I'm sure that's why he got asked to be an adviser to the stewards in World RX [for selected World Rallycross Championship events in 2019]. I think he was a little afraid to go into it because he's not a guy who wants to be controversial, but when we spoke before the season I said to him: 'I will be up there in the office

sometimes I suppose [with the stewards, as team principal] and we will not agree I'm sure, but the good thing is you're objective and I know you can do it well.'

In the first race of the year in Abu Dhabi we were in the office because there was an incident between Niclas Gronholm and Kevin [Hansen] and it affected who won. Tommy was very professional in the way he worked and I think the stewards were very happy to have him; they can't always trust people if you come from one side or another. He was independent and he had experience when perhaps they [stewards] have never been in a racecar, so it's not always easy for them to understand. I think it's very important that we have a driver there and it feels very good that we've come so far and we finally have it.

Left: Rustad leads Hansen and the rest of the pack in Germany 2006.
Above: Rustad returned to regular competition and won the European Rallycross Championship in 2015. Here he joins 2016 champion Kevin Hansen and Tord Linnerud in celebration in Spain 2016.

Eivind Opland

Norwegian Eivind Opland began his international rallycross career in 1987, at the same time as Hansen, and raced a similar Volvo 240 Turbo. Opland switched to a Ford Sierra Cosworth in the second-tier division a year before Hansen, and over the next four seasons became an event winner. It wasn't until Hansen had graduated to the sport's highest level that Opland really found his form, finishing second in 1993 with a Nissan Sunny before claiming four successive titles with various different Mitsubishis. It was with a car from the Japanese marque that Opland stepped up to the top category in 1999 and won a European Championship event in his first term. But, he couldn't repeat his lower-category championship success and called time on his career in 2002.

Opland on Hansen

At Lydden Hill in 1989 Kenneth had broken his engine. I was on pole position in the A final, Bjorn Skogstad was by my side in second and Kenneth was in fifth place. If Bjorn won, he was the champion. Kenneth came over to me before the start and asked: 'Eivind, will you let him pass?' I told him not to worry because I wouldn't do that. I didn't let Skogstad past, and Kenneth finished third and that year he was the champion for the first time.

We started together at the same time and we became very good friends. All the time we were traveling together and camping together between the races; Kenneth and I were like brothers, more or less. He was a tough fighter, but a fair fighter, and a very good driver. He was smart, I mean if you are champion 14 times then you are good.

We had many good races together. I came with [the] Mitsubishi to Supercar, that was the first Supercar like that built for rallycross, but it was so difficult.

Kenneth was very lucky when he got the contract with Citroen, at the end of 1992.

Citroen had a Group A car, they had done many things before, but it was very difficult for me to get the

big money to go racing. That was the reason I stopped in 2002.

Kenneth was lucky, but he did a brilliant job for Citroen, and he is still with the same company's cars, even if they are Peugeot now.

Kenneth and I had one fight in Holjes I remember, in the big class [Division One, in 1999]. We came over the jump before the last corner with one lap to go and he tried to pass me [on the inside, through the corner exit]. There was no more space to go and he finished standing in the sand. He nearly tipped over!

Also in Arvika once, I was leading and he pushed me out, and I mean he really pushed me! I was so angry I went to his bus, but his father stopped me going in. One hour and we were friends again. It was not harder than that.

I would say he's one of my best friends in motor sport. He was so fair, but he can be very, very tough. If you are a winner though, everybody is tough. That's how it is.

If I had problems in the paddock, I went and asked for something, and he gave me that. It was never a problem. And the same the other way around.

Hansen on Opland

At Hameenlinna in Finland [in 1999] we were sitting with Eivind. He said: 'You know, I will win this event.' My sponsor Lars, from Sachs, said: 'If you do that, I will walk to the ferry.' It was quite far to the ferry, but Eivind didn't quite have the speed. Eivind just said: 'You will see.'

In one of the qualifying races, he won the start, then through the chicane the boost pipe came off. He went to the right side of the track and back to the paddock and it seemed that everyone behind believed that it was a restart, so they followed him into the paddock. He was able to fix the pipe, and then he went on to win the event.

When he meets Lars now, he still reminds him that he didn't walk to the ferry!

Eivind was perhaps one of the mentally strongest competitors I ever met. He had such belief in himself. I really look up to him for having that mental strength.

He did it quite well in Supercar, but he based the car on the Group N Mitsubishi and then some used some Group A parts. It never came to be a very good car, he won some races of course, but it was a difficult period for him I think.

I always had a very good feeling with Opland and he's still a good friend, even if he is Norwegian.

Above left: Opland leads Hansen in Portugal.
Above: Opland eventually graduated to Supercar and raced Hansen again.

Kevin Procter

A successful businessman and rally driver from the North East of England, Kevin Procter began competing in national rallycross events with his converted Ford Puma rally car. He first came up against Hansen in the standalone Rallycross Superprix at Croft Circuit in 2006. Against all odds, Procter would win a qualifying race at the event against Europe's most successful driver, but Hansen later won the final.

Graduating to European rallycross in 2008, Procter was a midfield contender for the latter years of Hansen's career as a driver, and claimed a sole victory in the French round of the series at Dreux in 2012, where he was joined on the podium by Hansen Motorsport driver Alexander Hvaal.

Procter on Hansen

Kenneth Hansen has always been a statesman in rallycross. It was good to have him at Croft, my home circuit, and even better to be able to beat him in a race there in my old rally car. He chased me all the way; I got myself a little bit excited because I thought: 'God, I've got The Man behind me.' But I managed to win the race. The highlight for me though was what happened afterwards. Kenneth came up to me, shook my hand and said: 'That was a great race, thank you.' That will always stick in my mind.

People see Kenneth Hansen as this big name of the sport, but he's just a normal chap who goes racing because he loves it, has done very well and will talk to anyone. He makes a point of being nice to everyone, that's great for rallycross.

I moved into the European Championship in 2008 with the same Puma first of all and it didn't go very well, but then I bought an ex-Jos Kuypers Ford Focus and it went better from there.

I've always been used to rallying where you're mostly on your own in the stages, so it was quite surreal to be sitting on the start with Kenneth Hansen on one side and Ludvig Hunsbedt and Sverre Isachsen the other; the revs rising and the car doors rattling, it's quite an experience.

I'm just a bus driver, but we eventually managed to win a European round which was an amazing feeling.

Hansen on Procter

When you went to national races in France, Finland or Norway for example, but at Croft especially, you know that even if you are the fastest in Europe you don't just go and win a national event. Somehow the competitors that are there, like Kevin, just took two steps forward, or maybe I lost some. On paper, the competition shouldn't have been there, but it was always tough. Kevin was one of the guys that was a shock for us, with his speed and what he did there. That weekend when he beat me in a qualifying race, it made me wake up to how you can never ever go to a race half-hearted. You need to have full motivation and be determined to win, if it's European Championship event or a national race.

I also learnt something else with Kevin, at the Autosport Show Live Arena in Birmingham. He was driving, and I was in another car. Perhaps I shouldn't have been, I was a little under cover, but I drove one of Pat Doran's cars and after the show I was looking down for the switch to turn off the anti-lag. When I looked up, Kevin was there. We went straight into each other head on. It was not a huge crash, but the cars were broken. When I see him sometimes, I still say sorry. The lesson there is, don't ever take your eyes off the road.

Rallycross has long been a sport where amateur racers could surprise the professionals, as Kevin Procter did at Croft in 2006.

Martin Schanche

Martin Schanche first tried his hand at rallycross in the mid-1970s at which time gravel hillclimbs and ice racing were his main pursuits. In 1977 the Norwegian struck out and contested the European Rallycross Championship. He won his first FIA title the following year. Schanche won six European crowns, making him the second most successful title-winner behind Hansen, and claimed 74 European victories.

For most of his career he engineered and raced Fords; fitting a turbocharged Zakspeed engine created perhaps the ultimate MkII Escort, his role alongside British engineer Mike Endean in creating the revolutionary Xtrac Escort set new standards and he pushed the envelope by evolving Ford's Group B RS200 for rallycross. He returned to Escorts for 1993, and then ended his career by campaigning an Opel Astra from 1999 to 2001, a car that struggled with reliability and returned only two wins.

Known for a fiery temperament that often got him into trouble, including famously stopping the A Final in Finland in 1992 by standing in the track to block his rivals – one of whom he felt had pushed him off the track – when they came round on the next lap.

His engineering prowess matched his driving ability and Schanche developed his own transmission system for his 1993 Escort. Besides rallycross he raced at Le Mans four times, contested the Pikes Peak International Hill Climb and several rallies. After his racing career his became active in politics in his native Norway.

Schanche on Hansen

While other rivals were happy to discuss competing against Hansen, Martin
Schanche was unwilling to contribute his memories of competing against
the Swede, an unusual stance for the Norwegian who is renowned for
wearing his heart on his sleeve and telling it as it is.

The only exception was a brief recollection of one of the most famous
rallycross races in history at Lyngas in Norway, in 1994, where Schanche
and Hansen took their fierce rivalry over the limit in a battle for victory [see
chapter two].

*Previous page and above: Schanche and
Hansen became ferocious rivals after Hansen
graduated to the top class.
Above left: Hansen and Schanche both had
backing from Sachs and it was all smiles
when they were in different championships.
Next pages, left: Hansen avoids trouble as
Schanche crashes.
Right: Hansen, Schanche and Per Eklund
with their children on the podium.*

Hansen on Schanche

At Brands Hatch in the Rallycross Grand Prix in 1994 there was a bit of fighting at the start of the final. Perhaps I was a little hard with Martin at the start, but then we came out of the first corners and up the hill into the right-hander. Martin came up the inside and fully ran into the rear of Per Eklund in front of me. Per's car more or less blew up in a fire explosion. I think that actually that was not meant for Per, it was me that Martin was aiming for, but he missed the braking point or did something wrong. We never spoke about it, but I believe that that was the reason it happened, because perhaps I was guilty at the start of the race, then he saw red and he couldn't control it.

At one of the European Championship events in Wales, at Pembrey, I think me and Martin were on the back row of the grid and I braked a little later into the first corner, a very sharp right. Martin must have been looking at me and didn't want to let me in, because he didn't brake and he ran right over the top of Jean-Luc Pallier's car.

So sometimes perhaps I was part of the reason when the outcome was not so good for him, but that isn't an excuse for what he did.

It was a dream to be able to compete against him when I moved up to Supercar, then to beat him would

have been a very good dream. But when we went to Austria for the first race in 1993, I was in the final together with him. I was so happy just to be there. He was quite fast, I'm not sure if I stepped up or if he was trying to be more safe, but in the final I was able to follow him and that was absolutely fantastic. Then he slid out wide on one corner and I went on the inside and passed him. That was not in my mind, I was happy to be second in my first race, so I was just living in the dream really.

He was the big name and he deserved to be there because he was a big star, especially in Norway. When I competed against him, my name grew in Norway too. And of course, it helped when Martin did something strange, which could happen often, it would be on the television in Sweden that this is the strange guy Hansen is fighting against.

I think he was the best ever to race with because we were very similar in the way we believed to drive a car fast. When he was behind me, or the opposite, he was very fair. He could be 10 centimetres behind my bumper and never touch me. And that's not what a lot of people believe about Martin.

With Per Eklund it was different, but Martin was really fair, apart from when things went wrong. He could get

very, very upset, he saw red and you could not control him, or perhaps he could not control himself. But 95% of the time it was fantastic, except when he was out of his box. It was always interesting.

There was a lot spoken about the fights me and Martin used to have. When we were going to race in Norway for example, I often wondered what was going to happen.

Many Norwegians loved him and also in Europe, but there were also the ones who didn't like him, even in Norway, because he was so different. To go to Lyngas [in Norway] as a Swede to fight with Martin, was lovely but also a little worrying sometimes.

We never had our hands on each other or anything, sometimes we were upset and had words. We really wanted to beat each other, and the newspapers in Norway and Sweden created a lot of that as well. I think it was a good job that there was no social media at that time, then it could have been a mess!

Martin was more of a constructor than me, even though I built my own cars. He actually designed and made transmissions and he was more into the engines than I was. I took these units, built the car and tried to make them work together, so a little different but quite similar too.

One time I went to find him because I needed to talk to him about things we were working on to get better TV coverage, and he was having yet more problems with the Opel. He was sitting there in the bus, in his underwear and crying. So I tried my best to cheer him up. That was the opposite side to him, Martin was very sensitive, maybe that's also what made his temperament go over the top sometimes.

Competing against Martin helped me to really push myself and to try to be better, to try to develop the car and to get better parts. I really hate to lose, even if I think I'm still quite a good loser, but I really hated it when I lost, especially if I couldn't even challenge. If I made a mistake or if we knew that there was something wrong in the set up, then I was okay. But if I had the equipment and I couldn't beat my competitors, that was really hard.

That pushed me harder to find more, so really if it hadn't been for racing people like Martin and having to push myself so hard, I don't think I would have won so many championships. In that way I can thank Martin that I became so successful.

Marcus Gronholm

After national success and promising privateer World Rally Championship appearances, Marcus Gronholm landed his first big-time drive with Peugeot for the latter part of the 1999 WRC season and won a pair of drivers' titles in the next three years. He later switched to the Ford squad before calling time on his rally career in 2007, bowing out while still at the top of his game.

In early 2008 it was announced that Gronholm would race in selected rounds of the European Rallycross Championship with Andreas Eriksson's Ford Team RS Europe (later renamed Olsbergs MSE).

Making his debut at Holjes, Gronholm qualified on pole for the final and, while second-row starter Hansen battled through traffic, took a final lap joker to retain the lead and claim a maiden win. He made further appearances in the Netherlands and Poland, and later raced in the American-based Global Rallycross Championship, before ending his driving career completely after an accident at X Games in 2012, an event which Hansen's team won with Sebastien Loeb.

Forming his own squad for the World Rallycross Championship, Gronholm's GRX team later competed directly against Hansen's team together with former Hansen Motorsport drivers Jussi Pinomaki [team manager] and Timur Timerzyanov [driver].

Above: Hansen chases Gronholm in Poland in 2008.
Right: The pair faced each other again in a crosskart race at Holjes in 2019.

Gronholm on Hansen

I heard a lot of talk about 'Marcus cannot drive in traffic' but they didn't know I had done motocross. It was completely the same, I had done one World Championship [motocross] race with 40 riders on the line, and now you had something around you [in a car] so it was not so bad, I felt okay.

I went to test the car with [Andreas] Eriksson two or three months before and we decided 'Okay, why not do Holjes?'

I hadn't been looking closely at rallycross cars and I didn't know much about rallycross, so I was a little bit lost with the system.

It was raining on Saturday and I was out with slicks in timed practice. I'd been fastest in free practice but almost slowest in the timed session that decided grid positions for Q1. I told Andreas that I thought we should go home but he explained that I'd be with the slowest cars in the first qualifier, so I took the start, won my race and was second fastest to Kenneth. I built it up from there and eventually I was on pole position for the final. It was fun.

I was a little bit pushed in the first corner of the final but managed to keep the lead, then went to the joker on the last lap and came out in front of Kenneth.

We had met before at some sponsor things, and also here and there where we said hello but I didn't really know him. We spoke during the event at Holjes just a little, because I tried to understand a bit with the setup and the tyres and everything how it was.

I did two more races that year in Holland and Poland. They were not good. In Holland we came to the B final but then the race

was stopped because of Morten Bermingrud's accident, then in Poland I had the quickest roll in my life. I think it was four seconds or something, roll and go. It was not a good race at all. I had a break for a couple of years, I did Pikes Peak and then Andreas asked me to go to GRC and it got to be more serious again. In 2012 we planned to do the whole season. I won the first two races, we were leading, but then I had a crash in Los Angeles. After that I thought: 'Okay, maybe I stop competing now, just to keep the head still in one piece.'

Hansen's team is strong. They know what to do and he is always there, so it's not so easy and we have to do everything perfectly to beat them. I'm really happy that they made it to be on the grid in 2019. It was a last minute decision, but without them it would have been a nothing championship, in my opinion. I would say Kenneth is a very nice guy and fair, but on the track, they sometimes play dirty together with Kevin and Timmy. They use tactics, and Timmy never gives up; he is pushing. But it's okay, nothing to complain about.

Hansen on Gronholm

I'd met Marcus a couple of times at the Swedish rally, but the first time we spent some time together was in France with [sponsor] Total. We didn't know what it was when we were invited to go to Paris, then from Paris we had a complete plane with a lot of drivers and other people and we went to Pau in the South of France to visit some factories, go to some seminars and have a dinner. We spent two days there, and we had time to talk with each other.

When Marcus and I talk we speak Swedish, because he's from the Swedish speaking part of Finland. He is a little similar to the Kristofferssons, he is the kind of guy who is making little jokes all the time, he's enjoyable to be around.

He was fast when he came to Holjes, then on the last lap of the final he was going to the joker and I was on the normal lap. I wasn't too rough there [at the joker exit]. Marcus had shown he was a good racer and he didn't make a mess of things. Perhaps I could have made a harder fight when he came back onto the main track, but at that time I was racing for the championship and he was not, so it was not a big problem. Some people said I lifted off and gave him the win, that I let him go. That is not true, I was just clever. If I had fought for the position it could have been a problem for both of us.

Similar to when Sebastien [Loeb] went to X Games to drive our DS3, when rally drivers are out in front they know how to drive a car and it's difficult to beat them. But they don't have the knowledge of the racing, the contact. If they are fourth of fifth in the race, then it's a different story. That's the complete package to be a rallycross driver. I told Sebastien, and I think Marcus learned also, sometimes when you go into the first corner you need to show: 'Don't mess with me! This is my corner, don't even think of taking my line'. I don't mean push anyone off, but you can brake very late and show them that you will not give this away. That's a part of the game to try to learn.

It was when we were in LA for X Games that Marcus had his big crash [see chapter eight] in

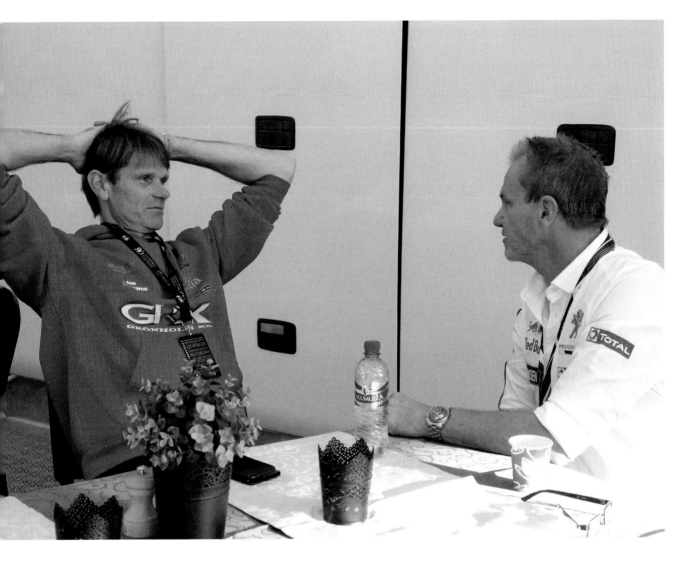

Gronholm and Hansen are now rival team owners in the FIA World Rallycross Championship.

practice. Everyone was very upset and we didn't know what the outcome would be. Marcus was in hospital and of course there were rumours. Andreas [Eriksson] spoke to us all and there were questions about if it was right to continue. Sebastien was ready to stop but we spoke about it and because we didn't know how it would be, we decided to do timed practice, because if we didn't and Marcus recovered then we would be done; we would never make it back from not doing timed practice. Later we got some good news about Marcus, and of course Sebastien won the race.

We talk a lot in person and on the phone about what's going now we both have teams in the World Championship. We need each other to be there. We spoke during the winter of 2018-2019 [when Audi, Peugeot and Volkswagen withdrew works-support from the series], because he said if Hansen was not going to race, it didn't make sense for him to be there with GRX.

When he saw the news that we would do the Titans series, he sent me a text saying that there was no point GRX being in the World Championship if we were not there. I called him to tell him that we were still working on World RX too and in the end he entered a team while we were still working on it. With Jussi Pinomaki as the Team Manager, his team is very good.

Sverre Isachsen

Sverre Isachsen graduated to the European Rallycross Championship in 2002 having twice won the national series in his native Norway.

Racing a Ford Focus in Division One, Isachsen claimed his first podium at the end of his debut season, then joined Hansen on the rostrum in his third podium appearance in Norway a year later. Isachsen's first win came in 2004 at Höljes where Hansen was second. He then earned his first championship trophy by finishing third in the 2005 series, behind experienced campaigners Hansen and Michael Jernberg.

The Norwegian built a strong team around him and was a regular podium contender until hitting his stride in 2009 when, using a chassis developed by Ingvar Gunnarsson and engines from Julian Godfrey, he took the first of three consecutive titles. Isachsen called time on his European career at the end of 2011, and stood alongside Hansen on the podium at the Swede's final Euro RX appearance in the Czech Republic.

Isachsen subsequently drove for the Subaru rallycross team in America.

Left: A puncture caused after a clash with Sverre Isachsen probably cost Hansen the win in Finland in 2010.

Isachsen on Hansen

When I did my first race in Europe, Kenneth was the king. He was winning everything. Everybody looked up to him and of course everything was nice around him, with the tents and the car, everything was 100%. That was the man you needed to beat.

In 2002 and 2003 it was luck if I got to the finish or not, I was quite crazy at that time so there were ups and downs, but I think from 2004 I was starting to do something. I took my first Division One win at Holjes, with Kenneth in the final and that was really good.

Things were a little better in 2005 and then starting in 2006 I was at the front more often and there was a lot of fighting and battles with Kenneth. We were not always the best friends, but in the end it was quite okay. I think Kenneth and I were really good friends, we talked a lot and had a lot of nice parties also.

I remember two races that were special; one in France, Kenneth was winning, I was second and I think at one point we were 30 meters off the track. That was a hell of a fight, it was a really crazy A final and a fight to the finish line.

Then we were in Holjes and I was winning, we had the same kind of fight but that time he was number two. After the finish Susann [Hansen] came over to Kenneth, she was quite upset and she said: 'Why the hell didn't you push Isachsen off the track?' Kenneth replied quite clearly: 'If I had pushed Isachsen off then we would have been standing in Trysil [40km away and over the border in Norway] with the two cars'. Then I thought: 'He is crazy!'

In 2008 we were fighting for wins, and I beat him sometimes, but in 2009 we were really good, we had sorted out our car, closed the gap and we were in the front. It was special. The first European Championship is always the best. That was fantastic.

Everybody said we were cheating. I think in 2009 I was 61 times to technical scrutineering during the races that season. There were a lot of rumours but I am an actor also, so I was building up the rumours too. That was the whole game, the same with Kenneth, he was playing a small game there too. We are clean players but you need to play a little bit around to make the racing more intense, boiling up all the people. That was the whole thing.

Finland 2010 was a special race. We had a hard fight then my car stopped just before the finish line so Liam Doran won with a car from Kenneth. The car did break down, but we agreed after the race it was the right result because we had a hard fight, we were maybe a little bit too hard and it meant we were in the same position in the European championship before and after Finland.

I am not the type who is going in the same line the whole time, I need a challenge to be hungry so after three years on top I felt I needed something new. Somebody like Kenneth, he was born with this thing. I have big respect that he manages to stay for such a long time but he has a serious team round him with serious people. That is his life.

Right: Hansen and Isachsen talk, while a young Joel Christoffersson [see chapter six] listens in.

Hansen on Isachsen

Isachsen was a little like Larsson, he came and learned the sport, and then, when he really got into it, he was very fast. He was also very determined, maybe not as strong as Eivind Opland had been but a little similar and he built up a strong team around him.

I think they spent quite a lot of money; they changed a lot of engines, they turned everything up to the limit more or less and many times on Saturday night they changed the engine, but he got it together and was fast. It was difficult for us because some races I couldn't follow. Like at Lydden in 2010 for example I had a very good run, very good when you look on the onboard – we still have them – but in the end it was not possible to follow him. Also once in Germany [at Estering] I was closing and was very close on the last lap when he went into the joker from the lead. It felt like I was on his bumper, but in those conditions, in the wet the time was more or less no difference and I couldn't manage to be in front of him over the finish line. That was hard.

There was some talk around that time that he was using some sort of torque control. We never knew if they did or not but we knew that the car was very fast and efficient with not a lot of wheelspin. It was very good, but if there was something wrong in the car, we will never have an answer. You can't say anyone has cheated before they are caught, so it wouldn't be fair to blame him to be cheating and winning.

At one race in Finland [at Kouvola] I was very disappointed with Sverre. I was leading and he hit me in the side at the right hander after the jump. I had made many races there and didn't have a win, so we felt like we deserved to have this success. But then, shit! I took a hit and got a puncture. I was not really angry that day, I was really disappointed and sad. I remember he came to talk and apologised after, but that was a hard one because of all that work and it looked very good, but no win again.

Liam Doran won with one of our cars. There was something strange there [when Isachsen slowed in the final corner]. I think Sverre felt quite bad about the contact, because he came to me after when I sitting in the bus. I don't think it was deliberate, I don't think he would have apologised that way if it was.

But I don't know what happened in the last corner. I was so disappointed with my own result so I didn't care about that. I've heard there are a lot of stories about what happened, but I don't know.

Per-Ove Davidsson

Having started his competition journey in Swedish stage rallies in 1976, aged 20, Per-Ove Davidsson, known as PeO, switched to the Volvo Rallycross Cup in Sweden in 1980, but returned to rallies again from '82 to '84.

Jumping back into rallycross with a Volvo 240, he won the Swedish title in 1985, then finished second in the European Championship in 1986, before claiming the title in 1987. He placed fourth in the 1988 defence of his title before quitting the series because of budget issues and with the Volvo being outclassed by the Sierra Cosworth.

Davidsson returned to rallycross near the end of the millennium with a Group N Mitsubishi Evo in a line-up with Dan Andersson, before departing the sport and competing rallies for fun.

Davidsson on Hansen

I won the Swedish championship in 1985 and that's when I met Kenneth for the first time, but I didn't know him. I learned to know him when he started to race the Volvo 240 in the European Championship. It took a couple of races before we got to know him well, I helped him a lot in the first year because he had not so many spare parts, so he had to borrow them. I let him take my spare parts and then he had to give it back for the next race. It worked very well together and we drove together to the races through Europe.

It was a big adventure because we had not so good vehicles to take the cars, so it was many very exciting trips. To go from Sweden to Barcelona is quite a long way.

Rallycross seemed very simple at that time if you compare with what it is today. I was the first in European rallycross that had a marquee [awning]. I put the marquee on my bus so we could work under it when it was raining. No-one else had it. I remember Martin Schanche telling me that it was cheating to have that over our heads.

I should have won the first year I drove in Europe in '86, I was just one or two points behind Anders Norstedt and I was leading two races when I had a puncture and I finished in sixth place instead.

In the final round at Estering in 1987, I was so nervous before the A final so I had to ask Kenneth to hold back and not overtake me, because it was so tight to Herbert Breiteneder in the points. I drove so badly in that final because I was so nervous, but everything went my way in the end, but it's good to remember that race.

Kenneth was prepared to help. We tried to help each other every time, if we could. Me and Kenneth were more pals than I was pals with Anders Norstedt. He didn't like me because I drove too fast. He didn't like it when I went to the first race in Austria in 1986, I had never been outside Sweden with rallycross before and it was my first race in the Volvo 240 Turbo, but I was 2.5 seconds in front of him in practice.

Kenneth was fair every time to race, of course we are both from Sweden. I was faster than him every time but we helped each other. It was very fair, maybe too fair.

He changed a lot when he was bigger with Citroen and I think not everyone likes him now as they did at that time. I can tell you that my money was on the Norwegian man [Andreas Bakkerud] in the 2019 World Championship final in South Africa [see chapter seven], and I think many Swedes don't like Hansen so much now. Sorry to say it, but that's the way it is.

It's because of the personality. It's too much. They [Kenneth and Susann Hansen] are extremely lucky to have two boys, such excellent drivers both of them, but it's too much family. They can have it that way but a lot of people don't like it.

But, every year I drove with him it was perfect and we had a lot of fun at every race. To the race and from the race we'd go together and it's a lovely to remember that time.

A couple of my mechanics started to go with Kenneth after I stopped rallycross and they said he had a very good set up on the car for every race. In '86 and '87 we had the same set up for every track, but he started to modify the shock absorbers and springs for different kinds of tracks. I think that was one of the successes he made, and also he was very good at getting the money. I was very bad at that; I tried to pay it from my own pocket.

Previous page: Hansen shares a ride with PeO Davidsson on a parade lap.
Above: Davidsson leads Hansen and Bengt Ekstrom at a Swedish Championship event at Alvsbyn in 1988.

Hansen on Davidsson

When we got the Lasse Nystrom Volvo [for 1987], Per-Ove was the guy we wanted to understand. We tried to look into what he was doing because he ran the same car. But, he was very difficult to beat. He was just better.

The last race that we did together was in the Swedish Championship in 1988 and we were a little better by then; I think we were a little more into the detail. He'd won some races in the Swedish Championship and then missed some, and I won those, so we were quite equal when we came to the final round. It was terrible weather, it was like floating with rain and we were a little more clever with the tyres than him and I beat him in the final to win the Swedish Championship.

He was someone you looked up to and it was really impossible to beat him in Europe. Sometimes I did but that was more luck. And then you went into the Swedish Championship and it was the same there; it was difficult. When he had a normal run you couldn't follow him.

So when I finally did that in the [1988] championship it was like I'd come over the edge and taken the next step. It was an important win, that one. Per-Ove was also a very fair driver from what I remember, but we didn't have a lot of fights, because when he was in front I couldn't follow, then if he was behind it was more protecting. He was just faster more or less all the time.

I think he was one or two years ahead with the equipment too. But during that period we picked up things, we learnt and it made us stronger in the end. Even if it was hard at the time and it felt really impossible, we worked hard, tried to be better and in the end, it paid off.

Left: Davidsson and Hansen flank
Englishman Trevor Reeves at Lydden Hill in
1988.

Morten Bermingrud

Having won five Supernational rallycross crowns in his native Norway driving a rear-wheel drive Volvo, Morten Bermingrud bought Hansen's 2001-specification Citroen Xsara in early 2002.

On his top-level European Championship debut at Holjes (Sweden), Bermingrud finished on the podium, behind Hansen and Ludvig Hunsbedt.

With his own team working closely with Hansen Motorsport, Bermingrud was twice on the podium again in 2003, won in Portugal and Czech Republic in 2004, and was again victorious in Poland the following season, each time joined on the podium by Hansen.

A consistent front-runner, the Norwegian started in all but two A finals in 2006, and also acquired a second Xsara to run for customers, but his driving career was changed significantly by a crash at Valkenswaard in 2008. As the cars launched away from the start grid in the B final, Bermingrud's car hit a wall to the right of the circuit and he sustained serious injuries, breaking both legs.

Although his team built a new Citroen C4, with guidance from Hansen, and Bermingrud returned to action late the following season, and subsequently continued racing at the highest level for several years, he was unable to match his earlier form.

Left: Hansen supplied cars to Morten Bermingrud, here he leads the Norwegian in Hungary.

Bermingrud on Hansen

We looked at buying [Jan Arthur] Iversen's Ford Focus, and some other cars too. We also tried to do something with [Eivind] Opland's Mitsubishi. But, we landed on the Xsara and for that we were very happy. In the first ever race for me in that car at Holjes, we were third. That was good.

The situation of having the car from Kenneth worked very well and it was the start of a very good friendship. He helped me a lot, I thought maybe that would be for three or four races and we wouldn't see him more, but that was not what happened. He helped a lot, actually I don't know if we could have done it without his help.

We discussed driving and compared starts, data and everything, but in the end a race is a race.

On the track he was clever, very clever. He knew the limits, where to push and where not to. I think he was a very good driver and the smartest one when I was driving. If he was not first, he was always waiting for the possibility to go by, and he did it in a fair way I think. Yes he was hard and used every opportunity to pass you, but he was fair; he wouldn't push you off.

In one of my best years I was in nine A finals, but I took three victories in the European Championship, that was the highlight. The first one was in Portugal, that was a big moment. It was at Lousada and with the huge crowd there, it was amazing. It was big moment for me to beat Kenneth. He was third.

We didn't expect to be up to the pace so quickly, but after that it was hard to get new money to update the car. Then in 2008 I had the big crash in Valkenswaard and that put me back a bit.

A car hit me at the start, I went off the road and hit the wall in the worst place possible. When they did the A final it was like a protest, the drivers just driving slowly after each other.

But, already in hospital, with both legs broken and everything, my team started to say that we must build a new car, so we did a C4. That was also with a lot of help from Kenneth, because he had already built one.

We went to him and measured everything and took lots of pictures of his car. That was many years after we started the relationship.

At the races in that time we had very good parties, and I always had the tie around my head. When somebody won, there was a party at that tent on Sunday evening. Whatever team it was, there was a party and we did it together. Then between the races, we go to big towns and had a nice time. That's stopped totally now. There's a lot more money involved now.

It was special then, and I couldn't have done it like the sport is now. I'm really happy that we started at the right time for me and we did what we could do. And for Kenneth he has a record that will never be beaten. That's amazing.

Hansen on Bermingrud

With the Citroen ZX, we built three. We kept one in the end, one we removed the shell – because the floor was the same as the Xsara – to build a show car, and the third one we took all the parts from. So we never had a car to sell.

It was something new to sell a car like that to Morten. I don't know why we did it at the time actually, I think we thought it would be interesting to develop the business.

We hadn't met many times before he bought the car, but after that we worked quite closely for several years. We helped him and supported him. It was successful, but he was very unpolite because he started to beat me sometimes. That was not what I had in mind at all!

Morten is a great guy, he is a lot of fun and can do things you don't expect.

His team was really good to work with. Perhaps it could be seen as a not totally good business way [to operate like that]. Normally you don't continue to help that much but they were a good bunch of people and we enjoyed working with them.

I don't think we had many big battles, from what I remember anyway. Perhaps we had some contact sometimes, but nothing bad at all. Morten was perhaps too fair many times, but he was fast so when he got it all together, he made in to the top of the podium.

His crash at Valkenswaard was very bad. At the moment there I thought he had died. We rushed out onto the circuit and it was a strange feeling. It was very good to see that he was at least okay, but it took him a long time to recover. Morten for sure didn't deserve that, it shouldn't have happened at all but in a strange way I think it was a good thing for the sport. We learnt a lot then about how you need to fit into and sit in a car, and about track safety. It was like [Ayrton] Senna's accident in Formula 1, it's just a pity that there should be a high cost for that.

Left: Hansen gets sandwiched by Bermingrud and Michael Jernberg.

Top: Bermingrud (left of pic) with Kenneth and Susann Hansen, and Stig-Olov Walfridson, in 2004 when all three drove Hansen-built cars.

Above: The crash at Valkenswaard in 2008 stalled Bermingrud's career but led to safety improvements.

Ludvig Hunsbedt

Having begun his motor sport career in 1978, Ludvig Hunsbedt was an almost ever-present force through Hansen's European rallycross career. He finished second to Hansen at Valkenswaard (Holland) driving a BMW M3 in 1990, then beat the Swede to victory in the second round of the 1991 season at Melk (Austria).

While the Norwegian, renowned for being a robust competitor on track, was a regular event winner, it wasn't until the regulations for the European Championship's second tier switched to Group N that Hunsbedt claimed his first crown. Driving a Ford Escort RS Cosworth in 1993, the year in which Hansen graduated to the top category.

In 1996, driving a Martin Schanche-built Ford Escort, Hunsbedt also moved to the top category, won the second round at Lousada (Portugal) and finished second to Hansen in the championship. He then won four times the following season to beat Hansen to the title. Hunsbedt remained a front-runner and took a three-year sabbatical from 2004, before returning with a Volvo S40 and resuming battle where he had left off. Having contested his final full term in 2011, Hunsbedt made a single World Rallycross start at Holjes in 2014.

Hunsbedt on Hansen

Kenneth had everything you need to be number one. I tell everybody, if you want to be number one, you have four different points you have to manage, and every point is 25% important. First is that you have to be a good driver, and Kenneth was a good driver. You have to have a good car, and Kenneth always had a good car. You have to have a good team, and he had a good team. And, you had to have a good budget. All of these are the reasons Kenneth managed to be the champion so many times.

Many times we were good drivers and maybe we had a good cars, but we didn't have the budget or the best team. That is the reason Kenneth won, and won.

He was a very clever driver, and he was one of the people who I trusted when I was going beside him. If we were going into a jump, over a jump or into a chicane, if I was beside I know that Kenneth would not touch me or push me into the wall or something.

He was a very good driver, but most important for me was that he was a very fair driver. Maybe if you ask Martin Schanche he won't say the same, but for me he was.

There was one time at Momarken that Kenneth and I were going together over the jump and into the next corner and we were going very sideways. It was stupid of me to put the car there, but I trusted him.

It was very good to win the championship against him. He wanted to win and he did everything to do that. He was very clever with all the rules, he knew how to make the right protest [for instance]; he was very clever with everything.

Hansen on Hunsbedt

At Montalegre when Ludvig came back [in 2007] after he had stopped for a while, I remember he went around the paddock and apologised to everyone before the race. There were some drivers who didn't know him so well and they asked why he was apologising and he said: 'Because I'll probably hit you or something, so it's better that I say sorry before that happens!' He didn't come to me, though.

I think a lot of people on the race track didn't like Ludvig because he was quite hard, but we had a very good relationship on the circuit. We had very hard battles but we gave each other space, it was never the intention to put the other one off.

Ludvig and me had many, many good fights. One time at Holjes he was a little hard to me in the velodrome, so when we came down the hill I gave him a little nudge going into the next corner and he was completely sideways. I was laughing in the car because I knew how he would have been at that moment. I knew if he had spun I would have got a black flag, but that's not what I wanted to do; I just wanted to give him something to show that I was not going take any of that kind of stuff from him.

We had a moment at Essay where we came out of the long second corner there and then down through the compression we were side-by-side, with Ludvig on the inside. You don't dare to do that with many drivers, but he gave me space, we survived the situation and I think I even won the fight. I knew when we went in it was not a good decision to go side-by-side there, but we did and perhaps Ludvig was also surprised that someone dared to do it.

I think together we both looked at everything like a complete season, or a complete race, and in the end, may the best man win.

You could really race him and try to do some stupid things, but it worked with Ludvig. That was so good, we had some very strange passes sometimes but we allowed each other to make those manoeuvres without putting a stick in the wheel, because we knew it would be the opposite next time around. Like the time we were side-by-side for half a lap in Momarken. He was in the Escort then, I gave him space and I think he won that one. He was hard but very enjoyable to drive with.

Outside the car he had a 'fox behind the ear' like we say, but in a good, positive way. He always had a card in his pocket, he tried things and he could trick you sometimes but in a fun and good way. I don't have any bad feelings about Ludvig.

Previous page: Hunsbedt chases Hansen at Essay in France.
Top left: Hansen leads Hunsbedt's BMW M3.
Centre left: Close combat in 2008.
Bottom left: Hunsbedt and Hansen have been the best of rivals.
Above: On the top step of the podium together with Hunsbedt.

Anders Norstedt

Having begun his rallycross career in the late 1970s, it was in 1983 – the year in which Hansen first competed in local rallycross events in Sweden – that Anders Norstedt had his first concerted assault on the Group A category of the European series with a Saab 99.

The next year he was never off the podium, and won three times to claim the title, before repeating the success in the next two years.

By the time Hansen arrived on the international scene in 1987 the Saab 900 Turbo was beginning to show its age and Norstedt finished third overall in his compatriot's first two seasons.

Norstedt's final Group A campaign was in 1989 – Hansen's first championship winning season – before the pair met again in the top category in the next decade. But, Norstedt's self-developed Saab 900 4x4 was never a match the top-flight opposition.

Left: At Lydden in 1989, Hansen gets the drop on Norstedt's Saab.
Next pages: Left: Norstedt jokes with Stig Blomqvist while Hansen and Eivind Opland mess around.
Right: Hansen leads Norstedt at Sils-Girona in Spain in 1987.

Norstedt on Hansen

Kenneth and I have more or less the same background because he has a family that was totally interested in making good results. I had the same in my career and I think that's very important that you have the harmony to do what you do. If you don't have support at home it's very difficult do what you need on the race track.

I was driving in the Swedish Championship when Kenneth first start in local races. I saw his driving and thought that he was like me, he was very serious with what he was doing, he wanted to have everything perfect, the car, tyres, development, people around him. I could see he was thinking in the same way about rallycross as me.

He was really competitive when he came to race in the European Championship. If you compared him with the people in the same age and the same step of the career, he was absolutely fantastic at that time.

It was absolutely the same hard races [in the late '80s] that they have today, but I think you needed to be more competitive at that time, because you had so many drivers in every class. Swedish events often had qualification races and it was just 20 or 25 drivers going through to the main event.

I think we had more fun, we worked together, we supported each other, we were more like a family,

even if we were competitors. You needed to fight on the track but off the track you were good friends.

When I was driving the Saab and was European Champion in 1984, '85 and '86, the reason that I got it three times, was the same reason that Kenneth did what he did.

I had the Saab factory behind me in the middle of the '80s and that means I had the technology, the experience, I had everything they knew from the factory to put into the car.

I think the big thing in his career was when he took the step up to the Citroen [in 1993]. He had huge contact with the Citroen factory where they had the rally cars. You can take a lot of things from their development, and I think that's the main reason why Kenneth was there for so many years. If you have a factory behind you, you can make good results all the time. Kenneth and I were the only drivers who had real factory support.

When he got the Citroen, I remember one time we were racing on Kenneth's home track at Kinnekulle. I took the start in front of him and I thought I had good speed but Kenneth was a little bit faster. That made me a bit confused because I should be absolutely at the top and Kenneth was on the way up. When he passed me

after a couple of laps and I could see the speed he had and I had no chance to catch him. That was the first time I saw him in race shape like that and it really was very impressive.

For Kenneth rallycross has been a lifestyle. I was an international driver for 15 years and it's a lifestyle, you're in that kind of bubble. I think he's going to have a huge problem when he packs up and sits at home. When you're doing it, you're just in the races, you live for it and you sleep for it. It's two different worlds to live in.

Hansen on Norstedt

Anders is an ambassador for rallycross and for motor sport. He did a lot of good things and I think he was a little bit unfortunate sometimes, because he deserved better than the results he got when he went into the top class, he had some troubles there.

He was a very sporting guy and like I said a very positive ambassador for the sport; not like Martin Schanche or Per Eklund.

When he did something, he did it very professionally. It looked good, he had good sponsors, and promoted things well. He was a guy you looked up to when he did things. It was the same as with Bjorn Skogstad.

Those two were a big part in why we became quite professional in our appearance. Nowadays when we look back at our bus and how it looked in our paddock and what we did for promotion, it's still very good that we were doing those things 25 years ago.

Anders was one of the front runners in the Swedish Championship and in the European Championship when I went there for the first time.

It was tricky for us to beat people like him, but of course during that period we learnt and learnt and learnt. I think it was good that we were not successful in the beginning, because we needed to work hard to get there and to try to achieve the dream. Even if the success wasn't there, that was the route to success, because if I would have been successful, I think I'd have suffered more later in the career.

Anders and I had a lot of hard races together, many times at Valkenswaard, but the Volvo and Saab were quite different on the track. The Volvo was more-or-less better at the start, but the front-wheel drive Saab was fast around the track, especially when we went to tracks like Lydden.

Lars Larsson

Lars Larsson entered European Rallycross Championship events in the top division from 1999, first driving an Audi Coupe for his debut at the Swedish round, before switching to an Audi A4, with which he claimed his first win in Poland in 2003, a country in which the Swede would win regularly.

Shifting to a more compact and competitive Skoda Fabia from 2004, a second win followed at Slomczyn in Poland, before Larsson ran Hansen close in the points through the opening half of the 2006 campaign. He then won twice in the second half of the season, notably again at Slomczyn, to take the title fight to the final round, where Hansen didn't make it out of the B final as Larsson took the crown.

Twelve months on, Hansen led the points into the final two rounds and only needed to finish ahead of Larsson in the season finale to wrap up the title. But victory for Larsson again at Slomczyn, before Hansen failed to score a single point in the Czech Republic – one of only two occasions that would happen in Hansen's entire European career – gave Larsson his second crown, after which he immediately hung up his helmet.

Like several of Hansen's former rivals on track, Larsson was later a rival in the paddock as a team owner and mentor to son Robin, who won the European Championship in 2014 and 2019.

Larsson on Hansen

It was hard to race against Kenneth in the beginning because we didn't have the same material. I'd met him at the very start of my career, I didn't really remember when the first time was but he was a nice guy, who was also very fast on track.

The more I got to know him, he was still very fast, but he could be hard on track too. We had a lot of good and hard fights, especially when I moved to the Skoda and was much more competitive. For sure we didn't get along all the time, because we both wanted to win and were hard competitors, but I don't remember any specific races where anything bad happened. Mostly it was good times, Kenneth was good to race with.

Our relationship didn't change when I got more similar equipment and experience to race against him directly, but of course it was much more fun to fight against him and it was wonderful to beat him and the other experienced guys like Michael Jernberg to the title in 2006. That's something I had been working at for a long time. If I'm honest, the second title felt easier to win. I stopped racing after that because I was happy with the results I had accomplished, and I felt it was time to end on top. I didn't want to keep on going for so many years like Kenneth did.

We are still both in the paddock now and we speak sometimes, but mainly I look back on my time racing on the European Championship against Kenneth with happy memories.

Previous page: Hansen leads Larsson at Kinnekulle in 2004.
Above: Larsson would eventually beat Hansen to the European Championship twice.
Above right: Close combat in 2003.

Hansen on Larsson

Lars came into the sport and he learnt very well; he built a good team, got a good package for the car and in the end he was able to beat me several times. He did the job very well.

We didn't have a lot of trouble and we got on well, but of course we did have some big fights on the track when we were not happy at all with each other, but that's the way it is when you are rivals.

Once in Strangnas he was coming from the joker and we had small contact, he gave me a touch in the rear and I couldn't turn-in to the hairpin. I don't remember if we complained or not, but we were called to the stewards, I remember he was very angry because he got a penalty.

He was also not happy when I passed him on the last lap at

Greinbach [Austria] when he was leading. I had a very good race, I think I was down to fourth at the start, overtook Jos Kuypers and Morten Bermingrud, then on the last lap I caught Lars on the fast tarmac section and overtook him at the second corner. He was quite angry at me because he said I had been completely on the grass. That was not true, I had two wheels on the grass and two wheels on the circuit. It was a correct move but he was not happy. I can understand that though because in the car it could feel to him that I was completely off the circuit, before you see any pictures or anything.

At the last race in 2007, when Lars won the championship for the second time, I had a big crash in the second qualifier. I was almost free after the start, but in

the middle of the start straight something happened with Sverre Isachsen and some other guys [Olivier Anne and Frode Holte]. Isachsen got pushed over and hit me in the rear so I got spun around and straight into the barrier. I was angry at Isachsen but of course it was not his intention to turn around on the straight before the first corner.

That was hard, it happened very fast. I had some pain in my neck after, which was strange because I was wearing a HANS device. But, the seat brackets had failed and when the seat goes down, the harness doesn't work and the HANS doesn't work either. We knew then we needed better mountings for the seat. Today the regulations for that are a totally different story. That's important.

Johan Kristoffersson

Much like Timmy Hansen, Johan Kristoffersson started his motor sport exploits in circuit racing, and with significant success. Having won touring car titles in Europe and Scandinavia, where he also dominated Porsche Carrera Cup racing, and with the lure of a World Championship on the horizon, Kristoffersson switched to rallycross and together with his father's Volkswagen Sweden-supported Kristoffersson Motorsport team, laid out a four-year plan to become world champion.

While the route that plan took changed over time – KMS joining forces with Marklund Motorsport in 2016 and subsequently Petter Solberg's PSRX concern for a works-assisted assault – ultimately the time frame was almost perfectly realised.

With Volkswagen Motorsport's Polo R, Kristoffersson won the drivers' title in 2017 and then won 11 of the 12 events the following year to secure a second title. The only man to beat the Swede that year was Peugeot driver Sebastien Loeb, who had Hansen as Team Manager.

Despite Hansen's record number of titles, his own best win rate in a season was six from 10 races, in 2002 and 2003.

Left: Johan Kristoffersson leads the chase of Petter Solberg, himself chased by Hansen brothers Timmy and Kevin.

Kristoffersson on Hansen

When I was young I spent most of my time in the paddock with Per Eklund. Then Per, my father and Kenneth were the Swedish guys really fighting on the track. So when I was doing some pranks, it was usually against Kenneth because I got ice cream from Per.

I remember one time Kenneth was sponsored by a meat company and he got free meat. Eklund was a bit jealous of Kenneth because they were eating nice meat, and Eklund was eating cheap sausages. Hansen had a big refrigerator with all this frozen meat and Per told me go there and unplug the cables. The next day everything was melted and the meat was destroyed, then I got ice cream from Per.

Another time I took a sticker from Per with his sponsor on and put it on the bumper of Hansen's car. There were a lot of things like that.

I didn't spend a lot of time with the Hansens, but of course I knew of what Kenneth did. 14 titles, unbelievable! He was the one that always had so much luck – if there was a bumper hanging off his car, he never got a technical flag because just before he was about to get it, the bumper would fall off. He never had a puncture, it was always things like that. But after all these years you realise it's not only luck.

I watch a lot of old videos because I was quite young when my father was doing rallycross, so I don't remember that much about it. But even in the videos you can see that Kenneth was ahead of his time, quite

smooth in the driving, efficient and I think he also had a car which was suited to his smooth driving as well.

In Arvika the news was always between my father and Eklund, but in the big newspapers in Sweden it was between Eklund and Kenneth, they had some really big fights, and in those days rallycross could be very rough.

Later when I was racing against Timmy and Kevin, it was nice to still see my father and Kenneth involved in the paddock and special because they have so much experience and you could see how much they enjoyed the sport growing so much.

You can recognise a few things in Timmy and Kevin, especially Timmy, from Kenneth. Timmy is smiling all the time but you know that he has some foxes behind the ears. Kenneth is still the same, if he is really, really angry you cannot see it on him because he's still smiling, but you know that he's angry. That's exactly the same as it was years ago when he was driving.

Hansen on Kristoffersson

When Tommy and I became friends we had the same sponsor and we did a lot of traveling together. Tommy was a master of jokes and playing games behind the scenes, but always in a good way. He was a lot of fun to be with.

Johan is so much like his father. When you have a discussion with him, the way he looks at things, it's so funny. He's a fantastic guy. On top of that, in the Volkswagen with PSRX, he was more or less unbeatable. The way he handled that Polo and, in all situations, even when he was in a difficult position, he managed to win.

It was frustrating to compete against him, but you also admire his way because it didn't look like he was stressed, even if he was in a bad position he took it very calmly and when he needed to do that extra start or that extra fast lap, he did it. Of course it was frustrating to see him winning all the time, but like Susann said to me: 'Can you imagine when you had your best years, how frustrating it was for your competitors?'

I never thought of it in that way. For sure it's not good for the sport when one person is winning all the time, but you can't go to a race and try to be average. It's just for the others to be better and try to beat you.

The best years I had when I had a lot of wins, not as many as Johan, but when you are in that position it's easy to not be motivated when you go to a race, because you have so much confidence in yourself. That could also harm you a little because sometimes you needed to wake up, if you weren't fast from the beginning, then you needed to catch up.

Johan managed to handle that very well. Even when his teammate needed to win to take third place in the championship [in South Africa, 2018]; of course, he tried to help Petter [Solberg] but he couldn't just disappear and in the end he won anyway.

His mentality must be very strong to be able to put it together even when he didn't need to, because even though he won the championship quite early, he continued to win events.

We should have been able to beat Johan. We had the resources and we had the people, but in the end we couldn't beat him. The complete package was not good enough.

Above left: Kristoffersson leads the Hansen boys at Holjes in 2018.
Top: Kristoffersson was World Champion in 2017 and 2018.
Above: Kristoffersson won 11 of the 12 events in the 2018 World Championship, in Canada beating Timmy Hansen and Sebastien Loeb to the the victory.

Manfred Stohl

For the majority of Hansen's time racing in the European Rallycross Championship, Austrian driver Manfred Stohl was competing in a wide range of classes and series around the world in rallying. Stohl's career culminated in winning the Production World Rally Championship in 2000, and finishing on the podium at the World Rally Championship's highest level six times.

Stohl is no stranger to rallycross and even spectated at Melk during his professional career.

Like Hansen, Stohl also formed his own team out of his driving career. He made his rallycross debut with Petter Solberg's squad in the final round of the 2014 World rallycross season, then teamed up with Austrian entrepreneur Max Pucher the following year. Stohl drove in the series full-time but without significant success, before ending his time behind the wheel to focus on leading his own STARD business, which has competed in World RX since 2015.

Stohl's research and development operation was also responsible for the world's first electric rallycross Supercar prototype.

Above: Manfred Stohl tackles Timmy Hansen on his rallycross debut in Argentina 2014.
Above right: As a team-owner, Stohl is now often alongside Hansen in the World Championship spotters' tower.

Stohl on Hansen

I am born into a motor sport family and my father visited rallycross when I was a child. I went to all the races at Melk, and I was a big fan of Kenneth, he was always like a star in this sport. I always looked up to him and his impressive career, and even when I was doing rallies, when I had time I would go to Melk to watch the European Championship races.

The Hansen family is 120% focussed on rallycross; they give their money, their private time and everything for rallycross and it's Kenneth who's at the front of the train pulling it along. I like that very much and I take my hat off to him.

He was absolutely the right person for Peugeot in the role he had. The relationship they had was not by accident, it was very, very important for Peugeot to have an experienced guy like Kenneth in the team to give advice to help them.

Even though our team has been in rallycross for a little time now, I still looking up to people like Kenneth with his experience. It's a pleasure to compete against him, but he is very hard to beat. Kenneth was here 30 years ago and he will still be here in another 30 years, and that makes him very different from almost everyone else.

Hansen on Stohl

I never drove against Manfred, but I was so surprised when I first met him at Melk because he knew a lot about the sport and me. Coming from the WRC, where he was a star name, and knowing as much as he did about rallycross, I didn't expect that.

I had the same feeling when I met Jean Ragnotti, I didn't believe he knew who I was and then it was the complete opposite.

That's an honour, especially when it's a person that you have looked up to and has achieved a lot and worked hard, and I know Manfred did that, he tried many ways to achieve a lot and to be there in WRC. In that way we are not very different I think, we share a lot of passion, not totally whatever it takes, but almost, to be there.

He has worked hard to make his view wider than a lot of people, especially with his work in China and with his development of electric cars and so on.

He has great experience, that shows in the meetings we have with other teams, he comes up with a lot of good ideas and suggestions. He's very strong in that way and his view from a wider perspective is very good. He's a clever guy, and I'm happy that he came to rallycross as part of his business.

Will Gollop

While Hansen was winning his fourth title in the European Rallycross Championship's second category aboard a Ford Sierra RS500, English engineer and driver Will Gollop claimed the 1992 European crown at the sport's highest level in his highly-evolved bi-turbo MG Metro 6R4.

With new rules introduced for 1993 – which replaced the Group B cars with a new generation of Group A-based machines – Gollop had to build a new racecar. At the same time Hansen graduated to the top class but, while the Swede battled fellow Citroen exponent Jean-Luc Pailler for the '93 crown, Gollop struggled with an uncompetitive Peugeot 309. That was replaced by a 306 for 1994 and Gollop raced Hansen on a regular basis for the next three years, but didn't win again at European level before he stepped back from the international arena.

Left: Belgium 1996, Will Gollop challenges Hansen's Citroen ZX.

Gollop on Hansen

I had a great deal of respect for what Kenneth did in the Volvo and then Cosworth before he moved up. We always got on well in those days, then when he came into our class, obviously rivalries spark up.

The incidents with Kenneth were maybe 25% my fault. It was a difficult time for us, after the Metro days, after 1992, we had to build a new car. We built the 309 for the first year [1993] which we knew wouldn't be successful because we never got the engine right. Then we gradually got the 306 better and better. In those days we were up against Martin Schanche, an engineer/driver, Kenneth Hansen, an engineer/driver and ourselves. Those are the days I really enjoyed. It was a double effort, the driving and the engineering of the car. Kenneth was always as good as any of us, I would say.

It was a non-contact sport like it is now, but rallycross is so intense that there's always going to be contact and controversy; just because you haven't got many laps to get it done. If you don't win the start you've got to find a way through and when you go off the start line with five or six other lunatics trying to make the first corner first, contact is invariably going to happen.

What happened between Kenneth and I at Lydden in 1996 was especially galling. We'd come a long way from winning the championship to getting the 306 competitive. We got pole position for the A final and I think Kenneth started at the back but there was some contact going into to the first corner that meant I ended up going off. The car got a broken driveshaft. I was never quite sure if it was the pushing and contact that broke the driveshaft.

They were tough times. It always seemed to me that it was the Scandinavians that could get a budget to go racing reasonably well and we always struggled. The Scandinavians seem to get money for motor sport more easily than I could in the UK, but I don't know if that's my imagination. I think there's some Scandinavian mentality about going out and conquering the world, like they used to.

Kenneth did really well when he came to the top class. I did not think he would get the Citroen ZX right, but he did and he was right on it the very first year. He quickly became the top man in rallycross and in my opinion still is. He's had numerous competitors over the years and he beat most of them before they dropped away. I'm sure if he got back in a car now he'd be pretty good today too.

Hansen on Gollop

Will was a very fair racer, and a very strong and brilliant driver. I feel a little guilty about what happened with Will, because a couple of times I was very bad to him, but it was not deliberate, it just happened.

Like at Lydden one time, I put him off at the start. And in Finland it was almost the same when he braked at a moment I wasn't expecting him to. Also, in Portugal, where I put him off the track because I didn't expect him to do the move he did.

We had some big arguments and I understand that sometimes he really hated me. I apologise for those moments, they were not deliberate.

Top left: Gollop and Hansen were European Champions in 1992.
Bottom left: Hansen leads Gollop at Mondello Park in 1993.
Below: Hansen on the podium in Belgium, flanked by Gollop and Per Eklund.

Bengt and Mattias Ekstrom

While Hansen began his rallycross career in Swedish national events before moving up to the European Championship, compatriot Bengt Ekstrom was following a similar path, only for him it was with BMWs rather than Volvos.

While Hansen claimed his first European crown in 1989, Ekstrom visited the podium in Germany the same year, before he claimed a pair of wins and finished third overall in 1990, his best championship finish. Ekstrom ended his full-time international rallycross career in 1992, ahead of son Mattias beginning his driving career in karting in 1993.

Mattias won the Swedish Touring Car Championship in 1999, before beginning an 18-year DTM career in 2001. Claiming two titles along the way, Ekstrom also won three annual Race of Champions events, before he made his rallycross debut at X Games Munnich and then the Swedish European Championship round at Holjes in 2013. With rallycross becoming an FIA World Championship in 2014, Ekstrom created his own team, EKS, fielding Audi S1s. He won his home round of the series at Holjes that year, claimed a second win after a controversial final corner battle with Timmy Hansen at the same circuit in 2015, then scooped the Drivers' and Teams' crowns in 2016. Having secured official Audi backing for 2017, Ekstrom ended his full-time career after Audi withdrew from the programme at the end of 2018.

Previous page: Bengt Ekstrom leads the final
in Germany in 1990.
Above: Timmy Hansen chases Mattias
Ekstrom in Portugal in 2017.
Right: Hansen congratulates Mattias
Ekstrom on winning the 2016 World
Championship.

Mattias Ekstrom on Hansen

As a kid my very first memory of Kenneth must be around 1986 when he drove a Volvo Amazon. I maybe remember his father more than Kenneth himself because at the time he was pretty shy and a bit 'new kid on the block'. I thought he was quite a humble guy and saw that he had big talent. Then my second memory is when he was dating Susann. It was so funny because he was the shy guy dating the girl in the paddock who also drove rallycross.

Then the next strong memory I would say was when he drove the Ford RS500 and all the battles he had with my father and with the Norwegians. Kenneth was probably the first guy to use proper launch control with rev limiters and so on, and had a car which had really bad noises on the start line. Today we all know that it's common in rallycross. He was famous for being technically ahead, one of the guys pushing the sport.

Then I remember the real battles he had with Per Eklund, which I thought were hilarious to watch because Per was the really verbal aggressive guy and Kenneth was really the well-educated, boring guy out of the car, but in the car both were the devil, those battles were always enjoyable.

As a team owner, racing with Timmy, I think the strongest memory of Kenneth is the last corner action I had with Timmy at Holjes [in 2015], when I saw Kenneth outside of the stewards' room, so I've seen him in many different moods and many different ways. I think he is a guy who will always search the rules to his own advantage, which is typical sign for a guy who loves winning. I really do respect him for being a guy who loves winning and his results tell that he has been doing a lot right. I think he can be proud, he has a very nice team with a lot of success, and you can see there someone who has done so much for rallycross as a sport. I had the joy since 1986 to watch him and what he has done, so I think everyone owes him some respect for what he has done for the sport.

When you put your team gear on, some people are ready to do whatever it takes, winning with or without 100% respect or honour or whatever, but everybody is different. I have been different in the early days of my career where I also didn't care how I won, only that I won. And I think to win a lot and to win often, you probably need to be less sensitive. But I felt for me as a person I'd rather win less often but with 100% credit. That's the only thing I sometimes struggle to understand [about] Kenneth, because when you meet him as a person, you would expect him to be different but the way he acts, he really wants to win badly every day and, in my opinion, not in a 100% respectful way. I do respect this because I have been there, but I would think that with time and age you would change your opinion. He is still the true hardcore race winner, which I love to compete against, but it's not a skill I would like to see in EKS. But still, I love to compete against them because they are the real hard fighters.

As a team owner and a driver, you want to compete against people with huge passion because they race differently. As I know from Kenneth, the only reason he does what he does is because of his passion. And I think his passion is what I respect the most in him, that he has so much passion and is able to keep going after so many years.

Hansen on Bengt and Mattias Ekstrom

We travelled a lot with Bengt when we started going to race in Europe, when he raced a BMW M3. My first memory of him was the first time I really met him. We had met before, but the first time we really met was in a car speedway in Gothenberg. I don't remember if it was a qualification race or a pre-final, but Bengt was leading. He got it a little bit wrong and had a stop. He had an old BMW and I was in the Volvo Amazon. You know, in car speedway you don't really have the chance to decide which side to go to try and avoid a car if it's stopped and I went completely into him. It was a hard hit so we couldn't continue.

We had a close relationship when we were in our buses in Europe, sometimes we had big fights on the track, but mostly I remember it was good, and of course I saw Mattias grow up.

I never drove against Mattias because he went circuit racing, then he came to World RX and created his own team. We had quite a good relationship in the beginning, but we are probably not the guys who will be the best friends.

I'm not the guy that plays the game like Mattias does, I'm different. You could say that he often has a fox behind the ear, that's a Swedish saying, that he has something else in his mind when you talk with him. Of course, that's part of the game also, you want to be a little psychological when you compete, but I don't like that way. Of course I can play the game, but not the same way.

It's difficult to say exactly what it is, but the personal chemistry is different. I have nothing really against Mattias, but when he started to play the games with Timmy, I didn't like that. Of course Timmy is our son, but I try to be quite opened eyed when sometimes Kevin and him are a little rough on track. If they blame something or someone, sometimes I ask them if we changed the cards, if they were in the other car, what would they have done. I don't try to defend every action they do on the track, Timmy and Kevin can sometimes do things you can't defend.

But, we had the thing in Holjes with Mattias [after the last corner of the final in 2015, when Timmy Hansen passed Ekstrom for the win]. It started because Mattias thought he was clear [in the lead], so he reduced his speed a lot, which made it possible for Timmy to make an attack and overtake. The Race Director said Timmy was off the track, so he got a penalty. When we showed the stewards that he wasn't off the track – because you need to have one wheel on the track and he had that all the time – they thought the contact was too hard, which I think is just a thing they came up with because the situation was there. If you really look into the incident, Timmy was trying to turn away from Mattias before they had the side contact. I think it was absolutely wrong what they did to take the win away. It was a brilliant rallycross manoeuvre, if Timmy had been off the track I would understand, but he was on the track and it was perfect.

That was also difficult because of what Mattias did after. He came with his team in the paddock and wanted to have the winners trophy. In the end he apologised for that, so that was fair. I don't think he thought about what he was doing at that moment, but it was a hard moment for Timmy.

A good part of Mattias is that he really put rallycross as a high priory when he came in, and he helped with growing the sport. He really likes rallycross, like Petter [Solberg] does too. He made it all the way, he drove himself, he ran the team and he took in other drivers. That was very important for the sport that people like him came in not only for work, but because they had a big passion, that was very good.

Above right: Hansen and Bengt Ekstrom were members of Sweden's Inter-Nations Cup team at Croft in 1990.
Below right: Hansen exchanges the event trophies with Mattias Ekstrom after Timmy Hansen was stripped of the Holjes win in 2015.

Tanner Foust

Excited by watching a video on YouTube of Marcus Gronholm racing a Ford Fiesta Supercar at Holjes, Sweden in 2008 when Gronholm beat Hansen to victory, American drifting star, television presenter and former rally driver Tanner Foust arrived in Europe to test a rallycross car for the first time in 2010.

He raced in four European Championship events that year with Olsbergs MSE, Hansen's last term as a full-time driver. The pair met on track again in 2011, when Foust took part in a full programme with OMSE and Hansen contested a pair of events in his team's new Citroen DS3 Supercar. Foust beat Hansen to victory on the DS3's debut at Holjes and later finished third behind the Swede in the Czech Republic season-finale, to date Hansen's last European Championship appearance.

Foust subsequently went on to win rallycross titles in America, and World Championship events with Volkswagen-backed teams.

Left: Hansen leads Foust at Holjes in 2010. Next page: One year later Foust won at Holjes and Hansen was first to celebrate with the American.

Foust on Hansen

Kenneth was the first driver that – and you have to remember that my coach was Andreas Eriksson who never came back with a tyre on the car, sorry Andreas – but Kenneth was the first guy I saw driving clean racing lines and making it work in a rallycross car. I remember very specifically being behind him at Lydden Hill going round the hairpin at the top of the hill and he was nearly straight and didn't use the handbrake and I thought: 'Okay, this looks much more efficient, there must be a better way to set these cars up; to be more like circuit racing cars.'

He was very unlike my team owner at the time [Eriksson] who was a passionate driver; Kenneth was a very cerebral competitor and had every strategy and every scenario worked out. He had a very thoughtful perspective, which I think helped elevated the sport to have that kind of professionalism. I admired him for that and watched him succeed with that method.

For him to have won the championship 14 times and to have turned his passion for rallycross into a business, I think he and Andreas were really the two pioneers in doing that, where they were racing but also renting cars and proving the speed of their cars themselves.

In my first year Kenneth had a good run for the championship and then he seemed to turn from being the racer to the team owner and started testing his new car rather than going for outright results. And that investment, he has watched it pay-off I think.

I love the act of driving a rallycross car in a rallycross competition. I think the tracks are spectacular and there's something about the old-school rallycross tracks in Europe and the capabilities of the cars that's a bit awe inspiring from a driving perspective. I think Kenneth and I share a dual personality when it comes to our lives out of the cars, recognising the business of rallycross and the importance for manufacturers to make small cars cool and appeal to young audiences.

Kenneth has an additional factor at play too, where he's been making a pathway for his children and having his kids there running in the sport must be incredibly rewarding for him.

Hansen on Foust

Tanner is a good guy, an ambassador for everything he does and he really raised the level in the paddock when he came to drive. Because of his work, and because he's American, he's very used to media and TV and he can market the sport very well.

In one way we are a little similar, because, I think, people think we are nice guys in the paddock but when you get into the race car, all hell can break loose. Tanner is a hard guy on the track and I think a lot of people looked the same at me, I could be quite hard on the track too. He's a rallycross guy. You need to be careful with him when you're racing against him.

But the most impressive thing about him for me is that he loves rallycross and also brought the American way of working. He is a big reason why rallycross has been in America for the last few years and he is a very fast driver too. It would be very interesting to see him do a full World Championship season in a good car.

Andreas Eriksson

Andreas Eriksson switched from rallies to rallycross in 2005 with a self-built Ford Fiesta Supercar. With an old school, maximum attack driving style, Eriksson could not be more different from compatriot Hansen in both personality and his approach behind the wheel. But, the pair's stories since Eriksson joined the fold have been intrinsically linked, as owners of arguably the two biggest rallycross outfits in the world.

An event winner, Eriksson's best championship position at rallycross' highest level was third in 2007, behind champion Lars Larsson and Hansen.

Like Hansen, Eriksson concluded his top-level driving career in 2011 to focus on his expanding team. Olsbergs MSE was the first European squad to fully embrace competing in America. With Ford support, Eriksson's team was also the first to win the World Rallycross Teams' title in 2014, which Hansen's Peugeot-backed squad claimed a year later.

The Eriksson and Hansen families were drawn closer than they might have been via the friendship of their sons who grew up together in the rallycross paddocks of Europe, and who have subsequently become accomplished drivers in their own right.

Eriksson joined forces with Turkish firm Avitas to form the single-make Supercar Lites category from 2012, and it was the Swede's team that gave Kevin Hansen his World RX debut in Argentina in 2015; the drive delivered as the prize for winning the RX Lites Cup. Eriksson later took on the promotion of the RallyX Nordic series and hired Hansen as expert commentator.

Left: Eriksson (left) joins Hansen and Lars Larsson for a parade.
Next page: Eriksson leading Hansen in Poland in 2009.

Eriksson on Hansen

I don't know so much about Kenneth's big time but he was the guy I called for advice when I was going to start rallycross. I called him, tried to get information how he did it but he couldn't really tell me anything. When I asked him why something was like this, whatever it was, he just said: 'This is how it's always been'. That's the only thing I remember.

It wasn't Kenneth, it wasn't Per Eklund, it wasn't anyone that drew me to rallycross. Rally was my big thing. But then I went to Holjes and thought it was pretty cool. I could see the potential. The kids were small, Maria [Eriksson's wife] didn't want to go to the forest to watch all the time. Everyone always thought I should do rallycross but I wasn't interested because you couldn't be World Champion, so why the hell would you go there?

That had always been my goal [World Rally Champion] but things changed with kids and family and so on, so when I started rallycross it was at the end of my career and it was a hobby.

It was a programme I had with Ford, building the fastest Ford Fiesta. It was me and Lars Larsson (Skoda Fabia) who had the smallest cars in the paddock. Everyone said it was wrong, that the cars were too small.

I did a lot of racing against Kenneth, but I was a little disappointed with the speed in rallycross. I was quite aggressive, not aggressive in pushing people off, but: 'Move out of the way, I'm coming, I want to go faster than you,' kind of way. To go fast in rallycross at some of the tracks, not all, was boring. Tight lines and being very tidy, I just wanted to go

flat out. The cars were very fast 550bhp monsters and I wanted to floor it. That's why I was never successful in the whole year because some of the tracks were shit. Boring, shit and shouldn't have been there. That was a challenge and Kenneth was very good at that; going inside on tighter lines, he had the experience.

Before I came people said he had better budgets but that was just jealousy, he just did everything better. When I started it was with Larsson and Sverre Isachsen it was a very good time, a lot of good cars and teams. At that time Kenneth was not always the fastest. He was among the fastest but he was not always the fastest.

I have a good relationship with Kenneth, much better than people think and I respect him more than anything because I know how hard he worked for what he has done. As a driver I was more of a Martin Schanche and Ludvig Hunsbedt fan because I believed in the show. When I came I thought it was a little boring, so that's why I've been trying to spice things up all the time. Not crashing cars, but I got a lot of fans very fast, not because I won races but because of who I was and what I did. I never went at the speed that was necessary for the corners!

Kenneth sometimes asked me: 'Why do you do this?' But I wasn't the guy who wanted to win everything because it was the end of my career, I wanted to enjoy it. I loved driving those cars but Kenneth was more of a championship guy, he always ran for the championship points.

In the Czech republic in 2007 Kenneth landed in the wall after

the first corner, before the little jump there. He came to me and asked: 'Why did you drive so aggressively?' And I told him: 'You were driving too slowly!' We had a little fight there. Many times he was probably angry with me, but he never told me, but in Czech he told me he was a little 'disappointed'.

That was the only big dispute that I remember from driving. Now I call him to help me. When I had a very short time to sort everything for RallyX Nordic in 2018 I needed to find the best expert commentator I could. There's a lot of people who think they're experts, but they are not, and the only name I could come up with was Kenneth's. The first on my list, I called him and I didn't know how to present it, so I talked about wind and water, and our boys, then I broke it to him and he said yes without a heartbeat. I really admire him for that, he did a great job, he sees all the details. When you listen to him doing that, you understand why he won all his races. Back then when I was driving I just drove because the car was super awesome to drive. Kenneth looked at all the details.

I think we have a mutual respect for each other and if you asked who I think is the best team manager and strategic guy, it's Kenneth. I haven't seen anyone better yet; even if other teams are winning, he is very good at that.

We respected each others as drivers in the end, maybe not so much at the beginning, then as team managers I always had my vision. Sometimes my vision worked, and sometimes not, but they [other teams] go with the safe card all the time. I'm not a safe guy, but I won a lot as a team manager, and Kenneth has won as well, so I think we're quite equal there.

We both have a lot of passion for the sport, which shows compared to the guys that don't have it and are just here to get paid. We're not here for the money, I can tell you that.

Hansen on Eriksson

For me Andreas is two guys. Sometimes I don't like the way he does things, and he knows that because I've told him, but sometimes he can be a wonderful guy, very thoughtful and very personable.

We have had our ups and downs, and we have had big arguments but normally we don't take them to heart. We had one argument in Germany in 2018 when Kevin [Eriksson] and Sebastien Loeb had a coming together. Before we went into the stewards room to defend our boys we had a big argument, but in the end when we walked out we had a much softer talk and it was good. That is often how it is.

For sure Andreas has done a lot of good things for rallycross and has a lot of good ideas. He's also had some bad ideas, but you need guys like him to mix things up. It would be boring if we were all the same.

Sometimes he suggests things which are quite stupid; he wants to get a reaction and to make things happen.

Many people that are similar to his character in other kinds of business, they try things and if it doesn't go well, they leave. That isn't him. Like with the Supercar Lites class, it hasn't been the golden route all the way. Yes, they have sold a lot of cars, but I think it's been hard to make money because they are supplying a very good service. In that way he has been steering a good course for his ship.

It was good to have Andreas in the car when we were racing because you learned that you didn't need to take what happened on track personally. He was that kind of hard race driver. We had some fights that we didn't agree about, but I don't have the memory that he was unfair. Perhaps I should, but I don't. We also have a very special relationship because our boys, especially Kevin [Hansen] and Oliver and Kevin [Eriksson] were playing a lot in the paddock. Sometimes me and Andreas could be very upset with each other but we needed to watch our tongues and not say the things in front of the children.

We are both team owners now and rivals in a different way. We know that some years are not the best, but we've always said that we need to keep the heart of rallycross in Sweden, and we do that by continuing to try to win, and to make things better.

I don't carry with me the first of Andreas' character. I can handle him when he's there, but I like the like the second Andreas much better, the gentle one. But I'm sure he doesn't like everything about me either.

Per Eklund

Probably best known for a successful and varied career in rallying, Per Eklund has never been far from rallycross. His debut was at Valkenswaard in 1971 and he won the first ever rallycross in Sweden [at Hedemora] later the same year. He raced for Saab in the mid-70s as the European Rallycross Championship became established and occasionally raced his own MG Metro 6R4 during the Group B era.

Towards the end of a rally career in which he drove for many manufacturers as well as running his own team, Eklund moved to rallycross full time in 1993, first with Subarus [Legacy then Impreza], before developing Saabs, first a 900, then 9-3. It was in this era that Eklund and Hansen – each of them team owner, car builder and driver – developed an intense rivalry.

Eklund won the European crown in 1999 and then headed to America to claim victories at the Pikes Peak International Hill Climb in 2000 and 2002. Eklund's final full European Championship season was in 2009, although he made ad-hoc driving appearances into his 70th year (2015). Since then he has, like Hansen moved to running cars, first the Saab 93s then a pair of Volkswagen Beetles, for customers.

Eklund on Hansen

It's a long story between me and Kenneth. When I came back to rallycross and he came with his first Citroen in 1993, from then we had fights until we both stopped really.

We were fighting everywhere in Europe, and there were a lot of black flags.

He was behind me in the last race in Germany in 1993 when I was in the Legacy, but he got a puncture and Jean-Luc Pallier won the championship in front of Kenneth, Tommy Kristoffersson and me. That was the start of the fighting between us.

He was very professional and had a good car with Citroen, and the latest engines. He was so good, but he was like a 'don't touch me' kind of guy on the track. He complained or made a protest more or less always.

In Finland one year I won the race on the track. At Hameenlinna there was a downhill near the end of the lap, a small left corner then tight right which opened out on the start line. I went inside him and was first at the finish line, but there was a black flag. I had passed him, and he told everybody there was no space. I told them there was space. Many times it happened like this. Then he was sitting on Swedish television on Monday morning saying that Eklund found a way but there was no space. It was forbidden to touch him.

Whatever he did, he would win. He knew the rules, he spoke with everybody, he knew all the Clerks of the Course and all these things. He never accepted anybody could beat him. He tried to find something. I didn't care, even if I had a black flag, I took it. I knew I was first to finish.

He was not rough on the track, but we are the same, all of us. One race in Alvsbyn in the Swedish Championship, Michael Jernberg, Hansen and me were in the final. There was a long straight then a quite fast right corner and a sand trap straight ahead. Nobody lifted off. I was in the middle, we were flat, all three door-to-door. Kenneth was on the right on the inside and Jernberg was on the left, and we just flew straight off, all three cars in the sand. I had no way to get out. Jernberg was absolutely crazy, he jumped out, ran over and tried to crash my windscreen. I had a glass window, and he smashed the whole window. Lucky enough he didn't manage to come in. Then there was a restart, and it was all three cars parallel into the first corner absolutely the same. The tractor had to take us out of the sand trap again and I think it was the third start we managed to do it. I don't remember who won.

There was me, Kenneth, Jernberg, and Martin Schanche sometimes, it was not easy and none of us were nice boys. It was really tough to fight. Kenneth won a lot but I took him sometimes, especially in the Swedish Championship.

It was a really big fight in 1999, I was already the champion before the last race and Kenneth had a crash, but it was not with me. I don't think he was happy when I won the European Championship, it was really good to win that year.

In 2000 we were in Poland with two races left. It was a big fight for the championship, it was very close and really important who was first there. I won. After the race Kenneth was in the parc ferme

and he found out that someone had taken a blade on my tyres. It was forbidden to cut the tyres. My mechanic had made some scratch just with his blade, maybe it was five centimetres. Kenneth of course made the protest and it was a big thing. They flew the tyres to Paris and everything. I lost the win.

He was always very friendly, when you talked to him he was like a nice dog, if you understand. It was a big fight from the first race to the last one, nobody gave up. Then always something in the race. But we have always been good friends one day after, even with the bloody protests.

The kids that are stars today were all like my children when they were small, Timmy and Kevin, Johan Kristoffersson and then Andreas Eriksson's boys were coming to me. I always gave them ice cream or money when they did some stupid things. Everybody liked this system.

Johan was the one to do tricks. Hansen had a new tent one time, he always had money and sponsors and so on for these things, and we were sitting under some rubbish setup. It was raining a lot, Johan came and asked what he could do and we were next to Kenneth.

I told him to go between the tents and take the back brace off Kenneth's. The sheet just smashed down and the whole tent was full of water. That was perfect, there was a lot of ice cream and money for that!

*Previous page: Eklund's Subaru Impreza leads
Hansen in the Czech Republic in 1995.
Above: In 2004 at Essay in France, Eklund
and Hansen battle again.
Right: The Swedish Championship benefited
from the publicity of the Hansen versus
Eklund period – and promoted the rivalry!
Following pages: Left: Eklund gives Hansen a
soaking in champagne.
Right: Hansen leads Eklund at Holjes.*

Hansen on Eklund

I didn't look at rallycross the same as Per did. I thought of it more like it was with Martin Schanche, close sideways racing. Sometimes it can go wrong, but Per was always rougher. We didn't have the same view on how the sport should be done.

We had terrible fights sometimes and we were far over the limit of what was okay. But, the fights me and Per had were probably the most famous things in rallycross in Sweden, maybe they still are now. People still talk about the fights we had, like the incident in Finland for example.

If he was behind you, it was not a question of if, it was certain that if he had the possibility, you would get a push. Perhaps he didn't push you off all the time, but sometimes he was very hard and did things over the limit, which I didn't like because it was not sporting.

We were the ones from Sweden who were fighting to win at that time, and because of that we both hated to lose even more. That was a lot of motivation to do well, there were a lot of mental games so when things went wrong, sometimes it really exploded. We didn't do things just to put on a show or be spectacular, in

those moments I could hate Per and his damn red car, and I believe he hated me too.

I must also say that I was not always fair to Per either. Sometimes I ran over the edge too, when I paid him back in an unsporting way, but it was just that I'd had enough. Especially once in Poland. I had got a hit from him in the Swedish Championship the weekend before, he had been completely on the grass on the inside and hit me off. And then more or less the same thing happened in Poland. I was so fed up, I went to the stewards and they said: 'No, it was no problem.' I replied: 'Okay, then we drive rallycross like that!'

I think we were in the B final, going into the second corner I was behind. I got into his bumper and decided that now he should go off now because he deserved it.

But, you know, to get him off the track, he was a real bastard. He braked so hard that I had to gear down and stay in the throttle to get him off the track.

It felt so wrong to do that but I had decided that he deserved it, because of what he had done and not got a penalty. Then, half-a-lap later, after the joker lap merge there was a right then a left before the last

corner. There I just saw something coming from the left. He had got up to speed again, so he came back, I think to take me off, but he missed the corner, ran completely over on the inside, went past in front of me and out into the sand trap. No-one saw that as an incident or an attempt or anything, but it couldn't have been anything else because he was really looking to pay me back again. We had a conversation after the race, I think I said some very hard words to him but nobody heard.

Of course, when there's a strong rivalry, like with Per or Martin or Bjorn Skogstad, you don't talk [to the other one] a lot and sometimes we went a long time without speaking. You wanted there to be some sort of wall, you don't want to be too friendly, because then it makes it different on the track; you can't just sit down and drink coffee together all the time. You can say a few words and perhaps have a coffee once a year or something, but then leave it like that, then after your career you can do something different.

Per is a good guy, today I love to meet him and talk to him. He's fun and enjoyable to be around in the paddock and he has given everything to the sport. I think both of us understand how things were. I think we have decided that more or less we would never agree on the track, but now, in the paddock it's different between us.

Some of our battles, especially in the Swedish Championship and some of the things we said probably shouldn't have been on TV, but we never did anything just for the television or for the papers. What was said, what I felt was right to say at that moment was what I meant and it just turned the boost up, but I think the sport gained overall from us fighting. I remember seeing the 'Hansen v Eklund, come and see what will happen at the first corner' kind of messages being used.

And that was quite true, because we knew that if we were together then something would happen.

In 1993 while Hansen drove the new Citroen ZX Supercar, Susann Bergvall raced the Group A Sierra in national events.

Best races, biggest incidents, driving technique, how one man's idea changed a sport forever, the creature that's always by Hansen's side and more. Fourteen stories that span Hansen's career.

2. FOURTEEN

Tyre dealings

Hansen's support from French marque Citroen meant that for the 2001 season, a deal was struck for the Kenneth Hansen Motorsport Citroen Xsaras to be run on Michelin tyres.

Following pre-season evaluation and testing, where Hansen produced solid pace on the radial tyres, the first round of the European series was held at Loheac in France, in front of a record 41,000 spectators.

In the heat of battle, however, neither the team's latest Xsara nor its Swedish driver were comfortable.

Disappointed with his pace on the opening day, Hansen requested that he be allowed to return to the more conventional Avon crossply tyre used by the majority of the field. Citroen's team manager Michel Perin eventually gained approval for the change.

Overnight, Avon tyres – with the branding removed – were fitted to the Xsara's wheels and Hansen was second fastest first thing on Sunday morning.

The reigning champion then went fastest in the final qualifier to net pole for the final, before leading the main event from lights to flag to secure an empathic win in Citroen's homeland, fending off a challenge from Peugeot driver Jean-Luc Pailler.

"That year we were doing the French Championship too and had good support from Citroen. They wanted us to be on Michelin tyres, so we signed to do that and we had a lot of tyres to use. We struggled a little in the beginning when we were testing, I think we had perhaps tested at some of the wrong tracks. The radial tyre was good when you were alone and we were fast. But in traffic in the races it was difficult to be fast with them.

Loheac was a huge, important race for us, with a lot of Citroen guests invited from the factory close by in Rennes. We needed to win there, but after practice and Q1 I just couldn't match the other drivers. I told

Michel (Perin), that we needed to change the tyres. I told him that I couldn't go any faster with the Michelin.

I don't think they believed it was the tyres, so they gave me the freedom.

We had to machine the Avon branding off the tyres; the awning was full of tyre smoke!

The team was happy and confident, but then before the warm-up on Sunday morning I started to think 'Shit! What if it's not the tyres?'

But, we went fastest after that. To win the final, to be king in Loheac, that was magnificent.

It's incredible to do that with a French car in front of all those spectators and guests, it was amazing.

After that we never needed to use the Michelins, we were free to do what we wanted."

While the European Championship's French round rotated between circuits for the following decade, it wasn't until 2013 that top-flight rallycross returned to the Breton venue. The Hansen name almost returned to the top step of the podium at the circuit in 2014. In the circuit's first World Championship event, Timmy Hansen qualified on pole position for the semi-finals but a poor start ended his victory hopes.

Hansen's eldest son made amends by emulating his father's Loheac triumph aboard the team's Peugeot 208 in 2015, then repeated the success in 2019 too.

"I told Timmy that to win in Loheac is something special, and of course he also knows that now."

Above left and right: Tyres were critical at Loheac in 2001.

Manufacturers

Hansen's driving career will always be associated with the plethora of red Citroens in which he achieved so much of his success.

But, as is so often the case in motor sport it could so easily have been a different story. Just as it might have been had he elected to race a Volkswagen Golf rather than being gifted the Lars Nystrom Volvo 240 for 1987.

With the European Rallycross Championship set for a regulation shift for 1993, Hansen was aided by Kenneth Andersson with sponsorship acquirement, in trying to secure a deal with a manufacturer.

Communication was had with Toyota, Ford and Citroen. Toyota had been ear-marked because the marque was achieving success in rallying, and its Celica was a 'good size of car,' according to Hansen. Ford, because 'they are good everywhere' and Citroen, because Jean-Luc Pailler had already been working with the French marque with his BX in top-flight rallycross and Hansen saw potential in the engine.

"We got a reply from Toyota, but I think it was quite cold. Then we were at Boreham [in the UK] to meet Ford and they offered me parts, mainly used parts, to build a Supercar. That would have been quite okay, but then the marketing chief from Citroen Sweden called me. He thought I was joking because he knew my name and was excited that we wanted to do something with a Citroen."

As with any relationship, Hansen's time with Citroen, in his own words, had 'it's ups and downs' and although the Swedish squad would field Citroens for 21 years, before a switch to sister-PSA brand Peugeot in 2014 [see chapter seven], there was a period around the turn of the millennium where Hansen looked elsewhere.

Still in touch with former engineer Benoit Bagur [see chapter six], that included a trip to Spain and the SEAT Sport factory near Barcelona. "We had some interest from SEAT Sport so we went there to present a rallycross idea to Jaime Puig [SEAT Sport Director]. There were discussions and in the end it never happened, but it was not far away."

Then, when Peugeot decided to stop supporting Hansen's team and take the World Rallycross Championship programme in-house for 2018 there was a period where Hansen didn't know if he would remain involved or not. At that stage he briefly entered discussions with Hyundai about running works-WRC derived i20s in World RX.

"I was in contact with Hyundai because we didn't know the future, we got the news that we would be involved [with Peugeot] later. When they decided to go by themselves, we didn't have a clear answer. We had a similar offer to what Marcus [Gronholm] had at the end of 2017."

Prior to that however, ahead of Volkswagen revealing its new Volkswagen Beetle for the American-based Global Rallycross Championship in 2014, Hansen's team almost ended up developing the new car for the Andretti Autosport team to run in the United States.

"Volkswagen visited some teams in Sweden and in the end decided to go with us. We had proposed a

plan to work quite closely with Oreca for both chassis and engines, but we would build the car, deliver it to America and help Andretti to run it. But, in the end we felt that it was not the way that we wanted to do it. There were some things that they changed that we didn't really agree with, so we said: 'This is not us, this is not Hansen Motorsport.' Perhaps we are stupid because they are the biggest manufacturer in the world, but we need to enjoy what we do and we are not here to work like that for others and to give everything away. That's not our passion. So we said no to Volkswagen and they were fully okay with that. The work we had done, they wanted to clear it; they paid for our hours. That was a very gentlemanly thing from them. There were absolutely no hard feelings."

Volkswagen subsequently developed its Beetle in house in conjunction with SEAT Sport, somewhat ironically given Hansen's contact several years earlier, and won three GRC titles with Scott Speed from 2015, before the series folded in 2017. The same team and car combination then won the Americas Rallycross Championship in 2018 and 2019 with Speed and Tanner Foust. Peugeot withdrew from World RX at the end of 2018, and Hansen's team subsequently took over the works-built Peugeot 208 Supercars to continue in the series in 2019.

Below left: Hansen raced Fords from 1989 to 1992 but began his long association with the PSA Group in 1993.
Below centre: When Peugeot pulled out of motor sport in 2018 Hansen talked to Hyundai.
Below: Bruno Famin was Peugeot Sport boss during Hansen's tenure with the marque.

Never Give Up

With rallycross races run over just a handful of laps, the first few metres are critical to the outcome. As such, contact in the intensity of first corner battles is often inevitable.

At the Dutch round of the European Championship in 2002, Hansen qualified second for the A final.

In the first attempt at getting around Valkenswaard's first corner, Norwegian Ludvig Hunsbedt was pushed into a spin, leaving his Ford Focus in the middle of the circuit. The race was red flagged and subsequently restarted, but in the melee that had resulted in Hunsbedt being turned around, the right-rear track-control arm on Hansen's Citroen Xsara had been broken.

With parc ferme regulations implemented ahead of the re-start, Hansen's request to return to the paddock was denied, but he didn't admit a reason as to why he wished to visit the team's awning before the grid was formed for a second time.

Aware of the damage he was carrying, the right-wheel able to change its toe (turn-in and out) by more than 50mm, Hansen elected to take the restart, with the intention of making it through the first corner then waiting to capitalise if any other competitors were to drop out. At the turn of the millennium, rallycross Supercars were not known for their reliability.

At the restart it was 1993 European Champion Jean-Luc Pailler – starting from pole position – who took the lead with his Peugeot 206, but Hansen managed to grab second place on the opening lap, then held on against the odds with Hunsbedt breathing down his neck to finish on the second step of the podium.

"I felt that something was definitely wrong after the first start because when I went into the left-hand corner, the rear went wide like a drifting car. I wasn't allowed to go to the paddock, so I thought that I would go to the first corner at the restart and then see. Perhaps there would be some crashes and I could get some extra points if someone else retired. But the start was okay, and the right-hand corners were okay too.

I knew the left-hand corner would be difficult but I managed that and continued. Jean-Luc was in the lead but I was able to stay second. That was, you know, you never give up. After the finish, this big guy who used to be Jean-Luc's mechanic came to me and said: 'Yeah we won, but you are the real winner.' He couldn't believe it."

Hansen managed a damaged car and held off the challenge of Ludvig Hunsbedt to place second at Valkenswaard in 2002.

War!

Lyngas in Norway played host to the penultimate round of the European Rallycross Championship in 1994 and Hansen entered the event knowing that victory would almost guarantee his first championship at the highest level.

Arch-rival Martin Schanche had to win if he was to stop Hansen taking the crown, and it was the Norwegian who qualified on pole for the final, a race that would go down in rallycross folklore.

From second on the grid, Hansen made the best start and took the lead on the long run to turn two, where Norwegian hero Schanche sent his Ford Escort up the inside of Hansen's Citroen.

As Schanche took the lead, Hansen was almost also overtaken by Will Gollop and Stig Blomqvist, but held on to second, as Gollop's compatriot, Barry Squibb, moved into third.

Schanche went wide at the final corner of the opening tour and dropped to third, before then re-passing Squibb and closing again on Hansen.

The Swede and Norwegian then traded places, and paint, for the following two laps, Hansen retaking the lead on lap four, before Schanche dropped back into the pack with a front-right puncture.

Hansen ultimately won the race in his battered ZX, spinning the car over the finish line as Squibb and Gollop completed the podium. Both Tommy Kristoffersson and Blomqvist also passed Schanche before the chequered flag.

Right: Before the war, Hansen's Citroen ZX is pristine but ended the event heavily damaged.

Kennet Nyberg

"When I don't have anything to do I put that video on. It was crazy. That car was very strong, so it was no problem with damage, it was really like stock car racing. I think it was lucky that Schanche had the puncture; it could have been worse for sure."

Will Gollop

"People talk about contact in rallycross, but I was in that race in Norway. They [Schanche and Hansen] knocked each other to Hell. The crowd absolutely loved it and Kenneth didn't seem to worry about it at all."

Martin Schanche

"We should have been disqualified, all of us. It sort of escalated and the judges let everything pass, so we did everything to each other. Especially Kenneth Hansen and me should have been disqualified and sent home. Both of us. But the officials didn't do anything. The spectators were chuffed to nuts, they had value for their money."

Kenneth Hansen

"That was special because that was not a normal rallycross race. I made a great start and Martin was furious. After that it was just boxing between us. We had some contact in the beginning and I came back after he went off. Then we were back again he continued to push me. I was quite upset and angry, I started to push back and it was a proper fight.

In the video you can see Barry Squibb was third and it looks like he's just thinking 'Okay, I'll leave these guys to it and probably I will win!'

Me and Martin were both very angry. We didn't speak to each other for half a year afterwards!"

New model success

Throughout Hansen's time driving for his own team, the Gotene-based squad had an incredible hit-rate with producing successful cars straight out of the box.

Having won immediately in the switch from a Volvo 240 to Ford Sierra Cosworth in 1989, Hansen's team created its own Citroen ZX for the Swede's graduation to the sport's top level in 1993 and claimed victory on the car's debut at Fuglau in Austria.

When the Xsara was subsequently introduced in 1998, Hansen again won on the new model's first outing at Melk (Austria), before achieving the same result on the maiden appearance for the C4 at Lousada (Portugal) in 2006.

That success was at least in part thanks to a considered and arguably conservative approach to development. Each car was constantly evolved through its lifespan and, when the new shape was introduced, the majority of components and philosophies were carried over into the new version; effectively a proven racecar in a new skin.

But not with the Citroen DS3. When Hansen ended his full-time driving career at the end of 2010, it was to focus on running the team and developing the new DS3 Supercar. Unlike its predecessors, which had been based around a longitudinally-mounted engine and transmission, with double-wishbone suspension, the DS3 used a transversely-mounted drivetrain and MacPherson struts.

The car would later win back-to-back European Rallycross titles for Hansen Motorsport in the hands of Russian driver Timur Timerzyanov in 2012 and 2013. But when Hansen gave the machine its debut at Holjes (Sweden) in 2011 he was – despite an eventual podium finish – ill-at-ease with the new car.

"It was a big risk to do the DS3 this way. Before that, when we tried new ideas on the existing cars, we knew that if it was not good, we could always go back. The DS3 was one-way, we couldn't turn back if it went wrong.

I spoke a lot to Citroen people in the construction side, and other people too, to ask for advice.

For example, it's easier to make better dampers if you go the MacPherson route; they absorb more with more travel and you have less moving points compared to double-wishbone.

We also thought to go transverse would be a good thing. For a long time transverse transmission systems were not strong enough. Perhaps you could go to Xtrac but that was too expensive, so when Sadev made a small, strong transverse system it became possible, and the way to go.

We had a short test, perhaps six-kilometres on a small rallycross circuit, we made a couple of starts and that was it. When we got to Holjes, it was very tricky because it felt like the car was driving me and I was just a passenger. It was nervous, not controllable, and I felt like I was above the circuit, not like in the C4 when you could count on it doing what you wanted it to do. This was different."

Top left: A Citroen Xsara shell in preparation at Hansen's old Gotene workshop.
Below left: The Citroen DS3 on its 2011 debut at Holjes.

Hillclimber

Rallycross cars, designed for acceleration and multi-surface performance, are well suited to the discipline of hillclimbing. It hasn't been uncommon over the years for top-flight rallycross cars, or machines developed from a rallycross concept, to be used in major hillclimb events, and it is not at all unusual to see rallycross cars on hills in Norway and Sweden.

Look no further than Martin Schanche using his Ford Escort Xtrac at the Pikes Peak International Hill Climb in 1984, fellow Norwegian Thor Holm driving a Ford RS200 on the famous mountain in 1988 and 1991 or Swede Per Eklund achieving success in Colorado in 2000 and 2002 with a Saab 9-3.

Hansen also took part in a number of hillclimb events. Having competed in a handful of rallies early in his career, the Swede had limited experience of having to read the road in front of him, rather than completing multiple laps around a circuit, and thus competing on hillclimbs posed an interesting challenge.

Making sporadic hillclimb appearances through his career, including a near full campaign in 1986, Hansen used first his Volvo Amazon and later his European Rallycross Championship winning Citroen ZX and Xsaras [see results, chapter ten].

"You have perhaps one kilometre or one-and-a-half kilometres like a rally stage and you need to be perfect because you know that if there's even a small mistake, then it's gone. The ones we did, they were too short to make mistakes on.

Sometimes it was a little challenging to drive in a more rally style, to be there against the clock, but I liked that. In rallycross you do four laps in qualifying and you need to be fast and clean from the start, but still there is a little more time, so you can often get away with a few small mistakes. Not in hillclimbs though.

We did quite a lot to change the car, to tune it up because they were very short stages, but also to make it more suited to tarmac, a little bit lower and stiffer. We also had some gravel hillclimbs, like one event we did in Lillehammer in 1998. That was more gravel, and we were competing against Martin [Schanche] and Michael Jernberg, so we had more of a rallycross setup.

We didn't go fully into it though, we didn't develop anything special, we just made the best out of what we had for it.

One time we were up in the North of Sweden, about 400 kilometres north from our place, in Gavle. It was a tarmac hillclimb and had a blind jump. You needed to be absolutely to the left on the road taking off so that you landed absolutely on the right. If you went 10cm wide you would end up in a huge ditch at the side of the road. There isn't a lot of practice, so you need to commit.

In one Swedish Championship hillclimb I was very determined to win, but Lars Larsson was quite a bit in front of me on the last run. I just let it go. That didn't happen so many times. I more or less went one gear higher in every corner. That shouldn't be possible. It was so risky but very enjoyable because I was in the flow. That was a moment when I really loved driving, and I gained a lot of time so it was fantastic. It was an incredible run, really on the limit, it was a little scary but I got away with it and won.

When we used the Xsara it had 700 horsepower non-restricted, it was just a bomb.

That was a lot of fun, I enjoyed those races."

Above: Hansen hustles the Volvo Amazon uphill in 1986.

Above: Norway 1989, Hansen leads the similar Sierra RS500 of Roger Sandberg but the event ended in controversy over fuel and Hansen's only disqualification.

Car Doping

VG (Verdens Gang) is one of Norway's most-read newspapers. In 1989 it had a daily circulation of over 360,000. Despite being a native of neighbouring Sweden, in that autumn of that year, Hansen was headline news in the centre spread of the publication.

But, the splash wasn't because the Swede was en route to his first European Championship title in his first year with the Ford Sierra RS500 Cosworth, this was a scandal.

Hansen was found to be using illegal fuel during post-event scrutineering in the eighth round of the European campaign at Lyngas in Norway, and for the first and only time in his 249 European starts, the Swede was excluded from an event.

"That's a very black mark. I made a mistake, or I didn't have the knowledge to read the regulations correctly. The Swedish and European Championships had different fuel regulations. I used the wrong fuel.

I got fuel delivered for the Swedish Championship and used it in the European. Of course, I should have checked that, or I should have known. Our distributor should also have known what they gave us but anyway, I was disqualified and that was correct.

Some weeks after the race I was contacted to tell me the fuel sample was not okay, then you have your own sample also. We checked it and it was the wrong fuel for a European event.

I don't think it made a big difference to the speed, because we just swapped one for the other and continued, but I remember we opened the middle sector of VG and it said 'Car Doping'.

There I was with my car and some guy taking the fuel sample. I was the doping guy, and that was terrible.

It took five or six years to get that stamp off my name because when I was successful, always people would say 'Ah yeah, but you're using the different fuel.' In the beginning people were angry, then it turned into more of a joke, but still it affects you when that happens. It was a rough time."

The result almost cost Hansen his maiden crown, the outcome of the Norwegian event further compounded by title-rival Bjorn Skogstad taking victory. But by the end of the year Hansen had secured his first European title by a single point.

Right-foot braking

Today racing drivers are brought up to brake with the left-foot, a technique that helps balance the car in medium speed corners and mitigate the time loss incurred when switching the right foot from throttle to brake. With older turbocharged engines, it can help minimise lag and maintain boost.

Left-foot braking is far from a new phenomenon, but Hansen began competing in an era where drivers, especially in racing rather than rallying, still used the more conventional method of right-foot braking, accompanied by the heel-and-toe technique of pressing the throttle when changing down gears under braking to maintain revs. When Stig-Olov Walfridson drove with Hansen Motorsport in 2004, Hansen frowned at his left-foot braking approach, and to this day, even when Hansen is testing the most modern World Rallycross Championship Supercars, he still brakes with his right foot.

"I tried left-foot braking sometimes but it's difficult when you're not used to something. I remember in Melk [Austria], there was a long gravel corner, so there it was difficult. I tried left-foot braking there but it was difficult to get the feeling. I would have needed to practice quite a lot, and perhaps I should have done in the end, by then it was much more difficult to win using the right foot. I tried using my left foot sometimes when we had throttle lag in the turbo cars, but when the anti-lag systems [ALS] came it wasn't needed so much for that reason.

Even today if I drive a racecar, I brake with the right foot. It's not the fastest, or perhaps the correct way, but if you are determined, it can work quite well. When I have driven the 208 [WRX Supercar], you can see the time difference compared to the regular drivers, because you need to move your foot.

It was always important for me to set up the pedals very carefully, we spent a lot of time on that, to be able to move my foot without much delay. When you do it perfectly you can be very quick between throttle and brake. The thing is, sometimes with the four-wheel drive cars, if you are too fast between the throttle and brake it can have a negative effect with the differential ramps, so sometimes it was an advantage that I would never have that problem."

Having plied his trade in circuit racing, Timmy Hansen experienced his father's driving first hand at the pre-event media day at Holjes in Sweden in 2010, where the then single-seater racer got taken for a passenger ride in the Citroen C4 Supercar.

"I felt that I had a responsibility in the team to give dad some advice and find some things around the track. My first feeling was: 'Wow, it's so fast!' Then I realised I had a job to do, so I started to focus as a driver would focus behind the wheel. Into the Velodrome corner he braked, released the brakes and then he braked one more time, to get the nose in and rotate the car. When we stopped dad turned to me, I think expecting me to be like the normal passengers who are just like: 'Amazing, I cannot speak any more', but I straight away said: 'Good, but you braked twice in the Velodrome, maybe we can work on that.' We went out again and he tried to change it, but it didn't really work because the car was understeering. That was interesting.

Dad had a very efficient driving style, to get the most out of the car, not always pushing the hardest.

He was one of the first who wasn't sliding so much and driving very cleanly. Being efficient is something we always talk about."

Relying on braking with his right foot means that Hansen pays a lot of attention to his seating position in the car and is very careful with the setup of the pedals.

On a roll

Putting aside teenage antics in a field with friends and a Volvo PV, Hansen can claim an almost unbelievable statistic of having only rolled once in his three-decade long rallycross career.

But, while in every event bar one, Hansen's car remained the correct way up, in the true fashion of not doing things by halves, when the Swede did have his one and only roll, at Momarken in Norway in 2007, it was a big one.

The sixth round of the European Championship was held in wet conditions, and Hansen started on the third row of the grid for the A final.

At the first corner, he followed pole-starter Tommy Rustad and champion-elect Lars Larsson into the joker lap, Rustad returning to the main circuit in the lead, such was the slippery nature of the standard lap, while Larsson and Hansen dropped into the pack.

Fighting to make up ground, Hansen made a move to pass Larsson over the circuit's jump in the middle of the race. The cars touched wheels and – as the bodywork of the cars at the time was ultra-thin to save weight, and did not fully cover the wheels – Hansen's Citroen C4 was sent into a violent series of rolls.

All four sides and the roof of the C4 impacted the ground at some stage during the accident, before the red machine came to rest upside down. Circuit staff and Hansen's team rushed to the scene as the race was red flagged. Hansen was fortunate to escape without serious injury. As a somewhat begrudging early adopter of wearing the HANS (head and neck safety) device, Hansen was later told by medical professionals that wearing the innovative device likely saved him from serious injury, or worse.

Lead mechanics Kennet Nyberg and Rickard Toftgren cancelled their holidays to repair the almost-destroyed car while Hansen recovered. The Swede returned for the following European Championship round in Belgium just five weeks later, driving the same car. Seven days after that Hansen claimed an emotional victory in the Dutch round at Valkenswaard.

Left: Wet weather made Momarken in 2007 a difficult event.
Below and following pages: The only time Kenneth Hansen ever rolled a racecar and it was a big one.

Kenneth Hansen

"It had been a difficult weekend, but I never give up and anything can happen in the final, so you always try to push.

A lot of that race you were a just a passenger because there was so much water and dirt on the track. It was raining like hell.

Me and Lars were going straight, side-by-side, then our wheels touched. I think my rear wheel touched his rear wheel and it just flipped my car up. When you see the ground from your seat it's not good, but I felt it would be okay, because it had always been okay. Then it started to roll.

The noise was terrible and I remember my first thought was: 'Ah there's a lot of parts broken here, this will be a lot of work.'

It went on for a long time, and it's quite stupid to think about that stuff when you could get hurt, but I'd never crashed like that, so I didn't really think about the fact that it could damage me.

I don't remember it stopping, but I remember being scared because I could smell fuel.

The first person I saw was Susann. I thought: 'Shit, what's happening? Am I dreaming? Why is she here, it should be a marshal or something.' But she got there and helped me get out.

Looking in the mirror, the race should never have been run. It was absolutely impossible to control the cars or to see anything. The data said I was doing 156km/h when I rolled.

I had been wearing the HANS, it was quite early for them and the first ones were not so comfortable. I didn't want to use it, but my crew said I had to. That day the doctor said to me that if I hadn't had the neck device, for sure I wouldn't drive anymore after that.

I was shaken and felt stiff for a couple of weeks, but I was okay.

But, it did affect me mentally. After that I knew it wasn't impossible to roll, and in a big crash I could also be hurt. I never 100% got back after that.

If I went off because I went too fast, I knew that was the reason. But we had just been side-by-side

and suddenly my car flipped. The wheels weren't protected because the wings moved a little. The regulations changed after that, but I didn't know exactly if or when a crash like that would happen again. When I had some fights on track after that, I backed off more often. Even if I got over it and didn't think about it, if you have a crash and cannot give a complete reason why it happened it affects you.

After Norway the mechanics worked day and night to fix the car, that was incredible. We went up to Kinnekulle to do a shakedown when it was fixed and I had a tyre explode. I went off again but there was no crash because there was lots of room, but the feeling that there could be a crash again came back to me.

Before that weekend in Norway, the car had always stayed on its wheels. It was on two wheels or one wheel sometimes, but after all those years, suddenly it was on the roof and it was a big surprise."

Timmy Hansen

"Kevin and I were standing with Oliver Eriksson, quite far from where the crash happened. Andreas Eriksson had just taken the lead, so I remember being happy for Oliver that his dad was leading.

Kevin started screaming and I looked up and saw dad's car in the air. Kevin started to cry a lot so I hugged him and I told him dad would be okay. As soon as he had calmed down a bit, we both ran as fast as we could, but we had to make our way all the way round to the opposite side of the track. We ran and ran, through the paddock, and around the spectator area to the side of the track. There were a lot of people there, I don't remember seeing dad; he was probably taken to the ambulance by then, and we met mum and she was helping to calm Kevin down.

Dad never crashed, so we weren't used to that. It was real Hollywood scenes of a bad accident, with terrible weather, everything dirty and you couldn't recognise the car."

Eric Faren

"It's one of those moments where you remember exactly where you were. I was just in front of the jump, watching the leaders and just heard this big bang, a really heavy noise. I saw the crash and remember thinking: 'Now it's over, he's not getting out of that'. It was so loud, and it was like your heart stopped while you were there watching. It was a quite strange experience, like you were not able to breath while you wondered what was happening. It was scary."

Kenneth Nyberg

"Me and Rickard had planned to go on holiday after that race. I was standing on the first corner, so it was quite far away where the roll happened, but I heard dung… dung…dung.

Kenneth had never rolled before. We ran there, Rickard was quite fast because he was on the start line. Then we saw the car, and it was incredible how he survived that crash. That's when it came over me what can happen.

We tried to get the car in the trailer, that was not so easy, so we worked quite late.

Kenneth was sitting in the mobile home and kept asking if it would be okay? Was the car destroyed? He was sure it was very bad but we kept giving him the same answer: 'Don't worry, we'll fix it!'

He went to some kart race with the boys I think. He was away one week, and we sorted it. When he came home, I don't think he believed it was the same car."

Tommy Rustad

"I went straight into the joker and was able to come out first because the joker was not much longer and there was a lot of traffic on the main lap. I was leading, but I caught up with Thomas Radstrom in the Hyundai. He was driving on three wheels and didn't have control of the car, I caught him two laps before the finish but he smashed into the side of my car because he didn't see me.

I got a puncture, and Andreas Eriksson overtook me, but on the same lap Kenneth crashed so there was a red flag.

There was a discussion about who was the winner, between me and Eriksson. It was not good to finish the race in that way, but finally Kenneth was quite okay, he was a little hurt but not seriously."

Susann Hansen

"I was waiting and waiting in the start area. There was a discussion with the Stewards that took a very long time and the rain was increasing a lot. I was getting worried about the fog inside the windscreen, the wipers not being able to clear the windscreen, the start RPM, the first corner, and the difficulty of being behind someone in that horrible weather. I was also worried about Timmy and Kevin standing on the grandstand getting soaked as we all waited for information.

I hoped and expected the race to be delayed until the weather got better. Maybe not until it stopped raining but at least until the worst rain had calmed down.

But the Stewards and Clerk of the Course said the race was on. I couldn't believe it. In that situation I only prayed it would go well, but it didn't.

There was so much water spray and mud, I didn't see the first few corners, but then I saw Kenneth side-by-side with Lars Larsson's blue car and that was a relief.

Then suddenly, like in slow motion, I saw Kenneth's car flipping up in the air. It was chaos.

My blood froze to ice, I could see fragments of the car flying all over, it looked like it had exploded.

While the car was still rolling I threw my umbrella away and ran. I wanted to run faster than my legs could move, it was like running in water, I couldn't move fast enough. I wanted to stop the car, I wanted to stop the unthinkable happening.

Just as the car landed on its roof close to the barriers, I arrived and went straight onto the track.

I just remember smoke, rain and pieces of car everywhere. Another car passed a couple of metres away at racing speed, but I didn't care. I only needed to see him, to see that he was alive and okay.

I fell on my knees at the drivers' side of the car, and there Kenneth was, hanging upside down in the harness. He looked at me with empty eyes. Confused, afraid and not fully conscious, but he looked at me. 'Thank you God' was my first thought. I talked to him as calmly as possible. People came to help and managed to get him out of the car before the medical crew took over.

A while later I went to the doctor to see Kenneth after he had been examined. The doctor said: 'This one might just have saved your life; as he pointed to the HANS device.' That was a big wake up call.

Kenneth hadn't been a big fan of the new safety protection, but this changed his mind forever with regards to safety work. No effort to make racing safer is too great.

I am still surprised that people that have never been in a racecar can judge when it is safe to drive or not. That day is a typical example of that. There are limits; if it is too wet or too dusty we can't simply say it is okay and safe to race.

I still get upset when I think about that day."

Russian connection

Hansen first visited Russia in 2005 to receive his 13th FIA European Championship trophy at the annual FIA Off-Road Championships prize-giving in Kazan. He then returned to Tatarstan's capital for three successive years from 2008 to compete in the annual President's Cup event at the Vysokaya Gora circuit.

Hansen's participation in the event was by invitation of Rustam Minnikhanov, then Prime Minister, and latterly the President, of Tatarstan, an autonomous republic of the Russian Federation.

Minnikhanov had switched from autocross and sporadic rallycross appearances in the European Championship to compete on a regular basis with a Hansen Motorsport-built Citroen C4 from the beginning of 2007.

Competing as part of an eclectic mix of cars in the President's Cup events, the Hansen Motorsport built Citroens, run by Latvian outfit TT Motorsport, were the class of the field, and Hansen claimed three successive victories. Notably, those appearances were the only times he raced a rallycross Supercar that wasn't adorned in the red-based livery for which is career is best remembered. And, aside from a one-off crosskart appearance and an outing in the Citroen Saxo Cup in Denmark, the only times Hansen was an arrive-and-drive competitor in his entire career.

"As a country Russia is not as different as I thought it would be. It used to be quite difficult to go to when I first went there for the end-of-season FIA prize-giving. Then people were quite poor, but over the years I went there, especially to Kazan, quite a lot changed; a lot of new buildings and having the Universiade [a biennial international multi-sport event, organised for university athletes] in 2013 made a big difference.

It was an adventure to go to Russia, but I must say it was a positive one, and when I went to race in the President's Cup, I was treated like a president.

Russians are Russians, that's the only way I can describe the people, but they were very friendly and very helpful. It was really like I was a celebrity when I was there.

The circuit was good. There were a lot of different cars and sometimes there was someone else that could fight with me and Rustam, but really, if I'm honest, it was just the two of us at the front.

Overall the event was not so different to what we were used to in Europe. The track was special because it had a chicane with a big compression, and if you hit it well, you came over a crest and normally you didn't jump. But me and Rustam had many good fights, then you needed to push everything everywhere that was possible to get out of that car,

so it meant a hard landing at the compression was part of that. Then after the hard landing, there was a 180-degree corner, where you were in the hands of the guy behind, so of course Rustam liked to push me there. That was fun.

We had some very good fights and Rustam enjoyed it so much. Especially one year when he was pushing me for all six laps in the final, really in the rear bumper and I just won it. He was absolutely delighted.

I always got the older version of the car, Rustam had the new one himself. I think they didn't have the support from engineers perhaps, especially engine engineers, so the performance was a little low and that made it different compared with what we raced with in Europe, but Rustam had a good level with his car.

I think for all of the races that I did there, Rustam gave a special invitation so all the children that came there got a lottery ticket, and every child won something, either a bicycle, skiing equipment, ice skates or whatever. It was a huge amount of presents and gifts for the families, that was a very warm side of Rustam.

Sverre Isachsen came to race there with us one year. He was in a Lada and I was in the Supercar, then afterwards we were offered to drive a tank with the army for half a day, that was different!"

Hansen won the President's Cup event in Tatarstan in 2008 and holds fond memories of his visits to the Russian republic.

The 2005 victory at Essay was a tactical masterclass from Hansen who managed to control the field despite a right rear puncture on his Citroen Xsara.

I hate to lose

'It's never over until you cross the finish line'. A commonly used phrase in motor sport that in rallycross, is as true as in any discipline.

Hansen entered the 2005 European Championship season on the back of five consecutive titles with the ever-improving Citroen Xsara, and qualified on pole position for the season-opener at Circuit des Ducs, at Essay in France. He then fended off the attentions of Norwegian Sverre Isachsen through the first sequence of corners in the final, before taking the advantage.

But, despite enjoying a comfortable margin at the front of the field, the right-rear tyre of his car punctured mid-race and Hansen came under pressure for the lead.

In a drive that ranks among his best ever, Hansen used all of the ability and race-craft in his locker to hold position ahead of Isachsen. With the pace having dropped, Isachsen in turn fell into the clutches of Michael Jernberg, but the Swede was hit by Guttorm Lindefjell from behind, dropping the Ford Focus driver down the order. Hansen held on for the second half of the final to secure an impressive win.

"When you're in that position, you know you need to be first. Before the joker lap was introduced you could drive very defensively and just be fast in the right places. Even with the puncture I was able to do that in Essay. I hate to lose, and when you are in that kind of situation you do everything you can to try to win. As long as it's in the regulations then it's okay, that's why I think it's good the joker lap arrived, because it can look a little ridiculous when someone has a puncture and they can keep the lead to the finish. But of course, I was very happy to win that race."

Hansen went on to claim the following two rounds in Portugal and Austria too, and at the end of the campaign wrapped up his 13th European crown.

An alternative route

Hansen's win at Essay in 2005, where the Swede defended his lead despite a puncture, would almost certainly be impossible in European or World Championship rallycross in the current era, where the compulsory joker lap has to be taken by each competitor once in every race.

Almost seven years prior to that Essay encounter, a new concept was pioneered in Sweden, after Hansen's father Svend started to come up with ideas during the mid-1990s to increase unpredictability in rallycross racing and promote excitement on track.

With the thought of pit stops swiftly dismissed, the initial iteration of the idea was to create an alternative optional route on the track, but it wasn't until later that the idea developed into each driver being required to take the alternative route once in every race.

The concept was first implemented at a one-off city centre race in Gothenburg, in 1998. That event, backed by the city and Swedish government, was held on a temporary track just 200 meters away from the city's main shopping street. Hansen finished second in the final, driving his Citroen Xsara.

The event was only held once, due to a lack of financial support, but thereafter the alternativ spar (literally 'alternative track'), which would later be called the joker lap, became an intrinsic part of the sport.

"I was a driver adviser in the FIA Off-Road Commission at that time, so I attended some meetings. A week after that event in Gothenburg there was an Off-Road Commission meeting in Prague, where I explained about the alternative route idea and how successful it had been. The delegates there just laughed at me.

I was furious, I couldn't believe the group of people laughing. For me it was a great idea, but they really thought it was a joke.

Now we can see what came out of that idea, and I like it. Some people still really don't [like the joker lap concept], but I think they are few now.

Before, if someone won the start it could be quite boring if the leader just blocked. Even if the driver behind was faster sometimes it was impossible to pass.

I think the reason my father started to think of it was because Per Eklund blocked me so many times.

It definitely changed rallycross completely though, because you can't take the start and be slow now. You need to be fast all the time."

Following that trial event, the concept was subsequently introduced at domestic rallycross circuits in Scandinavia and was approved for use by the FIA in 2006 for use in the European Rallycross Championship. Circuits around Europe gradually incorporated joker laps, and all new rallycross tracks created since the formation of the World Championship in 2014 are built with a joker lap section, which should be two or three seconds slower than the standard lap.

Other series also introduced similar concepts. The American-based Global Rallycross Championship used a shorter route for its temporary circuit jokers, while the Argentine Super TC 2000 touring car series sporadically implemented the concept and the FIA World Touring Car Championship used it for the first time in the Portuguese round at the Vila Real street circuit in 2017.

Top Right: The Gothenburg city race in 1998 was the first event to use what has become the joker lap.
Below right: Loheac, France. Three cars on the standard lap (left of shot) and two in the joker lap which is now a mandatory element of all World Championship rallycross tracks.

Spotting glory

A critical element to the joker lap strategy in rallycross is the spotter.

Standing trackside, or in World Championship races inside the 'Spotters' Tower', the spotter is in communication with their driver by radio, able to offer driving advice and encouragement, warn of any hazards on the circuit and crucially, inform when best to take the joker lap.

When the joker lap was initially introduced, it was used in a more random fashion, although the general consensus was that if a driver was at the front of the field, they should lead for as long as possible and take the joker at the end of the race, while if stuck at the back of the pack, they should take the joker early to try and run in clear air and close the gap to those ahead.

But, over time joker tactics have become increasingly important, both in gaining and defending positions, avoiding coming out of the joker in traffic and getting held up by slower cars.

The relationship between driver and spotter is an intimate and important one. Using his experience of being behind the wheel, and subsequently running other drivers within Hansen Motorsport, Hansen has been spotter for eldest son Timmy since 2013.

Kenneth Hansen

As a spotter you can mostly just do wrong, because when you do it right, it's just the normal job. It's easy to sit relaxed at home and look at the split times on TV. If the TV is showing the right car and so on, then it's not so difficult and often people say: 'Why didn't you do this or that?' But to be up there in the hot air of spotting, then it's hard, it can be really hard. But the feeling of pulling off a great strategy can be amazing too.

It's like being the co-driver in rallying, it's just that you're not in the car. Mentally though you are in the car because you're so focused and involved.

I think it's much better if you've done some driving, then it's easier to understand the complete picture. It's quite stressful, things happen so quickly and you need to take fast decisions, you have four or six laps and you need to make the call at the right time.

It's complicated, especially in finals when you have six cars and you need to play the game, like at Loheac in France where the joker is short. It's a little easier when it's a longer joker because you have slightly more time to play with.

Above: Hansen in the World RX Spotters'
Tower. He has been spotter for oldest son
Timmy since 2013.

The aim really is to get the driver in a position to be able to take the maximum out of themselves and the car without being disturbed.

Sometimes it's difficult to see all of the track, because of dust. We have some tools, we have some fixed cameras to guide us in World RX, but I mostly prefer to have eyes on the car instead of looking away to a TV and then back because you lose the contact for a little while and everything happens so fast.

It's the same with the timing screens, I use my own stopwatch. If you have a focus on one other car that you're directly competing with, it's much easier with a stopwatch. It's perhaps old fashioned, but that's the way I do it.

It's important to have a close relationship with the driver and to learn a system. Things like the level of the voice you use and how you pronounce words really tells the driver what you want them to do. It's not just advice, it's how much you're into it and pushing the driver. I have a good feeling for how comfortable Timmy is in the car, depending on the weekend. If he's

very together and is happy, then it's possible to push him a lot, but if it's a little tricky then I need to be more careful with him.

Timmy Hansen

Dad is so fully committed on the radio, like he's in the car, driving with me. Obviously I'm turning the steering wheel, but if I should be all-in or if I should hold back, or whatever I should do and where I should do it, that's him helping with that. He gives me a lot of information and speaks on the radio a lot too.

In some races he has really made the difference to help me to find the speed we needed to get everything out of it. In all of my great drives, he was also doing a great job at that time, delivering good calls when I needed them. We're a good team.

He has to read the situation though. If he can see there's more left out there and tells me that, then I'm going to give it to him, but if he pushes that too far, we can get into problems because I'm going to give him what he asks for. It's a really fine line.

Marsupilami

It isn't uncommon for racing drivers to be superstitious. In formula racing for example, some drivers climb into the car on the same side every time, while others always put a particular glove on before the other.

Despite his mother, Edith, being extremely superstitious by nature, never sitting at a table if she were to become the 13th person, never putting shoes or keys onto a table and never knowingly killing a spider, Hansen didn't have a specific superstition or routine that he carried through his career. However, he does admit to trying to continue trends, if he had been aware of doing something specific for an event which turned out to be successful; the way in which he packed his race bag for instance. But, those minor happenings eventually went forgotten, and often changed to something else.

In the latter stages of his driving career, Hansen regularly had a pre-race sugar fix. "I had a small Kexchoklad (a Swedish chocolate wafer biscuit). I always had one before the race; just a small one. I think it was also to be a little alert, to wake up a little. I remember one time when Joel Christoffersson was my mechanic. I had put the biscuit in the car, got in, put on the helmet and went to eat the biscuit, but it was not there. I looked out and Joel was eating it! I don't think it mattered really."

But, while wife Susann and mechanic Kennet Nyberg can lay claim to always being by Hansen's side

through his top-flight career, racing a rallycross car is a solo exploit. From the late 1990s Hansen always had a mascot riding shotgun, a gift from a then young Timmy. "He's Marsupilami, from a French cartoon. His tail is like a spring, which he can make do whatever he wants. If he's in a fight, it will be like a spring with a boxing glove! He was from Timmy, perhaps with Susann's help because he was still only young then. But, they brought him to me as a mascot and when I got him, I won four races in a row, so after that he was with me."

Some years later, when Timmy Hansen made his transition from single-seaters to rallycross with the family team in the European Championship, Marsupilami changed allegiance too, for a while at least. "After some time he [Timmy] took him out. I think he had some bad luck, but I don't think this guy is causing bad luck. Perhaps he was just not committing with Timmy, so maybe he is better outside. He was a little hurt for a while with no head and no tail, but I've fixed him now and now he's alive again. If I do some more races, he will be there again."

Today Marsupilami travels in Hansen's bag to every event around the world, but will probably guard the awning the next time Hansen drives, the small dog-like monkey creature's time of being strapped to the roll cage of a rallycross Supercar just a distant memory, for now, at least.

Left: Mascot or lucky talisman? Cartoon character Marsupilami rode in Hansen's cars for many years (he's in the left corner of the windscreen in the 2006 Citroen C4 above) and still travels to every event.

A young Hansen aboard his father's BMB President tractor.

From building mopeds to karting and folkrace, Hansen had varied interests and experiences from birth to beginning his rallycross career in 1983. Those exploits, his national military service and owning a fuel station, among other forms of employment before becoming a professional racing driver are documented in the next 14 pages.

3. BEGINNINGS

Danish couple Svend and Edith Hansen emigrated to the area around the Swedish town of Gotene in Vastra Gotaland County in 1955, along with three children; seven-year-old Rita, five-year-old Peter and three-year-old Erik.

Five years later, 40 minutes into September 29, 1960, Kenneth became the first of the Hansen siblings not to be born at home, but in the nearby Lidkoping maternity hospital.

Hansen first attended school in Gotene from the age of seven, but it was around his 10th year that his love for the internal combustion engine began, first with two wheels, attending local motocross races as a spectator with the family and together with best friend Morgan Persson.

Having managed to persuade his parents that he should have a small moped to ride at home, Hansen created a rudimentary course in the garden of the family home at Klenhult.

After wearing a path in the lawn, the young Swede worked on creating his own off road circuit through the undergrowth behind the house. Despite significant effort, the track never really materialised and it was largely the lawn and sometimes the vegetable patch, much to the disapproval of his father, that bore the brunt of Hansen's first motorised antics.

The next stage was to head into nearby quarries and forests with friends, where the riders became increasingly experienced, and brave. One overzealous moment lead to friends Hans Rytterstrom and Christer

Strand having a head-on collision and ending up in hospital. They were fine, their mopeds less so.

Speed was always a draw even from a young age for Hansen, as was the ability to improvise and invent, a skill that would aid him well through his later rallycross career. Tired of pushing the lawn mower around the family garden, as a young teenager Hansen built a wheeled trailer, complete with kitchen chair to attach to the mower so he could ride behind it in relative comfort.

Far left: On a family holiday in Norway
Above left: The oldest picture Hansen has of himself, aged three and on a tricycle.
Above: With the bicycle he got for his seventh birthday outside the family house at Klenhult, a property that has returned to the Hansen family.

Another of his early creations is what he refers to as a minibike. Developed using components scavenged from bicycles, mopeds and utilising some kart wheels, Hansen created his own machine, that he still has to this day, and which could reach 60kph.

It wasn't all about two wheels for long though. Just a few kilometres down the road from the family home, a pair of wealthy brothers built a kart circuit for their sons.

Persson's uncle gave him a new Swiss-Hutless BM 100cc kart for Christmas. For the first few weeks it didn't leave the young boy's bedroom and Hansen spent much time sitting in the seat pretending to drive it. Soon those dreams became reality as the pair started driving at the circuit. Hansen remembers his first experience of being on track as something he had only dreamt about from images seen in magazines.

But despite that early taste of karting, Hansen's thoughts were still on being mobile on the road, rather than racing on track. As such, his aspirations remained on two wheels. But, despite protests, his mother vetoed all such ideas.

The local kart circuit, dubbed the 'Eklund Ring' also hosted rental karting, and having joined the motor club while still at school, Hansen worked alongside his friends on the rental karting venture, and occasionally got to drive the karts. Built on cumbersome chassis and powered by lazy Briggs and Stratton engines, those machines were not high in the performance stakes.

Hansen's four-wheel endeavours would really begin in 1975 when elder brother Erik found a kart for sale in nearby Kinne-Kleva, and thanks to a summer job at the local Kinnekulle Ring with an agricultural company, Rosen and Sons, where he worked in the workshop, before later learning to drive lorry tractor units in the yard, Hansen was able to reimburse the machine's 450 SEK (45 Euro) cost to his parents.

That first kart was basic, and suffered from poor reliability, but Hansen persisted and would return to the family's garage to repair it after each failure to be back on track as quickly as possible, sometimes just with friends, but often with the kart towed on a small trailer behind his father's car. More often than not, completing a single lap was an achievement.

The following year, seeking a better option, Hansen located a Robardie kart built by Ronnie Peterson's father Bengt, complete with Parilla engine. The machine was acquired for 2200 SEK (220 Euro) and

Hansen took part in his first truly competitive race, the Fox Hunt in Storfors to the north of Vanern lake.

Initially travelling around 100km to races, Hansen's infrastructure was basic. In the absence of a paddock awning, a camping frame-tent was commandeered to work in when the weather was poor, but otherwise, amenities were minimal. It was a time for competing for the love of it, rather than targeting any specific goals. Hansen admits that racing against his friends, and comparing which of the group had set the fastest time in practice was more important than the outright result, but by persisting in both improving his driving, and attempting to extract more from the machinery, the results steadily improved.

Having completed the three required races to have the white 'novice' band removed from around the number on his kart, Hansen would claim his first race wins in his debut season. Soon though, the Robardie kart was not good enough to be competitive where Hansen aspired to race, and in 1977 he bought a new kart with spare engines from the Alvars Racing team to compete in the Class A, 100cc division.

Far left: The minibike Hansen built from various components and which he still owns. It's a restoration project on the 'to do' list.
Above left: The Robardie kart that Hansen raced in 1976.
Above: With Morgan Persson at an early race with a Category C kart.

In 1978, three months before he turned 18, Hansen started to learn to drive on the road, and within a fortnight of his birthday passed his driving test first time, the only complaints from his instructor being that he needed to calm down a little, not brake so late and remember he wasn't on track.

Before being qualified to drive on the road, Hansen's early car-related antics had already begun in fields at a friend's farm. On one occasion using Lennart Andersson's Volvo PV, and with five passengers on board, control was lost on a slope and the car rolled over. Everyone escaped without harm, and amazingly given his later career, that incident was one of few occasions when Hansen found himself inside an inverted vehicle, even though he had not been driving on this occasion.

Distracted by the usual teenage pursuits like socialising and partying, and without harbouring any real desire to become a professional driver, Hansen's karting activities slowed a little once he was on the road, although he was never far from a race track.

Having finished his nine years of compulsory schooling, he moved to the Skara Katedralskolan, college to the south of Gotene, for a further two years, to learn about the dairy industry; everything from how to make milk and cheese products, to servicing machines and fabrication.

With Gotene's biggest industry being its dairy, which still operates today, the aim was to be guaranteed employment at a time when work wasn't easy to come by. But Hansen didn't last long working in the dairy industry once he'd qualified. The requirement to work weekends didn't suit his desire to continue karting and he soon moved to a Gotene-based construction firm, working on house interiors.

In 1979 Hansen enjoyed his most successful year in karting, winning one of the season's biggest races, the Holiday Race, using a Class C 125cc geared Kalikart fitted with a Rotax engine. While he would never claim a Swedish title in karting, the Holiday Race was of similar prestige, attracting international names to compete alongside all of the leading Swedish drivers.

All the time Hansen was trying to improve his
equipment although not all of the developments were
a success, and he suffered a number of engine failures
as a result of over optimistic machining carried out in a
bid to gain performance. In his last full karting season,
he recalls leading seven or eight of his biggest races, but
failing to finish any of them because of poor reliability.

*Above left: As a young kart racer and motor
club member, Hansen took part in a school
event to promote and demonstrate karting
to pupils.*
*Above: For an ice racing event at Vanersborg
bandy arena, Hansen made tyre studs by
fixing screws through strips of metal that
were then fixed around the tyres.*

With national service still compulsory in Sweden at the time, Hansen was called for duty and spent the minimum required seven-and-a-half months at a base in Skovde in the tank regiment around his 20th year. His army education, Hansen recalls, was as cannon fodder; the role of Hansen and comrades being to vacate a tank in the heat of battle and take on opposing soldiers on foot. The average life expectancy for such a pursuit in war was three seconds from leaving the vehicle. Fortunately for Hansen, he was never dispatched to war.

That time in the army marked the first time Hansen had lived away from the family home. On his return to civilian life, he initially worked with brother Erik in the family water drilling company, before buying a BP fuel station in Moholm (50km from Gotene) with brother Peter for 40,000 Euro in 1981.

Hansen moved into a small apartment nearby, and also worked as a retrained fireman for the local fire service. The fuel station, where the pair serviced cars along with selling fuel, eventually failed to make money, but the premises provided the basis for the next step in Hansen's motor sport career.

Folkrace, an entry-level version of rallycross with low-cost cars and more rudimentary circuits that is still popular in Scandinavia, was first run in Sweden in Hansen's early 20s.

Using the facilities at the filling station, the Swede and his brothers began to build their own folkrace machines, usually Volvos; PVs, Amazons and 142s. In the first year of the discipline, 1981, Hansen made it to the A final in an event at Kinnekulle.

Above left: Persson and Hansen pictured with
their prizes for finishing second and third in
the Mer Cup at Kristianstad.

Top right: Facilities were basic and the tow
car was also the driver's changing room in
the karting days.

Centre right: Hansen was trained as 'cannon
fodder' during his national service.

Bottom right: Hansen worked with older
brother Erik (pictured here) drilling water
bore holes. In those days one bore could take
a week to drill, today it's half-a-day's work.

The Swede was an A final regular the following season, racing under the 'Team Hansens Bilservice' banner, and came close to securing victories, but either mechanical failures or contact in the heat of battle while leading meant podiums were the best he achieved.

The rules of folkrace, which still exist today, include a price-cap on cars and a bidding system that means every car is for sale at every event. With his equipment generally fast and well prepared, Hansen's machines were among the most desirable and in his two years in the discipline he got through more than 10 cars.

It was during the folkrace era that Hansen first sampled rallying, first as a navigator for friend Christer Strand, in a 100 horsepower, front-wheel drive Saab V4. Hansen's main memories of the experience involve 'testing' at night on snow-covered roads in the countryside, where he perfected his skills in snow digging, to extract the car from ditches or snow banks after various misdemeanours.

Hansen also got behind the wheel himself in some rally events local to Gotene after starting his rallycross career, using a Volvo 140 bought together with mechanic Tomas Gustavsson. Although satisfied with his pace on the stages, Hansen couldn't muster the same budget, or more crucially enthusiasm for rallying over racing.

By the end of 1982 Hansen was getting fed up with constantly having his folkrace cars bought and, with eyes on stepping up to rallycross, Hansen and Persson costed building a car. When they realised it would be a costly affair the plans were shelved.

The 22-year old then had a brainwave, and put an advert in the Idrottsbladet newspaper, offering his road-going Volvo P1800 in exchange for a rallycross car. After several days of silence, a proposal came in for an exchange for a Saab V4, which quickly fell through. Then, an owner of a Volvo Amazon rallycross car got in touch, and said he was interested in making a deal.

Travelling to Fagersta, 250km north of Gotene with father Svend, complete with the P1800 on a trailer, the Hansens met the owner of the Amazon on an industrial estate, and despite the appearance of the battle-scarred Amazon, a deal was done and father and son discussed the new chapter in Hansen's career the entire way home.

Previous page: Hansen moved from karts to cars when he started folkracing, a highly competitive version of rallycross that remains popular in Sweden today. Hansen is driving the number 46 Volvo 142 in 1982 at Brannebrona.

Above: The first rallycross car. In the winter of 1982-1983 Hansen traded his Volvo P1800 for this battled-scarred Amazon racecar.

While rebuilding and refining the car before the rallycross season got underway the following spring was going to be a challenge to Hansen who was inexperienced in such tasks, he had already decided that car would be painted in a similar fashion to Olle Arnesson's Hermetite Porsche. And, once the bodywork had been repaired, the red and white colour scheme was duly applied.

Following the financial failure of the fuel station, Hansen worked for a plastic moulding company in Gotene, making parts for car manufacturers and Husqvarna. While he was able to rent a small workshop to house his rallycross car nearby, he found the work monotonous, and again sought alternative employment.

He was interviewed and offered a job at a Volvo dealership in Skovde, but concerned that he may have oversold his abilities for working in the workshop, he initially turned the opportunity down, and instead went to work at a heating and ventilation company located to the south of Gotene.

However, he lasted only a few days in the job before returning to the Volvo dealership, where he began working in the quick service workshop, before moving into the main workshop, and liaising with customers.

The Volvo dealership would be Hansen's last place of regular employment. With his rallycross career taking off, the firm bought him the Volvo 240 in which he graduated to the European Championship in 1987 [see chapter nine], but with travel and competition taking up more of his efforts, and requiring more time away from work, in 1990 Hansen opted to take seven months off work to race in Europe.

He managed to secure sponsorship from BP in order to pay himself a salary and, having formed Kenneth Hansen Motorsport AB, he never returned to the Volvo dealership or conventional employment.

In 2016 Timmy Hansen asked his father to take a look at a house he was thinking of buying. The journey to view to property ended at the door of the former Hansen family home in Klenhult, which had been sold by Svend and Edith around the turn of the millennium. Hansen then had to explain the significance of the house to his oldest son, who subsequently bought it as the home he now shares with his wife Emma and their son Sam.

Family and friends have formed part of Hansen's team over the years, this is the 1994 entourage.

For a man familiar to hundreds of thousands of people around the world, and the acquaintance of many thousands too, Kenneth Hansen is a professional yet private character. He holds those close to him dear, from parents and siblings, to his wife and sons, and those close enough to be true friends.

4. FAMILY AND FRIENDS

Parents and siblings

From bringing him up at the family home at Klenhult to supporting his endeavours in karting, and later his career in rallycross, Svend and Edith Hansen were always staunch supporters of their youngest child.

Eight years younger than his closest brother, the Swede spent less time with his three siblings when he was young than he may have had they been closer in age. He grew up to work with both of his brothers at different times, each also serving time in rallycross paddocks around Europe.

Hansen has always enjoyed the support of his parents. His father, Svend (above), was a constant in the paddock until he could no longer travel to events. Mother Edith (right) enjoys the television coverage of current era of rallycross and is able to follow her family through it.

Edith Hansen on Kenneth

Kenneth was a very kind boy when he was young, and he still is. I'm very proud that he won a lot of times, but he's still the same boy. When Kenneth had success, when I was at work or in the town at home, there were always a lot of people asking about him. The newspapers wrote about him a lot which was very nice, like it is with Timmy and Kevin now. It's very exciting to read about them in the papers, it makes me very proud.

Kenneth was involved with engines from when he had the motorbikes at home and then karting. I didn't want him to ride a motorbike on the road, so it was good when he got a kart and did that. I didn't want him to be doing anything really dangerous.

In his career I have been worried about him many times, the same now with Timmy and Kevin.

It was a little strange when Kenneth stopped driving, because I was always waiting for the next season, but at the same time it was a bit more relaxed not worrying about him so much. But now it's the same with the boys.

I went to a lot of races but I'm not able to go anymore. I think the last race was at Holjes four or five years ago. When it got more difficult for me to walk, it wasn't so easy to go. Holjes was my favourite race to go to, but me and Svend also went into Europe many times and we made many friends when we had the camper travelling around to the races. It's very good that it's all on television now.

Because Kenneth is the youngest of the children, when he was young the older ones [Peter, Rita and Erik] helped him, they protected him.

Kenneth has always been a calm and positive person. Many times he came to me to ask what was correct to do, which direction to take. He was careful and clever to try not to take too many risks. When he was driving he understood if something was not possible to do, if there was too much risk. And he has been very careful in business too.

It's very nice to have Sam [Timmy's son] now too. He's very good, he's moving around a lot more now, but this is just the start. When Timmy and Kevin were young I told Kenneth that my mother once said: 'One child takes all of your time, so two children can't take more.'

Erik Hansen on Kenneth

Kenneth hasn't really changed much since he was a boy. He's always had his feet on the ground. We're quite similar, we've always had a good understanding and we work very well together. I'm eight years older, so maybe I should tell him what to do, but we are brothers and we can talk in a way not many people can.

I don't think there are so many people who are really close to Kenneth, but he has good friends. That's really good. I've seen so many drivers that you could not talk with once they got success, but not Kenneth.

Everybody knows him in Gotene. Our mother is in a home now, a lady was talking to us and suddenly she said: 'I know you, Kenneth.' We didn't know her, she was 80 or 90-years-old, but she said she had seen Kenneth in the newspapers all the time.

Many times we had a stage in the centre of the town and when they [Hansen family] came back after winning and many, many people came to see. That was really good. It was the same when Kenneth was driving, and when they won the World Championship [in 2019].

When we had a race at Kinnekulle, we had a stage in the centre on the Friday and all the cars came and there was a lot of people. That was just for the Swedish Championship, but things are not the same now, we don't have the famous profiles like that anymore in the Swedish Championship.

Kenneth was very quiet when he was young, he never did anything bad and was a nice guy.

When he was old enough we raced karts together for many years. There was no big competition between us, we helped each other, the same when we raced in folkrace many times. We were just racing for fun. That was a very nice time in our lives.

When Kenneth went to rallycross with the Volvo Amazon, I also drove in some races in a Ford Escort, but the difference between our families is that my wife doesn't really like motor sport, and when we had children there was not so much time. I've always been working with racing though, as Race Director at Kinnekulle and in Kenneth's team.

I worked in the team doing many things; as the cook, working with the drivers and sometimes a little on the cars, but not so much on that side. Sometimes we had 50 people to look after and feed all day, that could be busy!

If we had two races in Europe close together and we were in Portugal for example, we would go to the French Riviera before the next race and had a lot of fun.

I have many brilliant memories. It's good when you win and everything, and we did that a lot, but the travelling, when you are so close to everybody that was a really nice time. Driving to Portugal for 3000km, sitting next to each other, we had many good times.

That's what is best with rallycross, I have so many friends all over Europe. I'm not at the races as much now like Kenneth is, but I'm still in touch with so many people. That's really nice, it warms your heart.

Hansen is eight years younger than closest brother Erik (to the right above), but has raced and worked together with him.

The young Hansen was protected and encouraged by his older siblings. Here he is with Peter in a Volvo Amazon.

Kenneth on Parents and siblings

I could have been Danish, if things had been a little different. My parents moved from Denmark to the Gotene area in 1955. My father and his sister's husband came first for work, the families followed later.

We visited Denmark when I was young many times, but it was quite a big trip. Even to go to Gothenburg, you would stop once or twice to get a coffee, and that's only 150km. Today you don't think about just driving there and back to collect someone from the airport; it was so different then.

My mother and father had 12 and 13 brothers and sisters. We tried to count many years ago and there were 82 cousins. Perhaps I knew 10 or 15 of them, there are so many.

Me and Tommy Kristoffersson sometimes joke that Sweden had a lack of drivers so they imported us, because Tommy is not Kristoffersson, he is Kristoffersen actually, which is from Denmark.

My mother was in the war in occupied Denmark. She lost a child when she was very young, I should have had two sisters and two brothers. When a parent loses a child young like that, it's very hard.

I am quite a lot younger than my brothers and sister, when I was 10 my next brother, Erik was 18, so they took care of me and protected me a lot. But when I was in the first class in school, he was in the last. We didn't do so much together all of us, because when you are 18 or 20 and you have a 10-year-old brother, life is very different. I looked up to them a lot though.

My sister (Rita) was 12 years older than me and she was like a second mum. She lived not far away and I remember more about when she had her first daughter, Kristina, and we were not far apart in age, she was like my little sister. After a while they moved to the south of Sweden.

I started karting together with Erik and then Peter was also helping us do folkrace when we had the fuel station [see chapter three]. That was the time when we were closest, because we did the same thing and had the same mission.

Erik came to work for us at Hansen Motorsport later on, for many years, so we got closer again.

He has always been the guy who can take care of what you need him to do. He's very social, he loves to speak with people and he was always easy to work with. It was very rare that he could not fix a problem. He's a people person, like Peter is too. When Peter and I had the fuel station, we were quite close too. He

still lives there in Moholm. We are not so close now, he has three children and has been very busy with his business, but we stay in contact of course, especially with it's something to do with our mother. He was very involved when his son Magnus raced in rallycross, and they sold Cooper tyres in Sweden too.

Rita passed away in 2013 and that was very hard for my mother, and when my father died in 2007, that was also so difficult for her. She has had such a full life that it's difficult to get her life story. Sometimes when you are talking, something pops up that you've never heard before; it's so interesting. Her life has been so far away from all the electronics and phones we have now. She was scared about my racing, but she was always supportive, came to the races and helped.

It was my father who mostly helped me find sponsors. He even took over the kart circuit to run races for the motor club, then he moved on to rallycross in the club and ran the European Championship races at Kinnekulle.

I don't think he had any interest in motor racing before that.

He was always there, always supporting. He was perhaps like me with my boys now, you always want to try to make it happen, to try and find the sponsors. He could also be the guy that put on the handbrake if I wanted something too much.

My parents had their own camper later on and chose which races to come to in Sweden and Europe. I think when my dad understood that he couldn't come in the camper anymore, because he started to get too old, a part of him died already then.

Then we were racing at Kinnekulle about three weeks before he passed away. He was there, I won the race and he was very happy to have been able to be at a race again. That time it was a little like he was okay, he was okay that that was it.

He had quite often been up and down with his health, in and out of hospital and you always believed he would be fine. The last time we were there, I didn't understand that he would not come back. We were drinking coffee and we talked about how we had had wonderful times. Of course, when you talk like that you feel it's the start of the end. The day after that we couldn't contact him anymore, and me and my brothers were there when he passed away.

Without him and my mother I wouldn't have done what I have.

Wife and children

Susann Bergvall, daughter of Thord and Lilian, began her motor sport career in folkrace in Sweden, before graduating to rallycross in a Volvo 240. She and Kenneth Hansen met at a Swedish Championship race at Bergbybanan in 1988, and having entered into a relationship, the pair later began living together in Gotene, working towards a common goal of achieving the best they could in their discipline.

Their first son, Timmy, was born on 21 May 1992 and Bergvall continued to compete, racing Hansen's Ford RS500 in the Swedish Championship in 1993, scoring a podium in her maiden event, before graduating to the European Championship in the 1400 Cup for Group N 1400cc cars with a Citroen AX.

She claimed victory in the second round of the 1994 season, at Lousada in Portugal on her way to claiming the title in a final-round decider in Germany. In doing so, Bergvall became the first and so far only female European Rallycross Champion. On the same day at the Estering, Hansen secured his first crown at the sport's highest level. Bergvall also claimed the Swedish title in the same category that year, but hung up her helmet the following season to focus on running the team, by now her full-time occupation. The couple's second son Kevin was born on May 28 1998, and they married in Rome on 6 May 2000.

Timmy began karting in 2002 and claimed several victories in Swedish junior classes before stepping up to the KF3 category in 2005, then to KF2 in 2008 where he became Swedish Champion and 'Best Privateer' in the KF2 World Cup.

That karting groundwork led to single-seaters. For 2009 he signed for German team Mucke Motorsport to race in Formula BMW Europe and finished the year 13th. Remaining with the same squad for 2010, and competing against drivers who would later line up in Formula 1, Hansen took a pole position at Zandvoort (Holland), a fastest lap at Monza (Italy) and claimed victory at Hockenheim (Germany) on his way to third in the series. If a barometer of Hansen's level at that stage is required, you need only look at the list of names in the same series at that time, including later Formula 1 stars Pierre Gasly, Carlos Sainz Jr, Esteban Ocon, Daniil Kvyat and more.

Under the radar, Hansen also made is rallycross debut in 2010 with a one-off appearance in the British Championship's one-make Suzuki Swift category

at Pembrey. He moved to the Formula Renault 2.0 Eurocup with Austrian squad Interwetten Racing for 2011, but not without also making his rallycross Supercar debut in the French Rallycross Championship season-opener at Dreux.

One of 12 drivers to join the FIA Institute Young Driver Excellence Academy, in Formula Renault Hansen dominated at the Hungaroring to claim victory, while he also won three rounds of the Formula Renault 2.0 Alps series. However, his return to the series in 2012 brought a best result of 11th in the opening half of the year. Feeling the equipment under him didn't match that of his opponents, Hansen ended his circuit racing aspirations after the fourth round in Russia.

A few months later he deputised for Hansen Motorsport driver Alexander Hvaal when the Norwegian fell ill before of the Finnish round of the European Rallycross Championship at Kouvola, where he finished fifth.

Knowing the promotion of the sport was about to be taken over by IMG, Hansen switched focus to rallycross and subsequently joined the family team for 2013. In the sport's new era, Hansen finished on the podium in the opening event at Lydden Hill (Great Britain), won round three in Hungary and finished the year third overall. He signed to drive for the family team's collaboration with Peugeot for the World Rallycross Championship in 2014, and continued to race for the French marque until it withdrew from World RX at the end of 2018 [see chapter seven]. During that period, Hansen finished second in the Drivers' Championship in 2015 and won five events. He also gave Kenneth Hansen his first grandchild, Sam Hansen being born on May 4 2018. Timmy and partner Emma married in July 2019, mid-way through his best season that would culminate in winning the World RX Drivers' crown [see chapter seven] with four victories to his credit driving for the Hansen family team's private effort.

In the final round decider in South Africa, younger brother and team mate Kevin was also in the fight for the World crown. But, unlike Timmy, Kevin Hansen had always intended to be a rallycross driver.

He started karting in 2005, aged six, and claimed the Swedish Junior Championship in 2009, before winning the 2010 International Rok Cup Finale in Italy. His final karting season was in the 2011 German KF3 series.

Hansen's youngest son switched rallycross in the British Junior series the next year, driving a 1300cc Suzuki Swift, run by British engineer Graham Rodemark, the beginning of a relationship that would continue into the World Championship.

While racing in the UK, Hansen Jnr as he referred to himself, also raced in the JRX Cup – a short-lived series for juniors that ran alongside European Championship events in 2012 and 2013 – and bagged a pair of crowns. Stepping up to the new single-make Supercar Lites division in 2014, 16-year-old Hansen dominated at Arvika in the RallyX Nordic series, then won on his debut in the World RX-supporting RX Lites in Finland.

He won the Nordic crown in 2014 and the RX Lites crown in 2015, the latter carrying a prize drive in the final round of the World Championship with OlsbergsMSE in a Ford Fiesta. His start at Rosario in Argentina, where he qualified for the final, made him the youngest ever World RX participant.

Moving to Supercar as part of the Peugeot-backed Hansen team for 2016, running under the 'Hansen Talent Development' banner, Kevin emulated his father's success to win the European crown, becoming the youngest FIA European Rallycross Champion in history. He also drove in selected World Championship events and was awarded the prestigious FIA Rookie of the Year award at the FIA Gala the same year.

The youngest Hansen continued racing in World RX for the next three years, with the Peugeot-associated family team, before claiming a maiden victory in Abu Dhabi in 2019 and taking the title fight with his brother and Andreas Bakkerud to the very last race of the year.

Above and following pages: The great double act, Susann and Kenneth Hansen have earned success on the race track and in business through their dedication and hard work. Susann led the adoption of data logging after ending her own driving career, ambitions fulfilled. Bottom right on the following spread is Susann's first international win in Portugal in 1994.

Susann on Kenneth

Kenneth is the love of my life. I will never forget the first time I saw him. It was a round of the Swedish Rallycross Championship, I was there spectating with my parents and Kenneth was racing.

Like how it often is in a rallycross paddock on Saturday evening, we were having a barbecue, Kenneth and his friend came by and spoke with someone at the table. I remember I looked at him and he looked at me smiling with those kind eyes.

I'm a very shy person and would never dream of going and saying something to him, but then my dad and Kenneth's dad spoke and Svend said that Kenneth had been reading a book about sports psychology. For some reason they decided that I should borrow the book, so the first contact I had with Kenneth was when I returned this book called 'Best when it matters' to him. We never let go of each other after that.

We already had a common interest in rallycross and for me it felt like a relief to meet him, because then I knew where my future was; with him. Whatever he wanted to do, I knew I would be in on that. He never had to convince me to be in on rallycross with him, I was as much driven as he was from the beginning.

Being a rallycross driver myself, I knew that he was something extraordinary. He was not just a medium talented guy who could handle a car, he had something else. He had the understanding that it's not enough to be a good mechanic and good driver, but you also need to manage people, work together and make the most out of little money, because neither of us had any family fortunes.

Only a year after we'd been together, we started Kenneth Hansen Motorsport because we wanted to give rallycross a fair chance and see where it could lead us. Every year it was raw hard work from day to night. That was our fortune, the time we put in. I worked in the company all the time but without payment until 1995 when I came onboard properly because we had worked up a platform of sponsors and partners.

When we had Timmy in 1992, the maternity leave was combined with work, it was: 'Okay, now we have this wonderful little guy with us, and we will take him wherever we go.' It wasn't like: 'Now we can't race anymore, we need to go back to a more simple life.' That never crossed our minds.

Kenneth and me were a good match when it came to managing our little company, because we were good at different things. He was a good driver and mechanic, and had an engineering mind. I focused on administration, marketing and communications.

But Kenneth also has this ability to put on many different hats, with his jacket on in the office, his overalls in the workshop, drawing something at his desk, meeting sponsors and doing media activities, and obviously as a driver. That has been beneficial for him as the team grew, because he has the full understanding of all aspects. He knows exactly what it is to drive the truck or change tyres or whatever. He knows every detail. Sometimes that can also hold him back because he's so used to knowing everything and doing everything, he does things out of habit and forgets we now have someone doing it in the team.

I think a strong side that has been key to his success has been knowing how to control his emotions. He doesn't waste emotion. If he has a target to win, he doesn't lose energy for the sacrifice of missing the victory. If he's angry or upset at something, he's good at controlling that and just focusing on what is really important, he's not easily stressed. That makes his competitors very frustrated and annoyed because he smiles easily. If someone says something mean to him, he smiles and that just makes them even more angry. Then he knows he has won because they are wasting the energy they could have used to perform better.

Another of his strong sides is doing things that mean people want to stay with us in the team. He listens to others and makes them feel welcome.

Every time I have doubted myself, he has believed in me. I didn't think I was good enough to do rallycross. Maybe partly I did it because my father wanted me to, but Kenneth has always believed in me. To have those years racing side-by-side with him, it couldn't have been any better for me. Giving me the opportunity and support over the years meant the world to me and then when I stopped driving myself, it was my own decision. Kenneth thought I should continue but I felt it was the right time, I had done what I wanted.

I pushed that we should have the datalogging system and work more with data, he supported me fully. I'm not an engineer but he let me go on with that. It was a big investment for us, but he believed in me doing it, and I was quite good at it until we had other engineers coming in to do it later.

That is the part of him that I appreciate the most. He believes so much in me that I believe in myself. That is a very big gift to give to someone.

Timmy Hansen has progressed from being one of those children who grew up in the paddock to achieving the greatest success by winning the 2019 FIA World Rallycross Championship.

Timmy on Kenneth

My earliest memories are being in the bus, playing with toy cars in the paddock, and travelling in the bus to races. I remember the toaster smelt really strange, little things like that, but I don't have many memories of the actual racing.

I was doing what any other kid was doing at home, but I was in the rallycross paddock because for a lot of the time, that was my home. I was completely used to the cars starting and being warmed up but I don't have any early memories of dad being a rallycross driver or how well he was doing. He was just my dad.

Apparently when I got my first kart when I was four, I wasn't that interested. But I remember being able to compete when I was 10 and it starting to be fun. When I started racing, I realised what it was that dad was doing.

We did a lot of karting for a while, so we were either at rallycross or karting every weekend, and dad was really supportive.

When I got a bit older, I worked with data analysis for dad and the team and actually made a difference, before that I had just been cleaning the car.

I wanted to get to Formula 1. I have always been motivated by what's impossible. I'm a bit of a dreamer and it was so big, so impossible, I guess that's why I was motivated by that. There were two big challenges; to become a better driver and to raise all the money. I didn't manage all the money.

Of course dad bought my first kart and some small 80cc quad bikes that me and Kevin spent countless hours on when we were young, but it has always been my own choice to do everything I've done. Looking back mum and dad always gave me all the opportunities to do everything I wanted, but I've had to fight for it too. When I was going formula racing dad was a massive help when I was chasing sponsors and everything. Back then I was thinking I had achieved it myself, but looking back, without him I wouldn't have been anywhere near. He taught me that you have to work hard for what you believe in.

It was never part of my thinking to do rallycross, I just wasn't interested. Maybe I felt I had always been there, it was single seaters that I wanted to do. When I actually tried rallycross for the first time, I'd just gone through quite a difficult time in my racing career, I hadn't given up on the dream of Formula 1, but it was hard. Then you start to think about what it is that you really want to do.

My very first rallycross race was with Graham Rodemark in an almost standard Suzuki Swift in the British Championship at Pembrey in 2010. It was really fun, but I was incredibly mad at a guy called Dave Bellerby! He probably drove normal rallycross towards me, but I had only been in single seaters and you don't touch other cars there. The next year I got the chance to race a Citroen Xsara Supercar at Dreux in France. It was just for fun, but the car was amazing to drive and a lot of people enjoyed me being there I think.

I was really nervous when I lined up next to Jean-Luc Pailler because I'd seen him so much next to dad, it was big that I was lining up next to someone like that.

Dad wasn't there, he was running our team in a European Championship round at Lydden Hill, but he was on the phone a lot. I led the B final until a driveshaft broke. It was a good experience but in France the rallycross is quite similar to circuit racing.

I got the chance to drive with our own team at the European Championship race in Finland in 2012, that's when I really understood the size of the challenge to be fast in rallycross. I drove in the way that I had learned in racing, and it was a big challenge. I think I was a little bit lucky that it rained, I qualified for the C Final because I was not so good with the contact and stuff through the heats, but I won the C final and the B final, had a good run in the A final and finished side-by-side with Tanner Foust.

I didn't have a big plan, but after that race I knew what I wanted to do the next year; rallycross.

IMG had just become the promoter, so I thought it might be possible to be a professional rallycross driver, but I also wanted to have fun again.

I had been chasing that big dream in formula racing so much that I forgot to have fun. Then I went into rallycross and I could step out of the car with a smile, laughing with the people around me. I'd never had that much fun in my career before then. I'm very, very happy that I'm here today and not in Formula 1.

I'm proud when people say that they watched dad or they still have a cap they bought from that time. I'm glad that I get to carry that on. And then for the guys who are new to the sport, I'm just Timmy Hansen maybe without that link.

Maybe I'm a bit more like dad than mum. I'm calm and try to think before I act, but maybe a bit like mum with the emotions.

When we have guests with us in the team, they are all so appreciative at being welcomed just how they

are and I think that's down to what mum is doing. Not her actual tasks, but her amazing love and warmness. Dad is really good the technical side. He's very calm and never raises his voice or becomes mad. I think one of the reasons he's made it for such a long time in this sport is that he's always thought about the long term, while doing what he needs to today as well as he possibly can.

When Peugeot quit World RX, he was incredibly stable. The rest of the family were up and down, angry and sad, happy and positive, then back to sad. We all handled it differently but dad so positive and made the right choices, did the right things at the right time, even though we had nothing. He pulled us together, motivated us, made us believe it was possible to be back. He and mum work so well on pulling everything together, and me and Kevin are more involved in that too now.

Even now I am still understanding and amazed what dad has actually achieved in his career, what he is still doing and has been able to put together. I hope that one day I can be the same; doing the same things with the same values and giving the same things back to my son Sam when he grows up.

To have been together as a family and do what we did in World RX, I think we will look back at this time as a special one. It brought us very close and I'm very grateful for that. It's very easy for us to communicate and understand each other very well, but we don't act as family on race days; we're team manager and driver.

Dad is very good to work with, he has all the experience and he's a winner. He's very determined, it's a cliche to say, but he never gives up. It's very motivating.

When I tell my grandchildren about my young days and driving in the family team, those are the things I'll be talking about most. Not the wins, championships or the results, but the journey. The adventure.

Left top to bottom: Timmy Hansen between his racing parents. Timmy (number 21) waits for a kart race, Kenneth Hansen watches on as racing dad. Having matched and beaten future F1 drivers, Hansen's circuit career ended in 2012. Above: The future champion with an appropriately numbered kart.

Kevin on Kenneth

When I was small, I was obviously always watching dad drive. I don't remember so much, a few short moments, but I always had within me that he was the greatest driver and I wanted to do the same.

He and mum say it was never in doubt that I would do anything other than rallycross.

I guess I learned so much without realising it and combined with having one goal, to do what the guy I looked up to did, I managed to do the same. It was a bit different from when dad was racing, he had his own car and own small team but I think in a way I was a part of that and then I won the 2016 European Championship in the way rallycross was like at my time, with factory support.

It was just a dream to do what he had done, I had never cried so much as I did in the car that day in Barcelona. I don't know why it meant so much to me, it just did. I felt like I was born and raised to win that championship.

Even when I was small, everyone asked if I would drive. The Hansen name has a great history and I think I've got the passion and hunger to win from both dad and mum.

When I watch old videos sometimes, dad's just so diplomatic and professional and even when he won the first Swedish Championship, he was already then very professional so I just wanted to be the same.

Every time I went to my grandma's she had video tapes

of old races and I watched them about a billion times. I didn't put on cartoons when I went to hers when I was a kid, always rallycross.

I don't remember so much from when dad was driving, but I have some strong memories from Buxtehude (Germany). One was 2010, when he lost out to Sverre Isachsen in the final because Isachsen was so fast in the joker lap when it had looked like dad was going to win. I was really disappointed. I was crying because he didn't win, but he was quite happy because he had gone from last to second.

And again at Buxtehude when Swedish television was filming me and Timmy when Michael Jernberg crashed on the top section of

the track and dad won the 2005 championship. I only remember Jernberg crashing and dad passing by, but I strongly remember a really happy feeling.

I just love the sport and I love the way dad did things when he was driving himself. It's interesting to see how he drove, because I am very similar now. It was pretty cool to win the European Championship driving with almost the same style as him. Even if the cars are a lot better now, the driving styles are very similar.

When I was karting, in my first proper year I think there were three clashes with rallycross, but I missed the kart races because I much preferred to watch dad and rallycross than race myself.

The year after there were less clashes and I won the championship. As soon as I could stop karting and start rallycross, I did, in the Junior class in the British Rallycross Championship. I remember when that came up. I went to mum at home one day and said: 'I think I want to stop karting and drive rallycross.' She just said: 'Okay, then we stop and do what you want.'

In rallycross, Graham Rodemark [see chapter six] has basically been like my second dad, we have a very good connection. I've been lucky to have such experienced guys around me like him and dad. Timmy taught me a lot of what he learned from the engineers he worked with in formula cars too.

Feeling that he was always destined to be a rallycross driver, Kevin Hansen spent his childhood in the paddock absorbing every detail of his chosen sport.

Mum is very emotional and I think I'm quite like her, really happy when things are good, then really angry when something goes wrong. Dad is just a big smile. The most he can do is hug. He doesn't put his arms up and scream and run around, he's just really happy. Mum shows it everywhere to everybody, but dad is more within himself. It's the same at home, mum is a bit more up and down in emotions but dad is always a constant. He has taken a lot of shit in the past and he knows how to handle it. I think he's the only really stable person in the family. It's just who he is.

In 2017 me, Timmy and dad did the 10 Hours of Magny-Cours race together sharing a Peugeot 208 Cup car. Dad was really nervous at the start, he played himself down, but he did well. It was a new track to all of us and we're used to doing six laps, not hour-long stints. I think he was the most impressive of us all in qualifying. From his first flying lap to his fastest he was about five seconds different, but the fast lap he did was actually good, and the lap was about 2 minutes 20 seconds or something. Me and Timmy were on the radio pushing him a bit more and a bit more all the time. We were a bit quicker but it was impressive. It was really fun to do that together, and see he still has it!

Kevin Hansen won the FIA European Rallycross Championship in 2016, following in the tracks of his father and becoming the youngest driver ever to take the championship trophy (right).
Top right: After karting and a successful Junior Rallycross career, Hansen moved to adult competition in the Supercar Lites category in 2014, and won in Finland (pictured).

Kenneth on Susann, Timmy and Kevin

Even if I am very calm, I need to have my base and it needs to be good. When things haven't been good, maybe when Timmy was in formula racing and he was having a difficult weekend and we were not there, it's very difficult to perform yourself if you don't have support. I would never have been so successful if Susann hadn't been there supporting me because then I wouldn't have enjoyed it so much. That Susann has been there with me has been so important. She has been such a big part of everything, without her it wouldn't have happened.

I have good memories of when I was racing the Ford Sierra and she was using the Volvo 240. I got her a new car almost by accident. We were planning to build her a new car and in the workshop where I worked, there was a car, a right-hand drive 240 in very good condition, but it had British plates. The guys at the garage said that one or two years earlier, a guy had a problem and he left it there for repair, but he never came back. They said to me: 'If it disappears, it disappears, we don't want to hear about it'. I took it home and we stripped it down. I was working on the Sierra and she was working next to me on the Volvo, side-by-side. That was a special time.

I never intended to be racing at the top of the European Championship, it was just step-by-step that it happened. Then of course when you're there, you want to be the best at that time, you always want to be better. To have done that for so many years with my family is an amazing story

There was no question that we should keep racing when we had Timmy. Perhaps it was stupid sometimes, but it worked well I think. It was hardest for Susann and she did a lot, it was maybe most complicated when one of us had to change nappies when we needed to go to pre-grid for the final. Timmy refused to let anyone else do it, but we managed. And it worked, I mean Timmy is still in rallycross, and he's World Champion.

To start with he wanted to go away from what we were, he wanted to do his own thing. He loved karting and went to formula racing, he had his dream and he worked very hard. He also had some very hard years, which made him stronger of course. But in the end, we were in Russia and he said: 'I don't want to continue, because I can't do better. If I can't be faster, then it must be me or the car. If it's the car then there's no point continuing.'

Above left: Kenneth and Timmy Hansen.
Bottom left: Kevin Hansen sleeps in the paddock.
Above: Susann and Kenneth in 1988.

The equipment he had was a big thing, he had battled with guys like Carlos Sainz Jr and Daniil Kvyat and beaten them, so he is a good driver and we can see that today.

He really enjoyed it when he got the opportunity to drive with us in Finland [in 2012], he was smiling so much and decided he wanted to do rallycross. It was nice he wanted to do rallycross, but I mostly enjoyed that he was happier again. He did some Porsche races too with Johan Kristoffersson and enjoyed that, if he continued there, as long as he had been happy, that would have been fine.

It was difficult for me when Timmy was doing formula racing, Susann was with Kevin at a kart race and I was doing rallycross on the same weekend. I got used to it, but I never enjoyed it because I couldn't share their success or their disappointments. That's what makes it more amazing what we achieved together with the boys in World RX, it's like a dream. We are very fortunate to be able to work together like that. Of course, we have hard times, but it works so well. If we had normal jobs, it would be a completely different life for all of us.

Kevin was always going to do rallycross. He said that from the beginning, even when he had paper on the table at home and he'd draw a circuit and have races on there. He took his toy cars from the paddock to the grid, and did the commentary of the race. We could hear him doing that upstairs at home, he was so into it.

He and Timmy are very good friends and brothers, I don't think they would have achieved what they have without each other. But I always remind them to enjoy the moment, like when they finished one-two in Barcelona in 2019, because you never know if it will happen again.

They are also quite different, but together they are strong. Like me and Susann. I think she has the biggest winning spirit of all of us. If she goes into something, she wants to win.

And now we have Sam in the family too. It feels very strange to be called a grandfather, I still don't accept that. I'm proud, but it feels strange. A grandfather is an old guy, and I don't feel that way. But he is absolutely fantastic. I couldn't ever believe it would feel like that to have a grandchild. It's small things, I was at my mother's place and Sam came in through the front door with Timmy, ran to me and threw himself around my neck. You remember those things, it's lovely.

He makes a lot of 'brum brum' noises, and he's starting to be quite good with driving the plastic car. Timmy is a little worried though, because me and Kevin have said we will take care of it, his future is guaranteed. We will have a kart for him, we will fix it so he will get into a car very quickly, only if Sam wants to of course, but we will be there for him. And the great thing is we say: 'It's like always, the dad pays.'

Hansen struggles to think of himself as a grandfather but loves having a grandson. Like his father and uncle, Sam Hansen is beginning to grow up in the paddock.

Friends

Anyone that has largely dedicated their life to an international sport, and lived within it, will inevitably have countless acquaintances. But, real friends are a different matter altogether.

While Hansen has been close to many people throughout his life, sometimes the Swede has felt it was his success that some people wanted to befriend, rather than him as a person. He does, however, have a devoted group of friends, some of whom he has known since childhood, who he is able to totally relax with.

He has also become friends with members of the paddock too, both inside and outside his own team.

Hansen with Morgan Persson in their karting days. They remain firm friends.

Morgan Persson on Kenneth

When we were karting, Kenneth was always more successful and faster in races, but perhaps I was better when we were practising. We had so much fun with karting, myself, Christer [Strand] and Kenneth. My uncle [Kjell Ake Svensson] was working on a farm just by Kenneth's home when we were small and it was him that bought me my first kart, that was the start of it for us.

When we wanted to become more competitive in karting we ordered some Honda engines, but they didn't arrive. We got fed up waiting, so Kenneth and I went to buy two Rotax engines, but they were not developed for karting, they were motocross engines. The exhaust pipe was straight, but on a kart you need the exhaust to go through 90 degrees, so we did a lot of work to make that. On a two-stroke engine the exhaust is very, very important, we changed it with gas welding and it went very well in the end.

When we were racing gearbox karts, we had two groups, Team Gotene and Team Honda. Me, Christer and Kenneth were the Gotene Motor Club guys, the other group were the guys who ran Honda engines. Of course there were some guys from our club in that team too. If Kenneth or Christer were ahead it was fine because we were one unit, but the others we should have behind us.

I first met Kenneth when I was seven-years-old, and lived just five kilometres away from him. When we were karting, we competed with each other, but not against. The biggest competition was when we were practising.

There was a lot of fun too. Once Kenneth bought himself a fog free visor, and it started to rain before practice. He went out, and came back in and he was angry like hell saying: 'This shit doesn't work'. Then I showed him how to take away the protective packaging film. That was funny.

We had fun on the mopeds too. We were always tuning them, which was not legal, but we did quite a good job, so they were fast. We never took those ones to school, but Kenneth did once but it broke down. For the way home Kenneth sat on his moped and held onto my bike. The police stopped us, but because Kenneth's engine didn't run the police could not find any tuning, so he was lucky. If they had, it could delay getting your driving licence for a year.

One time his father Svend was following us and we didn't realise. The speed of our mopeds was not slow, it wasn't 35km/h, it was more like 75km/h, and he was really not happy with us about that.

After karting I didn't do much folkrace because I didn't like that you had to sell the car if there was a bid on it. I did some rallycross though, in a Ford Escort MkII with a 2.5 litre American Ford Pinto engine, that was fast!

I helped Kenneth as a mechanic too for some years. When he was racing the [Volvo] Amazon, we had rebuilt it to be beautiful before one season, and put a new engine in. Tomas [Gustavsson, see chapter six] wanted to try the engine, so he drove it on the gravel road where Timmy is living now, maybe 500 meters then turned around. He went slow, then for the last 100 meters, he wanted to try the engine, so he accelerated a little. That was fine, but when he braked the problem appeared. The Amazon had a what we called a flip front so it all came off the car together, and we hadn't put the bolts in. When he braked it came off and of course he ran over it. It lay there like a butterfly that had been killed on the road. Tomas was so embarrassed he bought the new parts himself.

I also helped when Kenneth was racing in Europe too. He's a very good friend and I'm very proud of what he's done.

Christer Strand on Kenneth

Kenneth and I had been racing in a rallycross event at Holjes. We were driving home very quickly because we were going to a Car Speedway race at Visby in Gotland and we needed to get the ferry, go to a party and then do this race.

Kenneth was driving his father Svend's bus, with Svend sleeping, and I was driving another car behind. We were going like hell and on one corner, Kenneth got it a little bit wrong. Svend rolled out of the bed and was angry. He asked what was going on, so Kenneth, with that smile he has, said: 'It's Christer. It's all his fault because he said that we must drive fast so we can get to the ferry in time.'

He didn't tell him that we had plenty of time to make the ferry, and that Kenneth had been driving in front anyway, but Svend never noticed that. When we got to a gas station, Svend came out of the bus yelling at me, and it didn't matter what I said, he didn't listen. Kenneth was standing there at the side just laughing.

We had been in the same school class from when we were seven-years-old. We were friends with a lot of people at the beginning but after we hit 10 or 12-years-old, we were not so interested in soccer like everybody else was, and we started driving small motorcycles, then we went karting.

I was very often faster than Kenneth in karting when it didn't matter, but when you had to be at your best, he was always better, because he has that mindset.

We drove our first kart race together and our first folkrace together, and, by accident, we found out how to win together.

When folkrace started in Sweden many people wanted to drive, so you were lucky to get an entry for a race. Sometimes Kenneth was lucky and I was his mechanic, sometimes I was lucky and he was my mechanic. Once when I was driving, we forgot the stuff that was in the boot of the racecar for the journey to the event. I took the start and won the race. We were surprised, then we discovered that we had forgotten the stuff in the boot and we realised we needed the rear of the car to be heavier, but it was an accident.

Kenneth continued in folkrace and I started rallying, but then we did some rallycross together. I joined him in rallycross in 1984, then in 1986 I was his mechanic and we designed our first tyre warmers [see chapter nine]. We did a lot of crazy things.

These days we are a small group of friends, now five people, and we always get together at a house, and close the door. Kenneth always says that he could have won any number of titles but when we're together we always tell him he still doesn't know how to drive.

When we're alone, I can say he is almost the total opposite to what most people see in the rallycross paddock. He is much funnier that most people know. When you're somewhere where people don't recognise him, he can be very funny, but as soon as someone says: 'Hello Kenneth' or he hears his name, he is directly back into work mode as a professional. To be in this circus as long as he has, you need to be professional 24/7.

He's in private or professional mode, but as he gets older, these two people are more and more the same.

He has a fox behind his ear all the time, in private we are always trying to cause each other problems. Just like his father, he cheats a lot when he plays cards, he's horrible to play cards with!

One of his big strengths is not showing what he is feeling. I would say rallycross is the most important thing to him, aside from his family and he's learned the game very well.

One of the problems he had, was that to get to his level and be a very good driver, he needed to be a little angry, to get in the zone. One time when he was in the Ford Sierra Cosworth at a race at Lyngas, Bjorn Skogstad beat him in the first and second qualifying.

I said to Kenneth: 'You're not there, you need to get very angry with Bjorn.' He said that just wasn't his way, but I told him to look at Bjorn and say: 'I'm going to kill you.' I said I didn't care what he did, give him the finger on the start line maybe, but do something!

Kenneth sat in the car, and didn't want me to see he hadn't done it, so he did a little fast one, but then after he did that, he won the start and the race. I think he could be a little lazy when he was driving, he needed something that took him up to drive at the right level.

I never sponsored Kenneth with my business, we never discussed it because we are friends. But, even though we were working in totally different areas, we had similar issues so we would discuss, together with Susann, how to do things in certain situations.

And then I sponsored Kevin in Supercar Lites. Kevin didn't like me when he was very young because he only loved Citroen and I drove a BMW. When we took my car to go somewhere, Kevin would not get in because it wasn't a Citroen. We could get Kevin into the BMW if Kenneth was driving, but Kenneth had a contract with Citroen and he was not allowed to drive anything else. One time, going to Holjes, when Kevin was about seven, it was dark so Kenneth drove the first 100km and when Kevin was asleep we switched drivers.

It was Kevin himself who asked me if my company, Inquire, could help him, because he needed sponsors. Kenneth wanted me to teach Kevin how to deal with sponsor demands, so I took that role and it grew.

I was not interested to give Peugeot Sport money, but then in 2019, when Kenneth, Susann, Timmy and Kevin were alone in the team [see chapter seven], two weeks before the first race I called Kenneth and asked him: 'So, when will you ask me to be a sponsor because you have a very shitty budget and you need some money.' Kenneth said he would not ask me, it was very late but in the end we did something. Kenneth is my closest friend and therefore his family are very close to me, it was important for me to help when they were struggling.

Even when we went to Holjes that year, and all out friends were there, people cannot understand how I can speak to Kenneth the way I do, I can be very bad to him and he just stands there and takes it. I love it!

Christer Strand (to the right of Hansen above and sitting with his great friend right) became a commercial partner of Hansen's team in 2019.

Ronny Larsson on Kenneth

I often say to Kenneth: 'You must thank me for you driving in rallycross. I fixed that.'

I worked with his father, Svend, in Gotene, for 10 or 12 years, so I got to know Svend very well. He worked for the city doing pipe work and I drove the machines. We would start a job in the morning and if we were ready by the middle of the day, but there was some more work to fix around it in the afternoon, Svend would say to me: 'Ronny, can you fix it this afternoon, I must drive to some companies and see if I can find sponsors for Kenneth.' That happened so much, so Kenneth can thank me for that.

The three brothers; Peter, Erik and Kenneth are all different. Peter talks a lot, and when he has something in his head, he just says it. Erik is a little in the middle.

He's always happy and whatever happens, he will say: 'No problem, we can fix it.'

And Kenneth, he always has something in his head but you can never read what he's really thinking. Svend and Kenneth are very similar in that way, but Kenneth is much quieter and in some ways they are very different as well. But, now when he wears glasses, he also looks like his father.

For a lot of years, me and Kenneth were both driving rallycross and living in Gotene, but I did everything on my own, until I stopped driving and my boys Johan and Erik did more.

I built a Peugeot 207 for 2007, which Johan drove in 2008 before Ulrik Linnemann called me a lot of times wanting to buy the car. We hadn't done the whole European season, so I sold it.

There were three races left, in Czech Republic, Poland and Germany. I was talking to Kenneth one day, and he asked when we would leave to go to Czech. I told him that I'd sold the car and we wouldn't go. Kenneth wanted to know what we would do next and I told him we would wait and see.

A week later we were talking and I told Kenneth I would maybe buy a Citroen or something. After two or three weeks, Kenneth called me and said: 'I was at Citroen last week. I bought a Saxo, a Super 1600.' I was a little shocked that he would buy a car like that. That's not Kenneth, normally he holds on to all the money he has.

A week or so later he asked me if Johan would like to drive it at the last race in Germany, just to see how it went. That was also a shock for me, because that is not normal for Kenneth either, he said: 'It's maybe two years since they [Citroen] drove it, so we don't know the condition.'

Kenneth said he would send the engine to Oreca, but he had promised that Timmy could drive the car first, so we went up to Kinnekulle for Timmy and Johan to try it. Kenneth said the car had been started in France when he bought it, no problem, so Timmy took the car first and drove full throttle. After a few runs we heard a strange noise from the engine. It turned out to be a problem with the oil level, and the engine was damaged. That's Kenneth sometimes. He is very serious and professional in almost everything he does, but can also be a little careless with some things.

Johan drove the Saxo in Germany, then in 2009 and that's when we started to go racing together with Kenneth. We said since we were living in the same town, we could help each other by me driving the truck and our car going in the trailer behind his bus.

One time I was really angry with him though. In 1992, I bought his Ford Sierra RS500 when he moved to the top class. I was at a race, at Tomelilla in Sweden and the turbo went. That was normal, but afterwards the engine broke.

I took it to a company in Gothenburg and a few weeks later the guy called me to talk about what was inside the engine, it was not the parts I thought it was.

I went to Kenneth's workshop and Svend was at the door. I was very angry, but Kenneth had a local TV crew there, so that was not the right time to be angry with him.

That evening, he called me and was annoyed because I had been angry with Svend. I told him exactly what I thought, about the shit he had sold me. It was not good and he knew it, but like normal he was just quiet.

I helped him when my son Eric [Faren] was driving with the Hansen Talent Development team, and I drove the truck to help Kenneth's team in Nordic and some World Championship races for a few years.

And Kenneth has helped us a lot too, he's is a good man. He's always been very closed, he hasn't let anyone in like he has with our family and that's special. His tent in the paddock is more open now than when he first started with Citroen, his team was always quite closed then.

He always says: 'If you're winning everyone says you're cheating', and: 'It's always windiest at the top.'

I think he became closed in those years when he was at the top with Citroen, and didn't have many people who he could really talk to. He has a small group of people who he really trusts I think. He's a mysterious man, he never lets anything out if he doesn't want you to know.

But we also talk sometimes a lot about things and the future, when he knows he can trust you. He's worked with rallycross for many years, it's his life. In the end he always comes out on top somehow. He doesn't come from lots of money, he has survived by being careful, and he always comes back. Like in 2019, after Peugeot stopped, he came back.

He's very clever, he's a strong man in that way.

Paulo Maria on Kenneth

When I first started shooting photographs, I used to go to Lousada in Portugal. Even then Kenneth was a legend in rallycross, so when I met him again in 2014, because we had a contract to take photos for Peugeot, I felt it was a privilege to work with him and his family.

I've worked in motor sport photography for 25 years and I've been close to some drivers, teams and people I've worked with. But in this case it's more than just work. I am always really committed with any team I work with, but with this team, the spirit and family feeling is amazing. It's much more than just people and drivers, it is really something unique.

I invited Kenneth and Susann for a holiday to Portugal in 2017 because I love wine and I know they belong to a wine tasting group in Sweden. They already knew of the wines from the Douro Valley so I wanted to create an experience for them there.

We also planned a surprise for Kenneth. Susann knew that something would happen and that I'd prepared a special surprise, but not what it was.

My wife and I collected them from Porto airport and we headed North. I said I needed to go to a small town to pick something up, but then Kenneth realised we were in the town of Lousada, and we were going to the city hall. The mayor and local press were there to meet him, he signed some books and his visit was honoured with a plaque. The mayor invited him to go see the rallycross track, he obviously said yes, but he didn't realise that we had arranged a car, a Citroen of course, and he would be able to drive there.

We just wanted him to be able to enjoy the track one more time, and he really did enjoy and remember it. He was fast. It was a big surprise for him and emotional for us to have him there, also as my friend.

During a surprise trip to the Lousada track in Portugal, where European Championship events used to take place, Hansen got to drive the track and was honoured with a mayoral reception and plaque.

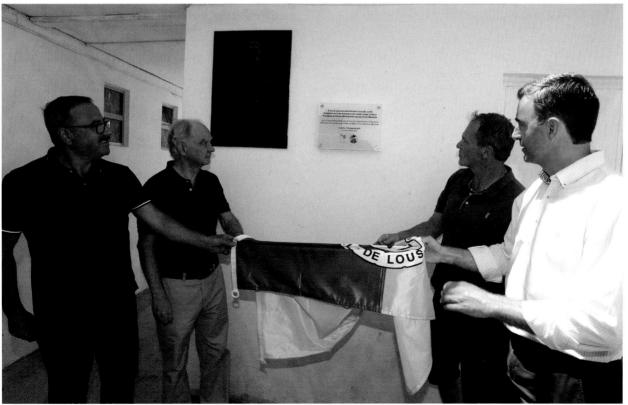

Kenneth on friends

When you become a little more known, or achieve something, I think maybe you also become a little suspicious. I have a lot of friends that I enjoy and like to talk to, but sometimes I have felt, after a while, that it was not the real thing. Maybe it was just because it was the name they wanted to be friends with, not because it was me as a person. Then you feel disappointed and I think you become a little more careful. You can still be friends with people, but I think sometimes you keep it at a certain level.

I have been lucky to have some very good friends though, like Morgan, Christer and Tommy Kvick. Tommy lived just two kilometres from me when I was young, we spent 11 years in school together and we're still good friends today. He was also important in my early racing. I have more good friends, but Christer is my best friend, one who I can speak about everything and that will never disappear. We can go without speaking for several months but then, when we call or meet, it's just like we saw each other an hour ago.

Once a year we meet together; me, Christer, Tommy, Tomas Gustavsson and Magnus Sturesson, who was working for our team for many years as a mechanic and truckie after he had worked with PeO Davidsson. There we have a few drinks and I feel very comfortable with them.

Those are guys that I can really talk to. We have done it for many years. For a while we went out to a pub or hotel or something, but we realised that the place wasn't important, it's more about us, so now we usually stay in the house or do some skiing. We can be quite hard on each other, but with a good feeling, of course we would never hurt each other.

When we used to go to a restaurant for example and someone recognised me and said: 'Hello, good result last year,' or something, then I was, and even Christer says he saw immediately, another person, in working mode. So much of my life has been spent in the rallycross world where you need to be professional so that's difficult.

Like for example with Tommy Kristoffersson. I feel very good with Tommy, we had the same sponsors, we competed against each other, and then later with our sons [see chapter one].

For me he's very close and a good guy, but it's also a competition so you can't speak to someone like that about everything. We are very open with each other, and from my side, I've always enjoyed spending time with Tommy. He's probably one of the people I've got closest to who was also a competitor.

When you are in sport, there are different pressures to what you might have if you are doing something else and that affects you. You need to succeed, you need the results and so on. You are also in the spotlight. I never enjoyed being there on the stage, or always talking with the newspapers, but it's a part of it and you have to be careful about what you say and who you talk to.

Friends are like family, you don't always agree on everything and there are some hard moments, but you can't continue like that forever and things usually work out in the end.

Top right: With Tommy Kristoffersson, the competitor he is closest to as a friend.
Right: Ready to go racing in 1989, Hansen's small team consisted of family and friends. Left to right the team are: Peter Karlsson, Morgan Persson, Svend Hansen, Tomas Gustavsson and Svend Dahlqvist.

Famous five. Kevin Hansen, Eric Faren, European Champion Timur Timerzyanov, Timmy Hansen and Alexander Hvaal stride out in Germany 2013.

As part of the self-built business that facilitated Hansen's racing, throughout his driving career the Swede sold on his successful competition cars and, over time, increased support to customers. Towards the end of his own time at the wheel, Hansen Motorsport began expanding to run other drivers at the sport's highest level.

That started in earnest with Finn Jussi Pinomaki in 2009, before Brit Liam Doran ran as Hansen's teammate in 2010. As the Swede took a step back from regular driving the following year, the team continued to grow and in the subsequent seasons it wasn't uncommon for the squad to be fielding more than five cars in international events, winning races and championships just as it had with Hansen in the driving seat.

With the team such a major part of Hansen's life, it's no surprise that the squad's first 'other' driver was partner and later wife Susann Bergvall, and latterly the focus has been on sons Timmy and Kevin, competing and winning as part of the family business under Hansen's leadership. That trio feature in chapter four.

5. DRIVERS

Jussi Pinomaki

A triple champion in the FIA European Rallycross Championship (Divisions Two and One-A), Finn Jussi Pinomaki graduated to the Supercar category in 2009. Driving a Citroen C4 alongside Hansen in the I Iansen Motorsport squad, Pinomaki's season started well with fourth place at the opening round in the UK. A maiden podium came by round four, but his campaign was marred by a huge accident in Austria.

Per Eklund's Saab 93 had come to a halt on the opening lap of a qualifying race at Melk. The leaders passed the stricken vehicle on the second tour, but with the stationary car hidden by dust on the unsealed section, Pinomaki ploughed into the rear of Eklund's machine, before being hit hard from behind by Rene Munnich's Skoda Fabia. Pinomaki escaped without injury and completed his only Supercar season, but arguably one of the brightest talents ever to make the step into Supercar didn't qualify for another final.

The Finn has subsequently worked for and run teams in the World Rallycross Championship as rivals to Hansen Motorsport and in the Hansen's time with Peugeot Sport.

Pinomaki on Hansen

2009 was the first year when Kenneth started to run the team for someone other than himself, so I was his first teammate for a full season. We were both in a new situation and I guess at that time he started to think about what to do after his driving was finished. He was the Supercar champion and I was the Division One-A champion, so it was a nice story.

We tried to do it as well as possible. From my side, things didn't go as I expected for several reasons but those had nothing to do with Kenneth. I felt he was helping me as much as he could, but it was new for him, I was there while he was starting a new beginning for him and his team.

I had a small budget, I never had anybody to help me with the sponsors and things. I had a lot of people who helped me, but to raise the budget myself and to race at the same time wasn't easy. I was on the limit from the beginning and then we had a big crash in Austria, and not all of the sponsor situations worked out like they were promised. Everything together made me give up on my own driving career really.

The crash in Austria wasn't a great thing to be involved in. It was a lot of bad luck. In those days for some reason we were not allowed to use radios, two years later it was mandatory to use radios. I just happened to be in the wrong place at the wrong moment. It was lucky that no-one was more seriously hurt. I still remember it like yesterday. I remember the feeling when I saw the car in front of me and I couldn't do anything – I remember the exact moment. It's passed now and it is what it is.

I've always liked Kenneth; he's been open and I felt that I could always trust him with whatever we did. He had really good guys working for him, it was a pleasure to work with them.

He's a gentleman, I think most people who know him probably feel the same. Unfortunately, things didn't last longer for me as a driver, but when I ended, Timur [Timerzyanov] came from my team [SET Promotion] to drive for Kenneth, so we had something in common after that as well.

Hansen on Pinomaki

Jussi is fast and when I look back I think we could have done it another way. We learnt during that year how to run a car for a new driver. You know, with the technical setups and so on. The way with Jussi at that time was not the best way. He chose to go his own way with the setup that he felt suited him, but it was not a success.

Since then we have been quite determined that we have a car and all drivers start to drive it and they learn the car really well before they start to change a lot of things, because we know the car is fast. That was a learning point for our team. Jussi is a really good guy. He is very Finnish; he is not speaking unless he needs to. It's a shame he wasn't able to do more because he could definitely have shown much better. The big accident in Austria affected him a little I think, maybe something mental.

*Previous pages: Pinomaki in the Hansen
Motorsport C4 at Melk in Austria and (right
page) the immediate aftermath of the crash
in the same event that led to the end of his
driving career.
Above: Simpler times, Pinomaki and Hansen
lunch together mid-event in 2009.*

Liam Doran

British driver Liam Doran, son of European Championship event-winner Pat Doran, graduated from the British Rallycross Championship and selected European outings for his first full international rallycross campaign in 2010 with a Hansen Motorsport Citroen C4.

He won two European Championship rounds, in Finland and Poland, in his inaugural season with Hansen's team and made an unexpected challenge for the title in the latter part of the year, eventually finishing third just behind Hansen in the points.

After the European season had ended, Doran persuaded Hansen to send a car to the US for the first rallycross races in North America.

He remained with the team for 2011 and secured Monster Energy support. He was joined by graduating Division One-A Champion Timur Timerzyanov in the squad.

Doran and Hansen also returned to America half way through the year, for X Games in Los Angeles, where they beat Marcus Gronholm to the Rally Gold Medal.

Doran split with Hansen Motorsport at the end of the same season to set up his own team. He went on to win further European Championship rounds and X Games medals, and became one of the first globally recognised rallycross names.

Left: Doran leads on his way to victory in Poland 2010.
Next page: Hansen and Doran in Hungary 2010 and, below, Doran leading Hansen in Germany 2010.

Doran on Hansen

I undoubtedly had some speed in my early career but had a lot missing. I was ragged around the edges. I had learnt a lot from my father, but Kenneth was the complete opposite to my dad and taught me things that I was never able to learn from him.

It was perfect because I got a completely different angle on how things should be done. It didn't all rub off, perhaps I should have picked up more. Kenneth's massively professional, a true sportsman, a legend in terms of what he's achieved. Whether it was going well or badly, he was always a gentleman and it's an honour to have worked with him. The two people that I owe everything to for what I've done and achieved are Kenneth and my dad.

When we agreed to race together [for 2010] it was the first stepping stone of me becoming a top-level rallycross driver. I was just lucky enough to have had that opportunity to work with him.

We got on like a house on fire. Not only were our personalities different but the driving styles were wildly different too. I was immediately faster than Kenneth in places, a very small amount of places, but in some places I was faster than him straight away, purely because of the style and aggression of my driving. But 75-80% of the time he was faster than me. I feel like I maybe helped him find speed at the end of his career when the pace was getting faster and faster.

It's hard to say what the expectations were going into that season because the car was good and Kenneth had always done really well, but it was Kenneth Hansen, so it could have all been him. I didn't expect to be on the podium so soon [in the second round], then to get the first win, that was very, very good. I got it handed to me [when Sverre Isachsen's engine expired], but racing's always about that and I've handed wins to other people since then too.

The second win [in Poland] sort of sealed the deal for me because if anyone thought I was a bit lucky to win the first one, the second win it put a stamp on it. I dominated that event based on driving style. The track was a bit awkward to get around, the best way was basically sideways and backwards. Back then there wasn't anyone who had done that and the guys who were in it weren't really comfortable doing that. People like Kenneth were watching and saying 'There's no way I'm going into that corner full throttle like that.' I was young, and probably a little bit stupid, but it went perfectly and I won.

Kenneth and I always got on really well because it was almost like a father-son relationship. When Timur [Timerzyanov] came into the team [in 2011], thinking he knew everything because he'd won the European Championship in a two-wheel car, we just butted heads. I had my way and I'd already achieved good results, but he had his own way. He was very good. It wasn't a massive problem but we were direct rivals all of the time.

I'd been happy for Kenneth to beat me and it was fine for me to beat him. But when Timur came in out of nowhere and was taking the piss sometimes, I wasn't having it. He had a good year and I had a bad year.

We're absolutely fine now, we were both a lot younger then. I'd say Timur was the main reason I left the team, which is a shame to look back at now. Looking where I've come with my career and where Kenneth went with his team, we could have gone a lot further together, we worked really well together and did a lot of big things.

Perhaps making the decision to start my own team at the end of 2011 wasn't the best thing to do, but at the time rallycross was still so small and there was such a small variety of teams that I really had no choice, it was his team, one other team [Olsbergs MSE] or do something myself.

Kenneth and I still get on. He's congratulated me about bringing up my own family because I was the wild kid in the team when he had his family around him, and he said 'One day it'll be you' and I said 'Never!' And here I am now with a family, which is amazing and he was right all along.

Going to America for X Games [in 2011] was the most important moment of my career, and huge for Kenneth too, I'd say.

We shipped a car – no, actually, I arranged to ship the car because Kenneth didn't believe in it. We had a little bit of a clash, but anyway, we shipped a car to X Games in Los Angeles [see chapter eight].

We turned up in America with literally nothing; we'd shipped out a car and a crate of spares and we won a gold medal. What we achieved that day with what we had, and what we expected against one of the best drivers in the world, was unbelievable.

That is by far the proudest moment of my career and it's mostly thanks to Kenneth. He trusted me, we took the risk and it worked out. That was really the making of the start of my career.

Hansen on Doran

Liam was quite young, very determined and hungry when he joined us. He had done the British Championship, did it well, and we decided that Liam and I would run together in 2010, and it was a very good year together. I think he felt he learnt a lot and it was successful. We finished second and third in the championship that year, even though I had wanted to fight for the gold, that was a good moment.

I don't know what I had expected really. I believed that he could be very good, but that we should fight over second in the European Championship until the last race, I didn't believe he could be that good in the first year. He handled it very well.

I had already been thinking about ending my career. It was not so easy to keep finding the motivation, but I still didn't want to leave rallycross and it was a good time to go with two drivers while I developed the new car [DS3].

So the year after, we signed Timur [Timerzyanov] and Liam stayed with us. That was a little harder. It's always the same when a new driver comes in, if they are fast it's sometimes difficult to handle and the pressure was on Liam. It was definitely not good at all the races, they got quite upset with each other a few times. We learnt a lot from that year.

We have seen Liam be controversial, but there was not a lot of that in the first year with us, he was quite calm and very into it. In the second year it was different, I don't know why.

It's different when you are chasing and you don't directly expect anything, and I think he was very happy to be on the podium in the first year. The way he did some races, like in Poland for example was very impressive. In the second year you are on a certain level and you need to show that again, that's when things changed. From time to time he can be a very different guy. The good side of Liam is brilliant.

Top right: Doran revealed backing from Monster Energy in Portugal 2011.
Below right: Hansen had to regain control after Doran and Timerzyanov clashed at Essay in France 2011.

Timur Timerzyanov

Russian driver Timur Timerzyanov won the European Rallycross Division One-A crown in 2010, driving for the SET Promotion team, and signed for Hansen Motorsport for his graduation to Supercar in 2011, joining Liam Doran in the team.

Racing a Citroen C4, Timerzyanov finished on the podium at the second round in Portugal, then claimed his first win in Belgium and ended the year third overall. Tensions ran high through the season as the teammates clashed more than once, but it was Timerzyanov that remained with the squad for 2012 to race the new DS3 Supercar and won six rounds on his way to the title.

A second Supercar crown followed in 2013, the start of the sport's new era under the promotion of IMG, but the Russian didn't win an event while driving as part of a three-car effort by the Swedish outfit alongside Timmy Hansen and Alexander Hvaal.

As the sport grew into an FIA World Championship for 2014, Timerzyanov remained with Hansen's team, which had secured Peugeot support to run works-backed Peugeot 208s, and led at the end of the first day of World RX competition in Portugal. But the triple FIA champion only scored a single podium (Canada) in the campaign and parted ways with Hansen at the end of the year.

Timerzyanov on Hansen

I remember the day that I was told the 13-time European Rallycross Champion was coming to a national race at our track in Kazan. I was not even driving in rallycross then but I knew who Kenneth was and he was a legend to me. Just to shake his hand at that time was already too much for me.

I saw a professional driver that knew exactly what he was doing. As a driver then and now as a team manager, he knows everything about rallycross – I think it is almost like he is one of the creators of what rallycross is today. Kenneth gave me a lot of experience and a lot of knowledge about the sport, not only with racing the Supercar, but everything.

When I joined Hansen Motorsport, he worked with me

like I was a son, not ever shouting at me or crying on me. If I did a mistake, he exactly explained what I'd done wrong and what I needed to do. Every time when we needed to talk about something he started with the words: 'Timur, let's talk – let's watch the video and discuss what happened'.

He is psychologically a really good guy. He can see exactly when the driver is ready, when the driver is concentrating or not concentrating, he can give the nod to you that you need to do something now or you need to do it later. When he is your spotter, it seems like he's a co-driver who is sitting together with you in the car. 'Timur, come on we can go faster. We can do this, come on let's go! Faster, faster!' It's like he was all the

time taking as much of the pressure on himself as he could.

2011 was a hard year with Liam [Doran] in the same team. Both drivers were fast and we had good cars. At the third race in France we crashed on the last lap. Kenneth said: 'Guys, we can't continue like that. We need to stop this or the team will disappear and you will stay at home.'

In Belgium [at Maasmechelen] I had my first victory, even though I had the second position on the start line – Liam was on pole, but I won. That was the first year they built the joker lap there. On the last lap of the final I decided I could push 100% in the joker lap but I got a puncture on the jump entering the joker. Except the exit of the joker, the track had only

right-corners to go and my right-rear tyre was punctured. The C4 was a car which you could drive with a puncture but not be so slow.

I never even dreamed about being European Champion in Supercar. Even when I was racing in Division One-A I was never thinking: 'Okay, I can go to Supercar and win the European Championship title.'

I was close to the title in 2011, leading in the middle of the year. After that I had some problems with the car. I was not allowed to enter England for the first race in 2012 [due to visa issues] and I was really angry. After that I was just flying on the track all year. We developed the new car and step-by-step we had six wins in nine races, and seven podiums. That

was a great season for us.

The last year was a little bit difficult. When Timmy started to drive I think Kenneth lost a little bit of concentration because his son was driving there for the first time. I needed to understand that his heart would always be with his son. And at that moment it was difficult for me to believe in everything; in all setups and everything. You start to think in your mind that there could be something; when your mind is like that it's a problem.

I love Kenneth's personality – even though our roads went separate ways, but I think Kenneth knows exactly where he's going and what he needs to do. I respect him a lot.

Previous pages: Timerzyanov leads the field at Valkenswaard in 2012, teammate Alex Hvaal to the right.
Above left: Despite a punctured right rear tyre in the last lap, Timerzyanov landed his first victory at Maasmechelen in 2011.
Above: Timerzyanov's arrival changed the dynamics in the team and gave Hansen a new challenge to manage two fast drivers who were rivals and teammates.

Hansen on Timerzyanov

Timur is a lot of fun, but not always easy to understand. When we were discussing the setup of the car he used to say: 'The rear is standing'. I think I knew what he meant in the end. He learnt how to drive the Supercar very quickly and was immediately competitive.

His season in 2012 was the most impressive. Yes, the car was good, but his performances were what won him the championship. That was a dream, to take another driver to a title, and we made that together with Timur. It was absolutely special.

The next few years were not so good for Timur, he moved teams a lot. I think maybe he didn't have the trust in anyone and I think his mind was too mixed. He needs something like he had when he drove for us in the first two years, to have someone you really believe and trust, and he can just drive and make his part the best he can. I enjoyed a lot of our time with him but for it to be Timur's day, not only did he have to be there as a driver with the right technical things, but he also had to be there as a person.

Above: Hansen worked with Timerzyanov to develop the Russian's skills and understanding.
Right: France 2013, Timerzyanov leads teammate Timmy Hansen and event winner Andreas Bakkerud in what would be his penultimate year with Hansen.

Alexander Hvaal

After time spent in the European Championship for Division One-A, and a brief foray into the Supercar series with a privately owned Ford Fiesta, Norwegian Alexander Hvaal joined Hansen Motorsport in 2012 to drive a Citroen C4. Hvaal's route into racing was via his father, Tom, a generous and staunch supporter not only of Alex and his younger brother Joachim, but of many drivers at all levels of rallycross.

Getting quickly up to speed, the 19-year old produced stand-out performances in Austria, France and Sweden, before switching to a Citroen DS3 for the renamed Citroen Hansen Motorsport in 2013, where he partnered Timmy Hansen and Timur Timerzyanov. Hvaal concluded the campaign with a pair of victories in Austria and Germany. He switched to Petter Solberg's PSRX team for the inaugural World Rallycross Championship in 2014, but the partnership was over before the middle of the season.

Hvaal on Hansen

I went to the first event at Lydden Hill [in 2012] and immediately, I think it was in Q2, I went into the wall and my day was over. I couldn't believe what I had done, but Kenneth worked really hard on me to stay focused and look forward, and in the next two events I was on the podium. At one point I was leading the European Championship. Kenneth has faced so many ups and downs in the sport and he knows all about it.

Some people call Martin Schanche 'Mr Rallycross', but I think the true Mr Rallycrosses are Kenneth Hansen and Per Eklund.

Kenneth is amazing, he taught me everything I know. Going from Divison One-A to Supercar was a big step for me and Kenneth made it much easier. The experience he brought to the table was amazing – to be able to learn from him first hand was just incredible.

In 2013 I felt that the dynamic changed a little bit when Timmy came into the team, but we still had a good feeling, at least from my side. I know Timur and Timmy had a couple of situations where things changed a bit around the dinner table but I was out of it. Kenneth was very much that we were one team, we ate the same dinner and drove against each other as if it was any other driver, but with little bit more respect.

I had been second in Austria behind Timur the year before, but in 2013 I felt we had a really good car and I liked the track, so to be able to bring a win to the team after Kenneth had been working with me towards that goal for nearly two years, it was incredible. The team tossed me in the air after the race and Kenneth seemed so proud.

When I left it was on good terms, I have nothing bad to say about Kenneth or anyone in the team; from every mechanic to the chef and the family. To see the passion they all have for rallycross is just amazing.

Previous page: Hvaal's first win came in Austria 2013.
Above: Hvaal won again in Germany at the end of the 2013 season, here pictured on the podium with Bakkerud and Doran.
Right: Flying high at Holjes in 2013.

Hansen on Hvaal

Our first contact about Alexander was his father Tom, after Alex did a race in the Czech Republic in a Fiesta [in 2011]. The agreement was for at least two years.

Alexander had some very good races with us, but the luck was never really with him [in 2012]. He had good speed straight away, I was especially impressed by Holjes, even though I was not there because I was at X Games with Sebastien [Loeb]. He was fastest there and should have won. He got ill and had to miss Finland and that's when we took Timmy into the team, and they drove together the next year.

When he won in Austria [in 2013], he did it with his own speed. He was lucky to win in Germany [where the final was stopped early], but he had a lot of bad luck too so for me it still counts completely.

When I think back, at least most of the time with the drivers we have had, we have been able to give them success. With a good team around him Alexander could be a very good driver in the World Championship, so it is a pity that things turned out the way they did.

I was a little sad when he went to Petter and it was a little surprise for us. But, we wished him the best luck because I understand that it was a good moment for him to do it, because of what Petter's profile and marketing could give him. Of course I don't know the full story, but what I can say is that Petter couldn't have given him the chance. It's never one person's fault when two are disagreeing, but you don't come from two race wins to nothing over one winter. Alexander is so much better than that.

I spoke quite a lot after that season [2014] to try to get Alexander and his family back into it. I wanted him to be in a good car so he could get some success because even if he stopped again, it would be with success. And he got that with Joel [Christoffersson] and our old DS3, and then again with Per [Eklund] too. That felt great.

Davy Jeanney

Davy Jeanney won the French Rallycross Championship in 2010, before graduating to an international programme in the European Rallycross Championship with a Citroen C4. He and his family team beat Timmy Hansen to second overall in 2013, and later signed to join the Swede in Team Peugeot-Hansen for 2015. At the undulating Estering in Germany, a track very different from his native French venues, Jeanney won his first FIA World Rallycross Championship event, then topped the podium again in French-speaking Trois-Rivieres at the Canadian round. Team Peugeot-Hansen won the 2015 World RX Team's title, but when Peugeot inserted Sebastien Loeb into Hansen's team for 2016, Jeanney's position came into question.

Hansen found a way for him to continue but Jeanney didn't achieve the same results in 2016 and left the squad at the close of the year,

Jeanney on Hansen

I met Kenneth properly for the first time in 2011 at the first race of the European Championship. He is the big man with many victories as a driver, and I got to know him more after this time. Even before I signed for Team Peugeot-Hansen, I had a really good relationship because Kenneth used Oreca and Sadev for the engine and gearbox like me, so sometimes I exchanged parts or transported the engines, and one time we worked on our car in Hansen Motorsport workshops.

After five races in 2015 we came to Buxtehude and directly from the beginning until the end of the weekend it was good, good, good, and victory. It was magnificent. I won Q1, Q2, Q4 the semi-final and the final. When I won again in Canada it was not the same because Timmy, Petter [Solberg] and [Reinis] Nitiss had crashed. It was not easier, but it was different. In Germany it was so special.

Kenneth's a good man and has managed a lot of people now, but I think in 10 years of managing people, he didn't change his system. He's very calm, very strategic. I like his philosophy and racing spirit, it's very much the same for me.

It was different in 2016, it was not so easy but Kenneth tried hard for me.

Previous page: Jeanney fans cheer on their man at Loheac.
Top left: Hansen and Jeanney.
Left: Celebration after victory in Canada.
Above right: Jeanney at full flight in Portugal.

Hansen on Jeanney

It was important to get that success when Davy's first win came in Germany. I knew how he was driving and I knew the feeling you need for that track, so I knew it could suit Davy. I was never very strong in Germany, I took some wins there of course, but it was not a circuit where I really felt it like Davy did that weekend.

The difference between the race before and Germany was that we had two days of great testing at Holjes (in Sweden). We learned a lot, not only about the car but about the differences in our drivers. We had a feeling that we could be stronger, but where that would lead when we got to Germany, we didn't know. Timmy was struggling a bit that weekend, if Davy hadn't been there maybe Timmy would not have been on the podium, but he [Davy] just dominated and Timmy found speed from him too.

It was very impressive. Davy is perhaps the most polite but very competitive guy I have worked with. He can be very hard on the circuit, but is a very clean racer.

We had a great team that year, and I mean a great team and to win the championship was very important. That was emotional, and Davy was an extraordinary team player. Then Peugeot came up with Sebastien [Loeb] and we understood that we would not have this team again the next year.

Of course it was a really great thing to have Sebastien, but on the other hand, the time we had with a great team and that team spirit, it felt strange to not continue that.

We understood, but there were two sides to it. We had already promised Davy a drive for the next season. Timmy and Davy got that message quite early [in 2015] so they could relax and focus and not

worry about next year … and then we had to change the team.

I said to Bruno [Famin, Peugeot Sport Director], 'If we have promised something, we need to do it because we don't tell a driver this and then we don't do it.' In the end we found a solution that he could drive 10 races with us together with Timmy and Sebastien. It was okay, but for sure it was not the same as if we had continued with Davy and Timmy together, but I'm really pleased we could do that for him.

But I think his motivation fell, you never saw that in Davy because he's such a great person. I think he mentally took a step down and didn't have the same goal, motivation, or the spirit to be there to fight for the wins.

Sebastien Loeb

Hansen and Sebastien Loeb first worked together at X Games 2012 [see chapter eight] before Peugeot Sport's increasing support for the Team Peugeot-Hansen partnership placed nine-time World Rally Champion Loeb into rallycross for the 2016 World Rallycross Championship season. The Frenchman combined the World RX season and his Dakar rally programme with Peugeot. Loeb took his first win at round ten in Latvia that year but didn't win again until the Belgian round in 2018, by which time Peugeot Sport had taken the project in-house. Matched on pace by team mate Timmy Hansen throughout the three years they drove together, Loeb, like Hansen, had expected to continue with Peugeot into 2019 until the manufacturer suddenly withdrew from motor sport at the end of 2018.

Loeb on Hansen

After X Games, I met Kenneth again when I raced at Loheac in 2013, but then we began a full programme together in 2016.

Before I started the season I didn't know really what to expect; to arrive in a family team with the grandfather, grandmother, Susann, Kenneth, the two sons, I really didn't know how it would be. But they took me just like another brother and the atmosphere was really good. I feel they were happy when we got good results, even if it was me and not Timmy.

Kenneth tried to do the best for every driver; it's nice to work in these conditions because you know you have the same chances as the others, you feel that. When

I won in Latvia I had the feeling that they were happy for me to win and that was nice.

I had my experience of different motor sports and cars, but Kenneth has the experience of rallycross. Timmy [Hansen] also had more experience in rallycross than me so to share all this information and my own experience is always interesting. I think we were quite a good team from the beginning with two fast drivers.

It's interesting to work with a driver like Timmy who is very fast because I had a reference in front. It wasn't that every corner I was faster than him; some corners he was better, some I was better and we could share the information

and try to improve the global level together for the driving, the set-up of the car and the feeling we had. Usually it was quite similar and so we had some good ideas where to go. Kenneth also has a lot of experience of these kind of races so for sure, we could still speak with him about some real driving feelings and lines and things like that, and he has his own experience to help us.

He is the boss now and I think in his mind he's not a driver any more, he's the team director and he's doing the job perfectly. I also created a team, Sebastien Loeb Racing, and we have different programmes, but for me it's much more difficult when I went to the race tracks to see the guys driving and I'm sitting there, it's not my place. I think Kenneth feels his place now and he tries to share his experience to help all the team, to always do the best and it was nice to work with him.

I enjoy rallycross a lot, it's really an exciting discipline. The atmosphere is very good, it's a lot of adrenalin and stress at the start, but for sure I'm not 100% happy with the results we got.

Previous page: Hansen and Loeb celebrate after their first win together in Latvia 2016.
Above left: Latvia again, but this time in 2017.
Above: Leading the two Fords and Petter Solberg in France 2016.

Hansen on Loeb

Sebastien arriving was an amazing thing for the team, but it was also a sad moment, not because of Sebastien but because Davy [Jeanney] is such a great guy and he contributed so much to the team and we were the Team Champions together.

Of course we were very honoured to have Sebastien because if he's not the best driver in the world, then he is at least one of the best.

When he arrived, I knew Sebastien, but I didn't 'know' him. Every year and every race we did after that we got closer and of course you start to know each other more.

We had great fun and we all found a different Sebastien, the guy with the glint in his eye who is a lot of fun and enjoys a lot of jokes. Even if I expected him to be a great person, after the years we spent together I think he's even greater. You could never know exactly where you had Sebastien, he always had a little joke in his back pocket.

It's not fair that people think he's not so interested in what he is doing. When you get a little closer to him, you know he is into it and I mean really into it. There could be some very hard discussions sometimes about things in the team, why things were going in the particular direction or whatever and he was very passionate.

It's true that Timmy and Kevin put a lot of time into the races before the weekends, Sebastien perhaps took less time to investigate, but he's a great driver and he can adapt very quickly and he can bring a totally different way of thinking. When he is at a race, he is determined, but of course if you have a car that you don't feel comfortable with or the starts are not so good, sometimes you could lose interest a little. That could happen with Sebastien, but that's not unique, many drivers are like that.

When you are as famous as he is, it can be too much sometimes. If he wanted he could do interviews, sign autographs and have photos all day. He disappeared quite often, but I think that's normal behaviour, if you're not American! I understood because he wanted time for himself, and to focus.

When Sebastien came to us he was very open. He said: 'I know quite well how to drive a rally car, that is not a problem for me and I will approach rallycross with the same type of driving as I know. But if that's not good enough, then I need to change my style.' That he could recognise that shows what kind of person he is, even with everything he has done. I think he really likes rallycross a lot, it suits him and he was ready to do another year before Peugeot stopped.

We need to understand that he doesn't need to drive. There are so many other things he could spend his time doing but he decided to spend it on rallycross. I do not believe the pay cheque is the important thing for Sebastien.

To make him feel more welcome I told him that he was like my third son, and he replied 'Well, you must be bloody old.' That is his sense of humour.

I was very proud about the way Timmy and Kevin worked with him. If you had a map of a circuit, you could pick things from all three drivers where they were fastest. It made me so proud that they could contribute to Sebastien being better too. Timmy and Sebastien were quite equal, but at the beginning Timmy had the advantage many times. Sebastien caught up and they were getting the maximum from the car we had. Sebastien was with the team in the transition between working as a small team and growing to have the huge manufacturer input [see chapter seven]. We didn't succeed as much as we wanted, but it was still a great time.

Of course we knew Sebastien is a star and is very famous, but he was one of us.

Left: Hansen guided Loeb through three years in the World Rallycross Championship. Above: Loeb sends it over the hill at the Estering during the 2017 German World RX event.

Janis Baumanis

Using year-old Peugeot 208 WRXs, Hansen's team ran the Hansen Talent Development programme in 2015, giving drivers new to the sport's top class an opportunity to test and race as a part of Hansen Motorsport. Latvian Janis Baumanis was the first driver to compete under the Hansen Talent Development banner, at Lydden Hill in the UK. He finished on the podium in the European Championship round in Norway and set good times in the Turkish World RX event before the car suffered technical issues. At the same time he was racing in Super1600 with former Hansen Motorsport driver Jussi Pinomaki's SET Promotion team and won the FIA European Rallycross Championship.

Baumanis on Hansen

In 2015 I did a total of 18 events and three of them were with the Hansen Talent Development team. We had quite a good year with SET Promotion in 2014 and I was in talks with different teams about doing the European Championship or World Championship races in Supercar for 2015, but we decided to go with Hansen because it was the best solution to join the team with most experience, and to learn from drivers like Timmy [Hansen], and Kenneth of course.

Even at the first test, just at an airfield I was getting knowledge and experience that I am still using today and that for me is really amazing. I remember the first time we tested at Holjes. I had only driven there in the previous two years in the Super1600 car, and in that you take the big jump flat out, no problem. Before driving the Supercar I asked Kenneth if I could do the same, and he said: 'Just try'. On my second lap I had a good exit from the corner before and tried it flat out. I flew 35 or 40 meters and almost landed in the barrier on the outside. I collected it but of course I missed the corner. It was really good that he allowed me to try things, but he also told me what to do, how to do things better and easier to be quicker.

There were also a lot of times when Timmy helped me with driving style and how to set the car up. It was great to be able to try things that were not better for time but better for the feeling and it was really interesting to work with them. I got a lot of information and knowledge then that nobody before or since has been able to give me.

The highlight of that year was definitely finishing third in the European Championship in Norway, where I did similar lap times to Tommy Rustad in the final but because I was held up by Joni-Pekka Rajala and his big Saab, I didn't get the best result I could. I was sixth after the first corner and was pushing like hell to be on the podium. It was really nice feeling. Also in the World RX race in Turkey I was second in practice and a lot of the big guys like [Petter] Solberg and [Mattias] Ekstrom were really shocked how I could do that with a 2014 car. I surprised myself, and it would have been a good race but we had some technical problems with the car. The important thing though was that I understood that I could be really fast when everything is there and the situation in the team is really good. I achieved 99% of what I wanted with the team that year.

Even now, Kenneth is always open and says directly what he thinks. When I'm doing well he always gives me more motivation to do even better, of course not telling me what to do but just for confidence. And it's amazing that he's always smiling, even if it's not going well for his team.

*Previous pages: Baumanis was fast in Turkey
before car problems intervened.
Left: Baumanis was a Hansen Talent
Development driver in 2015.
Above: In the Peugeot 208 at Lydden Hill.*

Hansen on Baumanis

It was interesting to work with Janis, especially in the testing we did together where I was really involved. You could see how he developed and I think the target he and his family had, and still have, was to go step-by-step to be better and better. That way Janis has grown into one of the top drivers, even if it has been a little bit of a longer route for him. Things were a little up and down between the best and the worst results, but year-by-year he has developed a lot.

We set up the Hansen Talent Development team not to just rent cars out or to try and sell them, but to see if the concept could be successful. It's back to the fact that when we are involved we want it to be successful and as good as possible. Of course it depends on which drivers you have and what they can bring, because all drivers are different and their routes are different, but if the aim and motivation is there then it's always possible to take it quite far.

With Janis it took a little while for him to be consistent, but now he is in the World Championship and he is absolutely there. I think it proves that it's good to have a development team like that to try to guide the drivers in their early career. Perhaps not to be involved in everything they do, but with what they need to do as a driver to be better, and today Timmy and Kevin are doing the same thing with their Yellow Squad team. In the end a lot comes down to the budget available and you have to try and make the best of what you have, but it was very good to work with Janis and his family when we did and I think he did well.

*Above: Larsson leads at Essay with the
Hansen Citroen Saxo.
Right: Johan Larsson.*

Johan Larsson

Having been a Hansen family friend since childhood, fellow Gotene resident Johan Larsson became part of the Hansen Motorsport team when he was loaned a Citroen Saxo Super1600 car to contest the German round of the European Rallycross Championship for Division One-A in 2008. Just missing the podium in that first event, he subsequently campaigned the car, and later a Citroen C2, until the end of 2011 and finished on the podium on a number of occasions. He also claimed the category title in the Swedish Rallycross Championship in 2009.

Following the end of his full-time driving career, having handed the steering wheel of the C2 over to brother Eric Faren, Larsson returned to Kenneth Hansen's team for a one-off appearance in a Citroen DS3 Supercar for the Swedish Championship showdown at the pair's home circuit, Kinnekulle, in 2012.

Twice faster than the sport's most successful driver ever in the qualifying races, Larsson went on to finish his only Supercar outing fifth, two places behind Hansen.

Larsson on Hansen

We had sold our own Peugeot 207 Division One-A car in the middle of 2008 and I actually had no plans to continue racing. Kenneth had bought a Citroen Saxo Super1600 so Timmy [Hansen] could try rallycross and he asked if I wanted to drive it in the final round in Germany.

I think that was best race of my career. With zero meters of testing I just missed being on the podium after a small first corner battle with Jussi Pinomaki, who was the champion.

After that we had very good cooperation with Kenneth and the team and we were always fighting at the top with the Saxo and later the C2. It was great to be a part of the team and we shared a lot information. Of course with Kenneth, because we always got on well, but also with the really good mechanics and the fantastic drivers that drove for the team through the years.

The last race I did with the team was at Kinnekulle in 2012, together with Kenneth. What a day! To drive that amazing Supercar at my home track, in my hometown was something very special; a dream come true really. It was so fun and we had so many people there cheering for us. I think I adapted to the car quickly but unfortunately, I got quite a lot of punctures during the day. Kenneth helped me a lot before the race, but to be honest with so many friends and sponsors there I just wanted to have a lot of fun and enjoy it. To be able to beat Kenneth in timed practice gave me confidence and satisfaction.

Below: With the Citroen C2 in Portugal.
Right: Larsson raced a Supercar on home ground at Kinnekulle in 2012, going head-to-head with Hansen.

Hansen on Larsson

I have been friends with Ronny, Johan's father for many, many years and we had bought a Citroen Saxo as a possible rallycross car for Timmy, or to use as a practice car and explore driving on gravel a little bit more.

We had the car, and Ronny had sold the car Johan was racing so we offered Johan the chance to race it in Germany. After that we continued running as a team for some time, and later with Eric. It's never easy to find the budget, but it worked well that we could help them with travelling and transport that meant they could do it. Even if we didn't directly work with them with driving and coaching like we did with the Supercars, they were a part of the team and could ask what they wanted and we were always there if they needed help.

When Johan and I drove together at Kinnekulle, that was fun but it was just a coincidence that we drove at the same event. I had wanted to do some races and of course when it was at my home circuit there was also some pressure from the club to do it. It was also good to be in the car to feel it and to understand what our drivers were talking about better. Johan had been wanting to drive a Supercar and we had some cars there, so Johan drove the DS3 that Sebastien [Loeb] had raced at X Games and I drove the car Timur [Timerzyanov] had just won the European Championship with.

We were in the same team, in the same tent but in a one day race there's not a lot of time, not like a two day race where you can sit down and look at the data and discuss everything. There it was more just to fix the car, watch the video quickly and get back in the car. It was a rush, completely different from normal.

I definitely think Johan could have done something really good if he continued to race in Supercar. What he was missing was the aggressiveness, sometimes he was a little gentle especially when he ended up in traffic. In some ways he and Eric were very similar but being in traffic didn't affect Eric so much. In that way they were quite different. Johan was very fast and I think he showed that quite a few years later when he did a race in RX2 and got a good result.

Eric Faren

Son of Hansen family friend Ronny Larsson and younger brother to Johan Larsson, Eric Faren joined Hansen Motorsport in 2012, taking over from his brother to race the team's Super 1600 Citroen C2 in the European Championship.

Choosing to race with his mother's maiden name, Faren, instead of birth surname Larsson to avoid confusion with his brother and the unrelated fellow Swede Robin Larsson, Faren was a regular front-runner in the front-wheel drive class. He had previously raced in rallycross as a junior driver before switching to the Swedish Touring Car Championship's Junior series in 2008 and 2009 where he raced a Citroen C2 under the Kenneth Hansen Racing banner.

First racing a Supercar in 2014, Faren was in contention for the RallyX Nordic title in 2015 when he raced a Hansen Talent Development Peugeot 208. He won the season finale at Solvalla and placed second in the series. He also qualified for the semi-finals in his home round of the World Championship, but ended his driving career at the conclusion of the campaign. He continued to work for Hansen Motorsport as a mechanic and spotter for Sebastien Loeb before focusing on his Team Faren squad.

Left: Faren in discussion with Hansen.
Right: Faren took over the C2 from older brother Johan Larsson and remained connected to the Hansen squad.

Faren on Hansen

It was a bit unlucky that I qualified for the same semi-final as both Timmy [Hansen] and Davy [Jeanney] in the World RX race at Holjes in 2015. We were running the car separately, in a different part of the paddock, and I got called down to Team Peugeot-Hansen, because I was also working there as a mechanic and Davy's spotter that year. They explained to me that if I was in the top three and one of them was behind, I would need to give up the place.

I felt like the only possibility for me to get into the final was for me to be third behind Timmy and Davy, so I kind of gave up a little bit before the semi had even started. It was a bit sad when they actually told me, but afterwards I feel it was more of a compliment that they had to have that discussion with me. I think they saw that we did something good in a year-old car.

In 2014 I was working on a budget to do four or five Supercar events and we ended up doing two. Kenneth was involved in those, not officially but the car was in the workshop and he helped me with it; like when we were racing in Super1600, but only behind the scenes.

For 2015 Kenneth had plans to run the Hansen Talent Development team and I told him early I wanted to race a Peugeot. I got a new main sponsor and did RallyX Nordic.

It helped that Kevin [Hansen] was also racing in that series in Supercar Lites. We took care of the transport and Kenneth came to all the races. He was generally quite involved with the Talent Development team and wanted it to be good.

That season was the most expensive and biggest risk we have ever taken and it was probably only possible to do it in that type of car because Kenneth was kind enough to let me handle it myself, to take care of the car instead of having to pay someone to do it, I just paid Rickard [Toftgren], who was my mechanic at the races, for a few hours in the workshop when I really needed his help.

Kenneth was very involved with me too, probably more than with the drivers who did the European Championship with the team, because there he was

also busy with the World Championship team.

We had decided to go very safe with the engine, we tried a few times in RallyX Nordic to turn it up and I gained a few tenths per lap immediately, but I couldn't risk it because I simply couldn't pay if the engine blew. I knew I was down on power a lot compared to the others at Holjes in World RX but I had good data from Timmy [Hansen] racing the year before, and he helped me with watching the onboard video a lot too.

That was a good year, but looking back, the time in Super1600 was the big highlight of my career. It was good racing and you always had to push to the limit. It felt like I was as much a part of the team as Alex [Hvaal] and Timur [Timerzyanov]. We did everything together; naturally we were a little bit outside because we took care of the car ourselves and it was not a Supercar, but we all travelled together and Kenneth really made no difference between us. Those two years ended with missing the overall podium in the European Championship by a point which was a shame, but in the Swedish Championship final at Kinnekulle I won. It was special winning at home – my dad and brother had done it there before – where you know everyone in the grandstands and I felt like I was properly part of Hansen Motorsport.

I had started with rallycross in 2007, but they changed the junior class I was racing in and at around the same time the STCC [Swedish Touring Car Championship] started a new junior class. Kenneth was involved with selling parts for Citroens, so he decided to build his own car too, together with the mechanical school in Torsby. Joel Christoffersson was in charge of building it. Kenneth asked if we wanted to try circuit racing, so we rented the car in 2008 then we bought it for 2009. Together with Linus Ohlsson we ran as Kenneth Hansen Racing, although dad and I took care of our own car and Linus and his father took care of his. Kenneth wasn't really involved but of course he helped with tips and advice, then 2010 was the first year I started to work for Hansen Motorsport as a mechanic on Kenneth's car.

Hansen on Faren

Eric is a very funny guy, and he's also very dedicated to motor sport, he knows a lot, if you have some questions about what happened at a race, he knows. He's very into it and he worked hard to try and find sponsors for his own racing, and now to run his own team.

He deserved to get a good drive and we worked with him to be able to give him a good base to work from when he did a season in Supercar.

I like Eric because he's a racer; if there's a possibility he goes for it, not all race drivers do that. You have to learn where the limit is, the balance is to do it at the right time so you're not the stupid guy who puts your nose in every time, but still you need also to try and to have a reputation that you are coming and fighting to the end. It's good to have that reputation, I think Eric had it and I also worked to have that myself in my own racing.

He was fast at Holjes in 2015. Many of the Swedes have done races at Holjes and you get a lift when you're racing on home ground, but he did a very good job there and surprised a lot of people.

It was good that year when he and Kevin were doing Nordic in two different categories and I tried with my experience to help engineer them. I knew the 208 very well and I tried to guide Eric in the best way I could. It was quite interesting to be involved in the Swedish side a little more too because we had been focused on international events for a long time, so it was good to be back on home ground.

Ada-Marie Hvaal

Norwegian Ada-Marie Hvaal joined Hansen Motorsport as part of a new venture for the team in 2012 when the JRX Cup was introduced as a first rung on the ladder for 14 to 18 year olds.

The concept was created in a partnership between French firm M-Technologies and Hansen's team, among others, and run under the MAKS Events banner at FIA European Championship events. The single-make JRX class was for cars with a purpose-built spaceframe chassis, weighing 700 kilograms and powered by a 140bhp two-cylinder engine with a Sadev four-wheel drive system. The cars arrived late and unfinished to the first planned event in Norway, so the first proper race was held at Holjes in Sweden a few weeks later, where Hvaal finished second to team mate Kevin Hansen.

The 15-year old – cousin of former Hansen driver Alexander Hvaal – finished three rounds and was second again in Holland to end the year third overall as Hansen became champion. Hvaal left the team at the end of the campaign, while Hansen won the title again in 2013 before the category was axed.

Hvaal on Hansen

Joining Hansen Motorsport to race in JRX was a gift from my mum and dad at my confirmation, and of course I didn't say no. Kenneth is a legend in rallycross and I looked up to him so much as a child.

It felt like we were one big team, even though the tents were separate, everyone ate together and talked through everything together in that year.

It was Timmy [Hansen] who followed me and Kevin most and helped us with the driving, but I have several good memories of Kenneth; the best thing was just getting the opportunity to be in the team together with him. He was so calm, very good at communicating and sharing his knowledge and experiences that you could learn from.

Unfortunately though the JRX car never really worked, which was very disappointing. The idea was good, but it didn't work so well in reality and we dropped out after the first year when we didn't feel the cars were where they should be.

Hansen on Hvaal

Ada-Marie did one season, it was quite early in her career and she hadn't driven much. If the car had been more reliable it would have been possible to test more and help her develop as a driver, but we didn't dare to run it because then we couldn't race. She didn't want to continue after the first year because they didn't believe in the concept, I think it was all just a little bit too early.

We thought it was a brilliant idea to have a junior category in rallycross. The problem was that we chose a two-stroke engine. We should have done it a different way, but the advice we got was that, to be able to run it for drivers from 14-years old, 600cc was the maximum engine capacity we could use. To get good power out of the snowmobile engine we chose caused quite a lot of issues.

There were a lot of difficulties in the beginning, but the look of the car, being about two-thirds the size of a Supercar with the engine in the front was good, and there was space to have a driver coach in the car too. It was a good concept but perhaps at the wrong time with too little testing and not enough investment. We believed in it a lot but unfortunately it didn't work.

We tried to run a two-car junior team, but we didn't expect the car to be so fragile. There wasn't the budget to have lots of mechanics but, with hindsight, we should have brought in more people, but then of course the car should have been more developed and reliable before we started racing.

Top left: Hvaal leads a JRX race at Maasmechelen (Belgium) in 2012.
Top: JRX cars were delivered to their first event incomplete and under developed.
Above: Hvaal with Kevin Hansen (left) and JRX co-founder Marc Laboulle.

Andrew Jordan

Having begun his driving career in the junior ranks of the British Rallycross Championship, aged 14, Andrew Jordan quickly graduated to the top-level Supercar category and only just missed out on the British title in his second year, in 2007, under the guidance of former Hansen rival, Will Gollop.

Jordan competed against Hansen in the end-of-season rallycross Superprix at Croft Circuit in the UK in 2006 [and finished fourth while Hansen won], but without options to become a professional rallycross driver, Jordan left the sport after the following season to pursue a career in the British Touring Car Championship, where he claimed the title in 2013.

Having taken up television co-commentary duties for the revitalised European Rallycross Championship the same year as his touring car success, Jordan returned to the wheel of a rallycross Supercar in 2014 and finished on the podium at his home round of the inaugural World Rallycross Championship.

The following year, through links with partner Red Bull, Jordan joined Team Peugeot-Hansen to race a Peugeot 208 WRX at Lydden Hill. He set a fastest qualifying time and only just missed a place in the final.

Above: Used to racing in a family-run team, Jordan was an easy fit at Team Peugeot-Hansen in 2015.
Right: Jordan raced a Peugeot in the British World RX event at Lydden in 2015.

Jordan on Hansen

I'd followed Kenneth since I got into rallycross, and then raced against him at the Superprix at Croft. I remember him being very complimentary because in the Superprix, qualifying lap times decided the starting position and I beat him to pole. That was quite a feather in my cap really and he was very complimentary. That was nice. At that point I wanted to try and do rallycross as a career, but there wasn't the profile in the sport. Kenneth was one of the few drivers that made a living from rallycross, so he was someone to look up to.

I knew him a little, but when the opportunity came to drive for his team I was very excited. Being the most successful guy in the sport you know he's good and you can tell by just being around him that he has huge experience. There were a couple of times, we were trying a few things on the setup of the car at the race I did with them, and even though Kenneth was the boss, he was in the truck working on differentials himself. He's been there and done it all, and can be very hands on when he needs to be.

He has that kind of aura about him where if there's a rush to get a car ready in a short space of time or whatever, he is quite calming and relaxing. When I drove with them they had a real family atmosphere in the team. I could see a lot of me and my family in them that way.

The car I drove was early in its development at that point, but we still had good pace and I was pleased to set a fastest qualifying time, that was really good. I think it was a very level playing field between me, Davy [Jeanney] and Timmy [Hansen].

Kenneth's an icon of the sport and he's been a bit of a trend setter of paving the way of making a career out of rallycross. I'm sure he's been very influential to a lot of people getting into the sport, and above everything, he's a nice guy.

I'd love him to do one more event to make 250 European Championship starts. I was trying to get him to do it, but obviously it's not simple. From what I hear he's still quick. I think that would be awesome.

Hansen on Jordan

Andrew and his family are such good people. Andrew is a very professional driver and the way he worked with the team meant it was a very enjoyable race at Lydden. He's a real team player and good character that you want to work with.

It's a shame that at Lydden we didn't have the specification of car we had at the next race – after we had done a very good test – otherwise Andrew might have done better than he did. I know he could be the same level with the right car, I know what he can do and has done, there's no question about that.

I understand why he chose to go down the racing line, and I think he is good enough to take that as far as he wants, but perhaps in the future he will come back to rallycross and I think he can be very good, but for that one race at least it was good to be able to work together. We joked a little that he's Kevin [Hansen's] brother. When you look at pictures with those two together, at that time they could look just alike.

Kenny Brack

A Swedish driver who conducted the majority of his career in the America, Kenny Brack competed in CART and IndyCar, and won the coveted Indianapolis 500 in 1999. He can be considered one of Sweden's most successful motor racing exports.

Brack mentored Timmy Hansen when Kenneth's oldest son was competing in Formula BMW, assisting with sponsorship acquisition and driver tuition, then seized the opportunity to join Hansen Motorsport for a one-off appearance alongside Kenneth and Jussi Pinomaki in a Citroen C4 at the Swedish round of the European Rallycross Championship at Holjes, in 2009.

While Hansen finished fifth, Brack made it to the B-final and was classified 10th. That year he also took part in the rallycross section of X Games 15 in Los Angeles and claimed victory in a Ford Fiesta.

Above: Brack raced with Hansen at Holjes in 2009.

Right: To prepare for his Holjes outing Brack visited the European Championship event in Hungary, here he talks to Jussi Pinomaki and Hansen.

Brack on Hansen

I think among the people who understand, Kenneth is one of the big profiles in Swedish motor sport, and is highly regarded internationally too. He was different in rallycross because he adopted more of a racing mentality. People in rally or rallycross perhaps sometimes didn't pay so much attention to the details like people in racing, where every hundredth of a second counts, but Kenneth did. He was always very neat in driving, with his lines and not sideways everywhere. Maybe that's part of his success – I think that he's one of the greats of course.

I can't remember how racing at Holjes came up, it was a cooperation between Kenneth and the track. I'm no stranger to any kind of car really, but at that point I'd never driven anything on gravel, of course I grew up on gravel but I'd never competed in rallying or rallycross of that sort. It was a fantastic opportunity, and also with Kenneth who I'd known for a long time.

I was on the pace lap time wise, none of that was an issue. Unfortunately, we had a bit of misfortune on the race weekend. I think we probably were the fastest car, but in qualifying something happened with the electrical or throttle system so I had to use the on-off switch to drive. When I switched the car off it didn't pull, and when I switched it on it was full throttle. I had to drive practice like that and it was hard to produce the lap times we were capable of.

That put us on the back foot because then you start the heats from the outside and I didn't have the rallycross experience to recover from that situation. It was a bit of a shame, but it was nobody's fault. As it was I got to the B final because I had to battle my way through the competition. But it was a great experience. I knew a lot of the rallycross fraternity, I grew up around it although I'd never driven it. That event is fantastic, there are a lot of people at Holjes and it's a big party.

I have also been very happy to see Timmy's development from racing in Formula BMW when I used to help him to becoming one of the leading lights in rallycross. That's a great progression and it's fantastic to carry that Hansen family heritage onto the next generation with Kevin too. He's a funny bloke and he's a good driver as well.

Hansen on Brack

We got to know Kenny because he was a mentor and helped Timmy for a couple of years in circuit racing, and that led to him driving with us. We just did one test day and I remember my first impression was that he was very professional.

The race was just for fun really, but he was very determined, learnt a lot and the speed was there. It's a shame that he had the problem in practice because he just needed to learn a little about rallycross competition; how close it can be, that sometimes you need to give space, but you need to take it too. As a team we learnt a lot from him, how he operated and the ideas he had. Because of his background he is very strong mentally, and has a great winning mind.

Fredrik Salsten

Swede Fredrik Salsten raced a rear-wheel drive Citroen DS3 in the FIA European Rallycross Championship TouringCar category from 2014. Based on a bodyshell acquired through Hansen Motorsport, Salsten used the car to win the 2015 TouringCar title. He graduated to the headline Supercar category during his title-winning term, making his debut in the European Championship in Spain driving a Hansen Talent Development-run Peugeot 208 WRX. He subsequently raced the car in a full Euro RX campaign in 2016, made the final in three of the five rounds and finished second in his home race at Holjes, behind Kevin Hansen.

Salsten on Hansen

I didn't discover motor sport until I was 17-years-old but when my interest turned to rallycross, Sverre Isachsen and Kenneth Hansen were my favourites. Then I met Kenneth for the first time in 2013 when I bought a standard Citroen DS3 bodyshell from him to build into my TouringCar. It came straight from the Citroen factory so there was a lot of work to do. I also bought the body panels from Hansen Motorsport.

After I won the TouringCar Championship we decided to do some Supercar races. I chose Hansen Motorsport because it felt like the team is one big family and everybody works for the same goal, and that is to win.

The first test I did was a brilliant experience. After I'd had about 30 laps in the car, Timmy [Hansen] did three laps to give me a lap time to try to beat. After some more laps and with good coaching I was spot on with Timmy's lap.

That was a great moment, and one of my highlights of the season was definitely finishing second at Holjes.

The Supercar is more forgiving when you make a mistake and you can almost save it every time compared to a TouringCar where there is no room for mistakes because if you make one, you will probably spin. Strangely for me the Supercar was easier to drive. I really think the TouringCar experience helped with racing the Supercar, especially in the wet because the driving has to be so smooth when there is so little grip.

The Hansen team is very professional and caring. You are always welcome, you almost get the feeling that you are at home. I have learnt so much from them, the difference in feeling between being with them and with my own team was really not so big.

Kenneth always has something to say that can help you move forward, and he also knows when it's faster to back off a little bit, which is important.

He is one of the kindest and most open-minded people in the sport. The whole family are like that.

Hansen on Salsten

Fredrik's situation is very similar to me and Susann really because his girlfriend [now wife, Veronica] also drives in rallycross. He's a very clever driver, he showed that a lot when he was racing the TouringCar, he didn't take big risks when it wasn't needed and he gained a lot from being clever.

When we tested with him for the first time I expected it to be quite different to how it was, but he's a very efficient driver. Normally you would think that Super1600 would be a more perfect way to come into Supercar because you have to be very smooth with those cars, but I think if you can drive a TouringCar really well then it can also be a similar style compared to a Supercar, because you need to take care of the speed and the lines. I was a positively surprised with his driving style.

Fredrik's a good guy to work with, he listens and wants to improve. At Holjes when he ended up second to Kevin he had very good speed, in the end the same as Kevin so he had the possibility to be up there. He became a father around that time and it was a big influence on him. When we stopped racing together he said that he would like to take a year off. He's a very personal guy and he thinks a lot about the people around him. It's not just work, business or racing, it's deeper than that. Of course we had hopes to do something with him again, for sure he has the speed and he was very good.

Left: Salsten used a Hansen Development Team Peugeot 208 to good effect in 2016 when his best finish was second place at Holjes.

Rustam Minnikhanov

An experienced autocross and rally raid driver, Rustam Minnikhanov first appeared in the FIA European Rallycross Championship in 2006, at which point he was Prime Minister of Tatarstan, an autonomous Republic of the Russian federation. For 2007 he acquired the Citroen C4 that Hansen had driven to second in the 2006 season. More a customer than a true Hansen team racer, Minnikhanov's car was run in a satellite operation by Latvian outfit TT Motorsport. Minnikhanov put in a full season with the C4 in 2007, before a new car was built in Hansen's Gotene workshops which the Russian drove in selected events in 2008 and 2009. Always torn between his political commitments and love of motor sport, Minnikhanov was elected as Tatarstan's President in March 2010, which effectively ended his international rallycross participation.

In the subsequent years, Hansen Motorsport provided Citroen DS3 and Peugeot 208 Supercars for Minnikhanov to race at home, notably in the President's Cup event held every August just outside Tatarstan's capital Kazan.

Minnikhanov on Hansen

I have only brilliant memories about Kenneth Hansen and his family. He taught me a lot about rallycross and how to handle those Supercars.

Kenneth is a professional in the sphere of motor sport not only as a driver but also as a constructor. His technical creations that I used for my participation in races were successful and competitive.

I'm glad to know him and that I had a chance to compete with such a legendary person.

As President of the Republic of Tatarstan I am proud to say that in the past Kenneth took part and won our historical President's Cup races.

Above: Minnikhanov and Hansen share a joke; the Russian politician enjoys his racing deeply.
Right: Hansen supplied Citroen and Peugeot Supercars for Minnikhanov.

Hansen on Minnikhanov

The first time Rustam came to a test was at Strangnas [in Sweden] and we planned to be there for one day. We were set up and ready, then his people called and said Rustam would be a little late. I think he arrived at the track at seven o'clock in the evening, so there was only time to do a short run, then I booked a hotel for them to stay the night. They said they would not be able to come until after lunch the next day because he had a meeting. He was the Prime Minister and that kind of thing would happen quite a lot.

In the evening they called again and said: 'We will come early tomorrow morning instead'. A little while later I got another call, and the tone of voice was quite different. It was a Russian guy but speaking good English and I felt that he was a little aggressive. He asked why I couldn't stick to the programme. I explained that we were trying to do that, but he said: 'You were going to practice tomorrow afternoon'. Then I understood. I explained that to teach and give good advice you can't say that it will take this amount time. You need a lot of time, as much as possible, and it's different for every driver, so of course it is good if we have longer. It ended there, but it was a strange call.

The next day, Rafael Bagautdinov [who has a role in the sports club, and was de facto team manager for Minnikhanov] explained that those kind of things were normal and that the phone call had been from a secretary in the government who was very upset because Rustam wanted to drive and didn't want to go to the meeting. In the end they had cancelled the whole meeting!

As a senior politician they don't like him to compete and they don't like him to go out on his motorcycle either, but he loves motor sport.

When we organised later tests he would come by helicopter, and he liked to have a motorbike there so he could also ride a little. For the tests, if they said he will come at 16.20 and he had 50 minutes to drive, at exactly that time the helicopter landed and at 17.10 it lifted again. It was very different to work with him.

On one Saturday at a race, he came in from a heat, changed his clothes, jumped on the motorbike and went. You could see all of his bodyguards thinking 'Oh shit!'. They didn't know that he was going and they jumped into a car and chased after him. I think he loved to do that, to be a little free.

What I loved about Rustam was that when he came to drive the car, for him it was like Christmas. It was the time when he really, really relaxed and just enjoyed himself. He didn't show every time how good he was, but that was because he had a lot of other things going on in his head. Sometimes though, he was very quick.

Once in the Czech Republic he put in a very good time in the timed practice, and he could do some good heats, but the best memories for me are that he enjoyed being at the races so much. That's the difference. Some drivers come to win, he came to enjoy and the best races he had were when he had fights with his friend Ayrat Shaymiev. When he could beat Ayrat, that was brilliant.

Top: Kiss leads Team Hansen Peugeot driver Jeanney at Franciacorta, Italy, in 2015. Below: Kiss had coached Timmy Hansen in formula cars but found the tables turned when he switched to rallycross.

Tamas Pal Kiss

Tamas Pal Kiss is one of the many drivers to get so close and yet so far from making it all the way to Formula 1. When prospects of achieving that goal faded, the Hungarian driver switched to rallycross at national level, then sought a competitive drive for his European Championship debut in 2015. He joined the Hansen Talent Development team for the final round in Italy and qualified second for the final, but was forced out with an alternator issue. He then bought a Peugeot 208 WRX from Hansen and challenged for the Euro RX title in the subsequent two years, finishing third overall in 2017 before calling time on his driving career.

Kiss on Hansen

I got to know Timmy Hansen before the season in 2011. I was about to end my single seater career for the first time, because I couldn't find a way to step up from where I was, but a team [Interwetten] in Eurocup Formula Renault 2.0 called and asked if I would do some testing.

At the first test in Barcelona I met Timmy, who was already driving for Interwetten. Of course I immediately recognised his name and his link to rallycross. My brother had won the Hungarian Rallycross Championship in Supercar and had raced against Timmy's father Kenneth at Nyirad. Kenneth was already the most successful driver ever by that time, but he was probably also the first to say hello, to shake hands and just be nice with everyone in the paddock. Because of that I had a good subject to talk about with Timmy and we got on well.

He was quite early in his career, so there was a lot of room to improve on data and track analysis, and driving wise, so because I had a lot of experience we ended up sitting together to look at the data and he improved quite a lot, at the end of the day we had only a couple of tenths between us. Then I went further in single-seater racing and in 2012 Timmy switched to rallycross.

I drove in rallycross in 2015, but in the middle of the season I was in trouble because I had submitted my entry to a round of the European Championship, but the team I was with seemed to be unprepared for that. It was such short notice but Timmy was the only person we spoke to who said it would not be no problem and

he put me in touch with Kenneth. Already the first phone call was 40 minutes long.

In the end it was a straight-forward discussion and we agreed that I would race a Peugeot 208 at the Italian round. Kenneth wanted me to test the car in Sweden to be sure we had good speed, and that went better than we expected. Timmy was there helping me out which I felt was kind of pay back for what I'd done before. It was amazing that four years earlier I was the experienced one, now, just a week after he won a round of the World Championship, here he was helping me with techniques.

The race in Italy was probably the most entertaining and the best feeling race I'd had in a very, very long time. Okay, we had a problem in the final, but immediately we were on the pace and qualified on the front row for the final. We had track walks together, shared some ideas and it all helped a lot. That really got my motivation for motor sport again, working with Kenneth's team and we decided to buy the car from them to run with my own team, but we needed their support.

It was never like they sold a car and that's it, the job was over. It was much more like a family-to-family relationship, there was a clear trust. There were several times when I realised too late that we needed parts, but Kenneth's team always helped us and without him we wouldn't have been able to be to have the chance to fight for the European Championships like we did.

Hansen on Kiss

I didn't know Tamas when he helped Timmy and they drove together in formula racing, and at that time we never believed that the good guys that were looking to go to Formula 1 would one day end up in rallycross.

When he was interested to drive with us, Timmy said immediately that he would be good and he was so right. It was wonderful that Timmy was now able to help Tamas get up to speed.

I liked Tamas as a person but I was very impressed by his first race in Italy and I tried to work with him in the Hansen Talent Development team as much as possible, our goal has always been to give our drivers the best possible chance, but of course I was not totally involved because we were quite busy with the World Championship team.

I think in some ways Tamas and I are very similar, perhaps we are both quite easy to work with as part of a team, but get him or me inside a car it's not exactly the same person at all. Tamas was hell to have as a competitor, he is fair but hard when he is in the car.

When he bought a car from us we were in very close contact during his European Championship seasons. He was good, he followed the advice we gave and of course he had his own ideas because he's a good driver but he didn't do things that we didn't agree on and he really wanted to follow the Hansen Motorsport way to run the car.

In the end he was not far away from winning the European Championship title, he was in the fight but sometimes it just doesn't work out.

Even Hvaal

Even Hvaal joined Hansen Motorsport for the final two rounds of the 2009 European Championship in Poland and the Czech Republic. Prior to this the Norwegian had made ad-hoc appearances in the series driving Division One-A cars over a number of years. Always impressive, Hvaal used a Citroen Saxo to beat category front-runner Jussi Pinomaki to victory in the Polish round in 2007. Graduating to a Supercar at the end of 2009, he joined Hansen and Pinomaki in a three-car Citroen C4 line-up. Third in the C final in Poland, Hvaal didn't qualify for the finals in the Czech Republic but showed impressive pace given his limited mileage. He became involved with the Hansen team again in 2012, when his daughter Ada-Marie raced a JRX car with the squad.

Hvaal on Hansen

I chose to drive with Kenneth's team for two races because he was known as one of the best in the sport. We did those races because that's what my sponsors wanted to do. Kenneth was very calm and welcoming, and it was good to be part of his team. We had some bad luck with the engine, otherwise I think it would have gone better, but we didn't do any more after that because it was so expensive.

We started again with Hansen's team for JRX with Ada-Marie, but the car and project didn't work as promised so we decided to stop.

Hansen on Hvaal

Even wanted to drive a couple of races with us and there was the opportunity to do that at the end of 2009. He's a good driver, especially as he didn't have a lot of experience in a Supercar when he came to us and the potential he showed in those races was really good. He took care of things on track, if you know what I mean – he was not a gentlemen! It's very difficult to just jump in at that level and do a brilliant race, but I was impressed by him.

I don't think it was ever in Even's plan to do a complete championship, he just did some races and then soon after that time with us, Ada-Marie started to race. When children arrive, it makes your life very different.

Left: Hansen photographs his team in Poland 2009 where he had the Larsson Saxo and C4 Supercars for himself, Jussi Pinomaki and Even Hvaal.
Above: Hvaal showed good form despite limited experience in Supercar.

Mats Lysen

Mats Lysen entered the FIA European Rallycross Championship for Division One-A with a Citroen Saxo in 2008 and took the title driving a Renault Clio for his family-run team the following year.

Graduating to Supercar for 2010, Lysen finished third in the German round, one place behind Hansen. He then drove a Hansen-run Citroen C4 in a one-off outing for a Norwegian Championship race at the end of the year as he assessed options for the future.

That event at Lyngas was a rare occasion where Hansen was absent from his team in European competition, away with Liam Doran in America at the time.

Lysen drove only that one race for Hansen's squad, in which he finished fifth, but went on to win his home European Championship event in 2012.

Lysen on Hansen

When I started driving in the European Championship it was in a Citroen Saxo, in Division One-A. From the start Kenneth was really kind to me. We were getting all the parts we needed from his team back then and he always helped with advice too. He's just a really nice man and going into the European Championship for the first time, he was kind to everyone.

When I moved to Supercar I always loved to drive against Kenneth. For sure he was hard to beat but you are not European Champion so many times if you are not doing the right things on the track. I did one event with his team in the C4. After one year in Supercar we wanted to try and drive for a team, and to try out the Citroen. I knew Kenneth and some of the guys there. When you see how much they have won, you can see how good they are, but that weekend we were a bit unlucky because only a small part of the team was there, Kenneth and the rest of the guys were at a race in America. We had some car issues but it was a good experience and nice to try to work with Kenneth's team.

We also tried a Renault Clio in the Czech Republic round of the European Championship. That team [Helmia Motorsport] was a lot closer and easier for us because they had everything in Torsby, and I live quite close, just over the border in Norway, so it was easier to deal with them.

Around that time Kenneth had started to build up his team by running other drivers as well, and they were always hard to compete against. Kenneth was always really good, but well prepared too and you can see the same with Timmy and Kevin.

Hansen on Lysen

We tried to help Mats where we could when he first started with the Saxo. When you see someone with talent like that and they are a good person of course you want to help them, and it was clear that he was a good guy and brilliant driver.

It was also good that we had the opportunity to have Mats in the car for that Norwegian race, even if I couldn't be there. Oskar Lund managed the team and we were in contact all day.

Sometimes I wasn't able to be at a race with the team. Of course it's difficult like that but if it's the only way then we always made it work the best we could. It happened a few times with rallycross, but when I was still driving it happened a lot when Kevin was karting and Timmy was karting and then in circuit racing. At times that was very difficult, they were at different races and I was at a European race somewhere else, but you learn from the experience and you learn that nobody is irreplaceable.

It would have been good to have Mats with us for more than that one race, but it was fine that he made a different choice. I really felt it was a pity in the end that he couldn't raise the budget to continue racing in Supercar because he really is a very good driver.

Left: Lysen (far left) celebrates with Sverre Isachsen and Hansen.

Stig-Olov Walfridson

Coming from one of Sweden's best-known motor sport dynasties, younger brother to successful rally and rallycross drivers Per Inge Walfridsson (the 1980 European Rallycross Champion) and Lars Erik Walfridson, seven-time Swedish Group N Rally Champion Stig-Olov Walfridson first made the transition to rallycross in the mid 1990s. Driving a Group N Mitsubishi he won three Swedish titles, along with making ad-hoc European Championship appearances.

He continued to compete in rallies, and in 2001 acquired an ex-Lasse Sallstrom Ford Focus 'Supercar', but met with limited success.

For 2004, 'Stecka' signed to drive with Hansen Motorsport in the Swedish Championship and the Norwegian and Swedish rounds of the European series. The highlight of the year was a second place finish to Hansen at Lyngas.

He again drove a Hansen-built Xsara at Holjes in 2006, before a serious rally accident put him out of action. When he returned, it was with his own Renault Clio Supercar, which he drove to a pair of Swedish titles and an empathic – and emotional – home victory in the Swedish round of the 2009 European Rallycross Championship at Holjes, just 100km from his Torsby home.

Above: Walfridson goes door-to-door with Hansen in a national event at Tomelilla.
Right: Walfridson raced with and against Hansen.

Walfridson on Hansen

I did the Swedish Championship with a Xsara from Kenneth in 2004. He was one of the best at that time, we talked about it and that was the way to go for me. I knew he had good experience and a good feeling for rallycross. He had been there such a very long time so it was easy to make a decision to work with him. It's easy to work with Kenneth.

I think I first met him when I started rallycross in 1995 with a Mitsubishi Group N in rallycross. It was some years later I rented a car from him.

There was one little incident that year [2004] in the north of Sweden at Kalix. It was raining and I got the better start, but in the first corner he pushed me. It was difficult to see because there was a lot of rain and mud there. We had a little bit of a fight there, but otherwise no problem.

He was very fair on the track. You know which guys you can go beside without them pushing you off. Michael Jernberg, Ludvig Hunsbedt and Kenneth were some of the guys who were no problem, it was easy with them.

I use my left foot on the brake and Kenneth was angry with me about that when I drove with him. He wanted to make a barrier [between the clutch and brake pedals] so I could not do that. I had that from 20 years in rallies, okay with rallycross it's not the best maybe. He told me: 'You must stop with this if you want to go really fast'. We had some discussion

about that. He tried to help me of course but it was hard to change. Kenneth was very helpful, I like him very much. I did some more rallies after the time with Kenneth, then I had the really huge crash on a rally with a moose. I could not drive for six months, and every morning when I went to our dealership [Helmia] I passed this standard Renault Clio Sport standing there. Every day I thought: 'Bloody hell it's a nice car and maybe it could be a good rallycross car'. That's where it started. So we built our own Renault Clio Sport Supercar.

It was a dream to be the winner in Holjes. It was a very exciting final, a lot of things happened there, but it was special with Kenneth, Jernberg, Hunsbedt and Henning Solberg in the race.

Now our children drive. I have one son who drives rallycross [Jimmie] and one daughter who drives crosskart [Felicia]. They have all been in the paddock since they were small children, playing together. Now Kenneth's sons are big stars, so that's good fun.

Hansen on Walfridson

Stecka is an enjoyable person to be around. He loves to go as sideways as possible, perhaps in the old-fashioned way. He was fast, his style was a little more like a rally driver. I remember after he was driving for us, we were in Belgium and I said to him, about the long downhill to the last corner at Maasmechelen: 'You need to go a little tighter because you know, this sideways, you lose a lot of time.' He was driving for his own team then, with the Renault. He just said: 'Yeah I know, but I don't want to. This way is so fun!' I like how he is and the way he does things. He's a very good, honest person.

When he won at Holjes, that must have been incredible. To be from the area, and to be a Walfridson with his brothers, with the history around them, it was a big thing. They have done a lot for motor sport and sport overall in Varmland.

Holjes, Sweden in 2004, Kenneth Hansen surrounded by his team.

Kenneth Hansen is the most successful rallycross driver ever, so it stands to reason that Hansen Motorsport is also the most successful team in the sport's history. Here are some of key players whose work has enabled that success.

6. TEAM

*Kennet Nyberg at work with Kenneth Hansen
in the team's old workshop at Gotene.*

Kennet Nyberg

Mechanic and engineer
1992 –

Nyberg on Hansen

I was working in a welding fabrication place in Gotene. It shut down and Kenneth's father asked if I could help him to repair an old bus. Then Kenneth asked if I wanted to go with him to some races. So I did, and I've been full-time since then.

Our parents were neighbours and friends so in the summer our families went camping together. My brother helped Kenneth when he raced a Volvo Amazon and won the Swedish Championship [in 1986] so we've known each other quite a long time.

When I started full-time it was just me and Kenneth, and some of his friends came to help in the evenings and at races.

My wife and I met in Norway in 1992. We have three children but she knows I always work here. Her father worked for Tommy Kristoffersson's team, so she understands. I always worked from 0500 to 1300, the children came home from school and I had the afternoon with them. It worked very well and Kenneth and Susann were very good about that.

When Kenneth was driving it was like a small family, but you always want to win, it doesn't matter who the driver is.

The first victory we took in Supercar, in Austria, when we had built the first ZX for 1993 was special. Martin [Schanche] came and looked at the car. We had a quite strange steering rack, he looked at it and said: 'That's not going to work'. During the weekend, something happened and Kenneth went off and I began to think that Martin was right. But that was not

the failure, it was something else and Kenneth won the final in the end. That was a good moment.

Even when Kenneth won a lot, when you went to a race, everything can happen, even though you know he is very fast. Maybe a driveshaft could break, anything could happen.

Sometimes he would come in and was maybe second or third. We'd ask if he had a problem. 'No, I don't believe I need to drive so fast to be first,' he'd reply. That was funny, that he knew he didn't need to drive as fast as he could the whole time.

But, when Lars [Larsson] and Sverre [Isachsen] came in properly [in earnest from 2005], it was much, much harder.

We tried to build the cars in a good way. When we built the Xsara and C4, we did nearly everything. We got some parts from Citroen and rebuilt them, but most of the car was made by us.

Later we had a lot of help from Peugeot, they did the biggest work, and we only put the car together [circa 2015-2016]. Then it changed quite a lot.

Before then it was much more welding and fabrication, we made transmission tunnels and everything. In that time you were always black. Now it's just your hands that get dirty, so it's much better.

Also by 2015 we had a lot of people. I always enjoyed it, it's no problem to work with a lot of people, but when we were used to only have a small team and then people were coming from England, Denmark, France, Latvia, that was a change.

Hansen on Nyberg

Nyberg and I must have spent a big, big part of our lives together when I think about it. He's been with us for over 27 years, and for many of those we were driving the bus together around Europe.

He's a very calm guy, who's not talking a lot but he's so into motor sport and rallycross. He started with me in 1992 and we built my first Citroen together. We had some support from Citroen but not like it was with Peugeot later. We didn't have a lot of engineers, it was our own work; we thought about things carefully and were realistic about what we could make and so on. We've come a long way together and he's been in the company and he works on the World Championship, sometimes on other things, sometimes on cross-karts, so it's difficult to put the finger on but he's a big part of Hansen Motorsport.

Nyberg has always been the guy who had the eyes to see everything. It could be a crack in something, or the clearance in something else, so he saved quite a lot of reliability problems. And it's not only on the car but also in the paddock. We call him hawk-eye because he sees everything, that was crucial to our success and

he's very special. He didn't only see things in rallycross, in other motor sport too where we picked up things up. That was so important when we were such a small team in the beginning.

We got some support from Citroen, but we built the cars and it was important to pick up things from other disciplines to understand what the cleverest way to build the car was. When we went to the Citroen Sport factory for the first time in 1993 it was like going to another world. We had very big eyes; it was like Christmas for us to be there.

The first time we went to the factory with the ZX we took it out of the bus at the workshop outside Paris [at Trappes]. We had done all the work at home, then we went down there to fit the engine and do some test days.

When they saw the car arrive all the guys in the motor sport department were interested to see it. They came out of the workshops and looked all around the car. Perhaps it was 20 guys there and they said no words, but gave us a spontaneous applause. That we will never forget.

Of course we were not like a factory team, me and Nyberg were also outside in the garbage containers looking for stuff that we could use. That's how it was.

When we first built the C4 [2006], we were at Oreca to do some last tests. We had a problem with a valve [in the engine], so we needed to take the cylinder head off and engine out to fix it. We were quite short of time and not completely finished, but we needed to rush down to Portugal [Lousada]. On the way, Nyberg got ill in his stomach and I was the only one that could drive the bus.

We were 24 hours away, not a good situation but we needed to be there. There was nothing to do but for me to drive. That was my worst trip ever. We couldn't stop and sleep because we were so late, it was terrible. When we arrived Nyberg got better and he could start to work on the car.

Top left: Nyberg (under the car) was also called "Spanarn" by the team because of his eye for spotting details.
Above: Nyberg at the wheel of Hansen Motorsport's first Supercar.

Oskar Lund

Mechanic
2009-2015, 2017

I first got involved with Hansen Motorsport when Morten Bermingrud bought his Citroen Xsara from Kenneth in 2002. I thought Kenneth was very nice and helpful. He is sincere and interested in what you do and how things are going. When I worked for Kenneth I was responsible for gearboxes, clutches and engines mainly, and I was also spotter for Alexander Hvaal when he was driving in the team.

The best moments were when we took silver and bronze overall in the European Championship in 2010, and when Timur [Timerzyanov] took the championship in 2012. Also for me it was very exciting that we managed to change an engine in Sebastien Loeb's car in 2017 in Norway, we did it in 50 minutes!

But there were big challenges too, like some engine issues we had with Hvaal in 2013, and repairing Timmy's car after his Q3 crash in Norway in 2017.

I started on [Jussi] Pinomaki's car in 2009. In Hungary [round four] we had a problem with the engine, so on Monday evening Joel [Christoffersson] and I drove from Hungary to Citroen Sport in Paris to get some parts, then to Oreca [Magny-Cours] and back to meet the team in Austria for the next race on Thursday. In total we drove 3000 kilometres. That illustrates the willpower of Kenneth Hansen and his team. On Friday we got the new engine in and on Saturday Jussi had a big crash and the car was very bad.

Kenneth's team is 100% professional and they have a winner's mentality. Like when we changed the engine for Loeb in Lanke, no-one thought we could manage it in such a short time, but this was team Hansen.

Tomas Gustavsson

Mechanic
1985-1989

I was a mechanic for Christer Strand in rallycross and that's when I met Kenneth. Christer was really into his normal work so didn't have so much time for rallycross, and that's why I ended up going to work with Kenneth.

I was chief mechanic you could say, but we didn't have a lot of mechanics so I didn't really have anyone under me.

I lived for the sport, it's what I did; work, sleep, eat and rallycross. After work on Monday to Friday I would eat then go up to the workshop at Kenneth's parents, until 2200 or 2300, then at the weekend if there was a race we would go there too.

We tried to be very precise with everything we did, even if we didn't have the economic resources. Because of that, we needed to solve things ourselves, sometimes in an agricultural way if we didn't have the money to buy a new part. It was a lot of cutting and welding.

The highlight was definitely winning the Swedish Championship in 1986 and the European Championship in 1989. That year ['89] we were in Ireland with the Sierra Cosworth and we had a water leak from the head gasket. We took the water out once the car cooled down, cleaned it and I put epoxy glue all around the cylinder head and the block. Just before the start of the next race, we put water in and started the engine. We didn't have any budget and no experience about the Cosworth engine and how difficult and expensive it would be to open it. Because it worked, we continued to the end. We finished second that day.

When we opened the engine after the season and it was 100% crap. There was so much leaking, the cylinders were like ovals, it was absolutely shit.

We had a very special rear diff with some springs inside that didn't work all the time. In Holland, the weather was very hot but we had some problems with the diff. We waited until 2300 and worked for a few hours. When we finished we went for a walk around the paddock and many of the other teams were also still up working. It had just been too hot to work during the day.

Ingalill Sandin

Chef
1994-2008

As Susann's aunt, and because we have a strong bond, the interest in their professional efforts in motor sport became increasingly obvious. In Autumn 1994, they asked if I wanted to attend an event and help with cooking and other household tasks for the whole team. After that, I was on the team for many years, it was brilliant. The kitchen area was my place.

The atmosphere was very good, it was a lot of fun with a feeling of community that we all worked together. We all felt needed and welcomed.

There was such happiness when the team was doing well and was satisfied, and I really remember the joint meals we had after a hard day working.

To have been one in the team for several years was a lot of fun. Many nice and fun moments were experienced, and you could be sure something would always happen that was interesting.

I first met Kenneth sometime in the early 1990s on a visit see Susann and him at their home in Gotene. My first impression of Kenneth was his calm and nice way of receiving people, whether he knew them or not. He has always been a wonderful person to spend time with, but during the races he became a bit like a lost devil behind the wheel, so focused. Once he got back to the tent, the same calm Kenneth talked and greeted everyone.

The fact that Hansen Motorsport has managed to get where it is today is simply because of a very professional job from the entire team. Kenneth has a leadership trait that makes people around him listen and work in the same spirit that is the best for the team and Susann can take a lot of responsibility for that too.

Top: Oskar Lund moved from working with Hansen Motorsport customer Morten Bermingrud to work with the Swedish team. Centre: Tomas Gustavsson together with Hansen and the 1988 Volvo 240 Turbo. Bottom: Family is a recurring theme and like any good family the Hansen team eats together.

Rickard Toftgren discusses details of the
Citroen Xsara Supercar with Hansen.

Rickard Toftgren

Mechanic and engineer
1997-2016

Toftgren on Hansen

I was working with another driver, Christer Bohlin and I'd known Kenneth for a long time because my father had done some jobs for him. In 1997 Christer didn't have any big plans so I did one race with Kenneth. The next year I did all of the races but still worked with Christer, then in 1999 I began with Kenneth full-time.

There were a lot of highlights, but it was really fun when we went with Liam Doran for the first time to X Games in 2011 [see chapter eight]. Liam organised everything and we had no idea what to expect. We'd already done couple of races in America but he drove badly and didn't get good results. At X Games he was in a good flow.

And then also at X Games with Sebastien [Loeb, in 2012], it was the first time we met him. I went to the first test, the first day we were with Phillipe Bugalski and then after Sebastien.

We had some problems with the car when we got to America, we worked all night to get it ready and went back to the hotel at about 0430. Most of the team stayed in Sweden for the European Championship event that weekend, and when we got to the hotel, because of the time difference, we put the internet radio on and heard the warm-up from Holjes.

Sebastien was quick. After one heat, when he won by 12 seconds or something, Kenneth said: 'When you have that big a lead you don't have to push.' And he just said:

'I didn't push.' It was like that the whole event, he just drove and drove. He was very happy.

With Kenneth driving I think my biggest memory is when we came back from a big crash in Norway and made the car good for him again and it was even quicker [than it had been]. That was really nice [see chapter two].

Me and [Kennet] Nyberg had our wives with us at that race and they'd never seen anything like it. We were working until midnight after the race just to get the car in the trailer and they were helping. We were supposed to be going on holiday but we had to cancel that.

Another big crash I remember was with Liam in a British Championship race [in 2011]. It was unbelievable. We were so scared because we heard Liam was unconscious and so on. It was crazy. Now we can joke that he has the rollover lap record at Lydden Hill – eight! The car was not repairable, so we took that one to pieces.

Kenneth was a very good driver, so he didn't get involved with those kinds of crashes. Okay, people put him into the tyres and so on but apart from that one in Norway, there were no big crashes.

In 2001 when he was doing the Swedish and French Championships, one weekend he went in a small plane to France [from Sweden, see chapter nine] and on Sunday morning had to do his practice, then two heats before the finals. I was alone with all the

French guys at the event in France that weekend.

I could maybe put the best parts of the job in three categories. When me and Nyberg started in the autumn to build a car and we did almost everything by ourselves with some Citroen parts.

Then when you went to the first race, you've maybe done some small tests, and you see what you've done during the winter. Maybe not every time we were winning, but with the C4 we won the first race directly, that was fun.

Then like what happened in Norway and there is some trouble, or you need to change the engine in 45 minutes, you do it and come out like: 'Yeah, we did it!' It's never fun to change an engine because you know there is a problem, but you solve the problem to go further in the race.

People used to ask me why I did it for so long, but all the time you're focused to get a little bit quicker and you get more experienced. You are always learning in rallycross.

Hansen on Toftgren

Rickard's father had done some rear axle and gearbox work for us, and we got to know Rickard better when we needed more people. He is quite the opposite to Nyberg because he's not so quiet. He's always pushing and Nyberg is calmer and about the details. When it needed to be fast work, Rickard just threw himself into it and fixed it. It was a good cooperation between them for many years.

Rickard was really into it; when he was there he was 100% all in. That you need in rallycross many times, for example if you've had a crash and you need to fix it in a hurry, like with Timmy's roll in Finland [in 2014]. Then it just happens and in one hour the car is back out.

Nyberg used to start little earlier then Rickard on the mornings at the workshop [at 0500], but in the end they were quite similar. That was also good, it's quiet in the morning so they could get a lot done, and then also got more out of the day because when they started to have children they had more time to do things with them in the afternoon.

Our work isn't like having customers in a shop. It's about sponsors and the achievements out in the field. On the race weekend it doesn't matter if its six or 22 hours work, it needs to be done. So then we could give more space and free time when we were back home. We tried to be flexible on both sides. Of course being a motor sport mechanic is not an easy job, it takes a lot of time away and it's not so easy to have a family too. That was a big the part why Rickard stopped, it was too much time away for him when he had three children growing up.

Left: Toftgren at work.
Above: The whole team is engaged in
repairing Timmy Hansen's Peugeot 208 after
his roll in Finland in 2014.

Benoit Bagur

**Citroen Sport engine development engineer
1994-1996**

I arrived in Citroen Sport in 1994 and in the beginning I was giving some support to Kenneth with the engine, the relationship between Kenneth and Citroen Sport was for the engine and some parts.

Because I worked in chassis too, quickly in accordance with Citroen Sport, I helped Kenneth with all of the car.

Kenneth was using an evolution of the old [Peugeot] 205 T16 engine that Citroen also used for rally raid. We developed the engine for rallycross. That was before the restrictor limitation [introduced for 1997] and we reached very close to 800 horsepower.

But I would say more or less 20% of my work was going into Kenneth's programme.

Kenneth and his wife are fantastic people. What I liked was on one side it was a family team with very few people, but with a very high level in technology. I like that mix of very simple organisation but very high level technology.

With Kenneth it was my first experience in rallycross, but what I can see very clearly was when he was on the track he was very aggressive to win; it was not the same man in the car as outside it.

After three years with Citroen Sport I went to SEAT Sport, but I continued to follow Kenneth, and gave him some advice as a friend, but nothing officially.

We tried to do something with SEAT Sport because I was convinced that the architecture of the World Rally Car was much better for the rallycross than the classic architecture that everybody had in rallycross. It had a transverse engine and transverse gearbox, with the centre of gravity much lower compared to the longitudinal engine [see chapter two]. We tried to do something but at the end it was not possible.

Far left: Benoit Bagur works with Nyberg on the Citroen ZX.
Left: Hansen in deep conversation with Citroen's Michel Perin.

Michel Perin

Citroen Sport Team Manager
1999–2003

I was a cross country rally co-driver when I met Kenneth and Susann for the first time.

Then I became [Citroen Sport] Team Manager and I was in charge of rallycross. I pushed a lot to help them. Sometimes I felt that I was a little alone, but one year I was able to help them do the European, Swedish and French Championships. Kenneth was flying between countries on Saturday and Sunday in one weekend [see chapter nine]. We didn't win the French Championship, but what a year!

Guy Frequelin [Citroen Racing Team Principal] was also a supporter of rallycross and Kenneth. It was a big change in my budget to help them, but I tried to do my best. Not because it was a friendship, because rallycross was a good idea for Citroen with the amount of spectators and everything, and Kenneth was definitely a good choice of driver. We were not in the situation where he had to prove himself, he was already one of the best.

It was a stupid idea from my side to ask him to use the Michelin WRC tyre [in 2001]. After two or three laps, the handling was fantastic, but the problem was the starts. Michelin behaved absolutely perfectly, and we managed the situation very well [see chapter two]. I phoned my boss from Loheac, he called the boss of Michelin and they agreed that Kenneth could use unbranded Avon tyres.

I had also managed a situation where I was asked permission to give Kenneth a Xsara kit car chassis; we helped as much as we could.

Later together with Susann and Kenneth, we discovered that we have a passion for wine. Susann started to go to learn about wine, now she's an expert and we have been to many different areas of France together to try different wines.

We were not only professional team mates, but also very good friends. If I have to talk about my personal career in management, and about the human connection with people, the Hansen family have a very special place.

Joel Christoffersson

Mechanic
2004-2009, 2011, 2013

Christoffersson on Hansen

It was horrible. Andreas Eriksson called me at the end of 2009. The season was over and he told me that Ken Block, and I had no idea who Ken Block was so I needed to Google him, wanted to do Rally America with Ford and Andreas. I was into rally and I was interested in working in more sports than just rallycross so I went to Kenneth and told him: 'I promise I will never do any rallycross events with Andreas, because that would not work.' But, like always happens in this sport, there's so much to do and everybody needed to be everywhere at the same time, so I needed to do one race as a mechanic for Andreas in the European Championship. In the end I did two, the rounds in Sweden and Poland. It was really hard to be at the events with a Ford shirt on but I'm really, really happy that I did it, because it's helped me a lot to be a better mechanic and to get to where I am today. But, it was

really, hard to leave Kenneth and it was worse because I understood it hurt Kenneth a lot – he was very angry with me at that time.

We met when Timmy did his very first karting event and we became good friends. I went to some rallycross events with them and because I had the feeling that I wasn't going to be a Sebastien Loeb, I quit karting. I had a good feeling for the technical side and I really wanted to work on that.

I asked Kenneth if I could come to some events and help them. I first went as the broom pilot, cleaning tyres and sweeping up when I was 13-years old. First to some Swedish events, then in the winter holiday I went to the workshop to try to help, to look and learn. Then when I was 16 I did the full European Championship with them. I remember my first European race very well, because it was the first event with the C4 [in Portugal, 2006] and we won, which was quite amazing. I got to go to Citroen Sport and everything – it was really cool.

I was living with Susann, Kenneth, Timmy and Kevin in their house, I think I was almost like an extra son for them, well they were like extra parents for me anyway. It was a great time and the passion they have for the sport is so amazing, I try and give that to my guys now.

After I had finished going to school as a race mechanic, I started to work full time for Kenneth in 2009 and I was running Jussi Pinomaki's car, then I went to Andreas the next year.

At the end of 2010, I called Kenneth and told him I had quit working for Andreas, but he was like 'yeah, yeah', nothing more than that. I told him that if he needed someone I would be interested.

I got some work in touring cars, but Kenneth called me and told me that they would do the first race of the season at Lydden Hill with Liam [Doran].

I was very, very happy because I knew Kenneth hadn't forgiven me, but he understood that I had stopped working for Andreas. I remember Susann saying: 'It was really hard for Kenneth to call you back.' But it was good that he turned around because I would never be who I am today without Kenneth.

Liam had a big crash that day, but I spent most of the rest of the year in touring cars, apart from when we went to X Games with Liam, and won.

Then the option to go to another rallycross team came up again. I called Kenneth and explained that they wanted me to go and work with Dodge in America. I told him I knew Andreas had built the cars, but I was speaking to Dodge, not Andreas. This time Kenneth said: 'You need to do it, it's a really good option.' Kenneth helped me a lot with some things during that season and I helped him a lot with contacts and arrangements when they came over to the US with Loeb for X Games. It was good.

Then the next thing I knew I was back with Kenneth for a full season in 2013, working with Timmy. It was brilliant to be back with old friends and it felt like family. If someone had asked me two years earlier I would have said Timmy would never do rallycross because he was just about racing, racing, racing, but he proved he did have the passion for rallycross.

Today Kenneth and I are good friends. 2010 was not the best year, but if I hadn't taken the option to go to Andreas then I would still be in Gotene working for Kenneth or in my father's car dealership, so that move

gave me the contacts I needed. When I started school I just wanted to be a race mechanic, but when I started to work I wanted to be bigger, a team manager, and where I am today with my own team [JC Raceteknik].

Kenneth has all the driving experience, that helps him so much with his team. That is one thing I am missing. He knows exactly what it means when a driver tells him what feeling they have in the car. He also has this way of keeping the team as a big family with everyone working for the same goal. Of course, everybody says that about their teams, but Kenneth's team really is like a family.

Joel Christoffersson grew up with Hansen Motorsport and progressed from schoolboy 'broom pilot' and collector of broken parts (below), to lead engineer (left, changing an engine on Jussi Pinomaki's car in 2009).

Hansen on Christoffersson

Even though I had done karting many years before, when we got to the first race Timmy did it was quite strange that we did not know very much. Joel and his father were very nice people and helped us a lot, and that's where it started. After that, Joel was just always around really. He was a good driver too, but his heart was to be a mechanic, that was his thing and if you look back it was the right thing because he is running a good team of his own now.

But you can't decide how someone's heart makes them behave. He got the offer from Andreas Eriksson and went to work there with the Ford team in a period where we were fierce competitors. That felt very hard for me. I understood why he did it, he got an offer he couldn't refuse, but it still felt hard and I wasn't very pleased about it because Joel was part of the family. We needed some time, but old friendship never dies and it felt really good for our team when he came back to us. It was special in 2013 that he was with Timmy, even if I knew in the long term he wanted to do his own thing.

Left: Christoffersson as spotter with Hansen in 2013.
Top right: Christoffersson the kart racer (centre) with Timmy Hansen (with garland), Kevin Hansen (right) and Kenneth Hansen.
Below right: Christoffersson and Kevin Hansen celebrate with Timmy Hansen after his European Championship victory in Hungary 2013.

Nicolas Gueranger

Constructor and engineer
2014-2018

I was born in Le Mans, during the 24 hours of Le Mans, but rallycross is very near my home. I went to the races [at Essay] with my family, they are big and good memories. We went there with an old Peugeot 504 and a tent. Rain or snow, with no electricity, nothing, we were there.

I think I was three years old when I met Kenneth and he took me up in his hands. I have a picture with my family around him from that time. He won one of the European Championship races there when I was young. I didn't speak English at all, but I remember Kenneth's face with blue eyes and smiles and I knew his family were very nice people.

Then I worked in motor sport very young; I worked in rally with PSA from 2008. They asked me: 'Do you want to do rallycross, we will see what we can do in some races?'

I said: 'Yes of course, I'm born in rallycross.' My brother and father did rallycross themselves in the French Championship, so no problem.

I went to Loheac in 2013 with Bruno Famin where we were proposing to work together [Peugeot Sport and Hansen Motorsport] to do World RX. We started the next season in Portugal, and after five years I was still there to push the team and help them win some World Championship races.

It was a lot of fun to work together. Kenneth is not always a quiet guy. There is fire inside, he can burn and he has energy. He has a lot of knowledge, he listens a lot, he teaches and explains very well and there's never any conflict. It was lovely to help him, he's like my father in motor sport.

Top left: PSA Engineer Nicolas Gueranger
(seated next to Hansen) felt that working in
rallycross was a sort of homecoming.
Below left: Lars Andersson worked closely
with Hansen on the development of Ohlins
dampers.

Lars Andersson

Suspension engineer
2012 –

I met Kenneth for the first time when we got talking about suspension. He realised that suspension was a big factor in how rallycross was progressing, and he wanted to have a closer partnership than what he'd had before. It grew from there.

At that time he had other suspension sponsors [Sachs], so we were doing a lot of work together but in a development phase, which was very okay for me. There were some people at Ohlins who thought this was not okay, but in the end they saw it became a good relationship.

It's very hard for racing drivers to be proper team managers because they usually have quite a big ego. But Kenneth puts that aside and always puts his drivers first, and always tries to give them the best tools possible. He's the only team owner I've worked with who always wants his drivers to have the same material. If we built suspension for testing, I needed to build suspension for all of the cars. I could not show up with just one set, because if it's better, he wants all cars to have it. That's quite unique.

We did a test in 2017 and Kenneth took his helmet with him. The goal was for him just to see if the drivers said the car is understeering, how bad was it? Is it just a small issue or something bigger? But he was as quick as the regular driver there.

He gives good feedback. Other drivers compare the lap times a lot between each other, but Kenneth can put that aside and just give technical info.

We were at a test once where Timmy was coming in and complaining about understeer in a certain corner. I asked Kenneth if we should help him to sort it out?

Kenneth said: 'No, we will teach him to drive first.' Kenneth talked to Timmy about the way to approach the corner, being patient and then getting on the throttle when he had settled the car.

Timmy made three more laps, came back and told us the understeer had gone. That is a very good strength Kenneth has.

Martins Zulis

Mechanic
2009-2017

I was working with TT Motorsport when they bought a Citroen C4 from Kenneth. Then, when Kenneth ran a car for Kenny Brack at Holjes [in 2009], they needed some extra mechanics and we already knew the C4, so they asked if we wanted to come.

That was the first time I joined Hansen Motorsport. I also worked in Poland for them at the end of the year. I suppose they liked what they saw, so the next year I did a bit more and after it was full seasons.

Every guy has dreams in life, so when they asked me to join the team, I didn't need to think about it, just say yes. That feeling was unbelievable.

Winning the 2012 European Championship with Timur [Timerzyanov] was incredible. Then when we joined Peugeot, things were on another level and completely different.

For Kenneth and Susann, it's always family first. When I was staying and working in Sweden and told them I had to go home, it was always: 'Okay, you do that.' They knew if I was happy at home, I was happy at work. My own family understood the other way too because I am so passionate for what I do.

I was number one mechanic on Sebastien Loeb's car in 2016, and he won my home race in Latvia. Afterwards he gave me his helmet and race suit. That was amazing. I will never forget it.

Kristian Ceder

Mechanic
2013-2017

When Kenneth was a big driver, I had no interest in motor sport whatsoever, so I never really knew about him until I started with the team. I soon realised how big his success really was.

That's something I really admire, but it's not the first thing that I like about him. He's a really good person.

I got a scholarship through a mechanics organisation in Sweden to be a guest mechanic with the team in 2013. I worked with Kevin in JRX [see chapter five] in Germany, but then we ended up working together much more. I had started with standard cars, so I had to learn everything about motor sport, but everyone in the team was very helpful to me.

I started to be more involved, looking after Kevin's Supercar Lites car between the races, and working at races in Sweden with the Lites and in World RX on Timmy's Supercar.

It's amazing to have had the opportunity to go around the world as friends, have a good time and to compete in a World Championship.

A lot of people don't like to go to work, but I got paid for doing what I love. It's like a hobby as well as a job for me.

Mads Sorensen

Mechanic
2013-2017

I was working with Ulrik Linnemann in Super1600 but his budget was low and he was speaking about not doing the European Championship anymore. I started thinking about going to another team, so I contacted Kenneth by email. The first reply said: 'No, they had enough mechanics.' Then, 10-minutes later he replied again and said: 'Maybe we need one for our next race.' I had only spoken to him once before, when we broke a part on Ulrik's car and we needed to borrow something, but he didn't know me at all.

So I flew to Portugal [in 2013] to meet the team and it was really special. That was also the first time I flew in a plane.

I was at motor sport school in Denmark, but then after that I started to work for Kenneth all the time. It was a dream come true to go to Peugeot Sport, looking at the Dakar and Pikes Peak cars, it started to become normal but it's something you dreamed about.

One time we were staying in Italy, me, Kenneth and Joel Christoffersson from JC Raceteknik, waiting for the boat to arrive with the trucks from the race in Turkey. We went out and had some beers and some fun. There was a guy selling drums in the street. He came to me but I said it was too expensive so I made a bid that was way too low. 20 minutes later he came back to Kenneth and the price was already half what it was to me. In the end Kenneth bought this drum and was playing it. He could make some noise but it was not like any song! We were laughing about what Susann would say when he got home.

I never dreamed what I'd get to do when I sent that email.

Far left: Martins Zulis (right of group together with Kennet Nyberg, Eric Faren and Hansen).
Centre: Kristian Ceder and Hansen in Canada after Timmy Hansen's 2016 World RX victory.
Left: Mads Sorensen escorts Timmy Hansen's battered car back to the paddock after his 2017 crash in Norway.

*Graham Rodemark and Hansen celebrate
Timmy and Kevin Hansen's one-two finish at
Barcelona in 2019.*

Graham Rodemark

Mechanic and engineer
2010 –

Rodemark on Hansen

I was 16 or 17-years-old when I started working in European rallycross with Martin Schanche, and Kenneth's team always came across as the most unapproachable people in the paddock. They were all polite; if you said hello they would say hello back, but that was it.

I was working with Pat and Liam [Doran] when Pat told me that Liam was going to drive with Hansen in 2010, I thought: 'God, that's going be hard work.'

But I was completely wrong. What I found was that without doubt, they are nicest family I've ever met in a rallycross paddock. When I went there with Liam, Kenneth was still driving and it didn't really matter what happened on track or how good or bad the result was, he always got out of the car with a smile.

Kenneth was an exceptionally good driver, especially on the fine details. The team had a fairly good base set up for the [Citroen] C4, but he could just feel and sense so much. He'd make a change that you'd think would make no real difference, and he'd go three or four tenths faster.

The way he managed Liam at that time was impressive too. Even if Liam lost his rag, which all drivers can do under pressure, Kenneth would speak to him with a calm voice and a big smile on his face. It's the same if he gives any of us a bollocking. You can't help but take it because he says it so nicely.

That first year there with Liam, we were at a particular track, and I cannot for the life of me remember where it was, but there was a long gravel section with a chicane and a bump. Watching the videos, Liam was flat out through that section and Kenneth wasn't, so Kenneth thought he would try it. When Kenneth came back in, and I asked if he tried it he said: 'Yep, once. But I won't do it again. It's dangerous and not necessary.' The way he said it, it was genuinely as a scared, there's no way I'm doing that, kind of way.

Later, for some strange reason Kenneth and Susann put trust me in to look after Kevin when he started racing in the Junior Championship in the UK. None of it was ever planned, none of it was ever spoken about any more than a month before the first season started.

I suppose I feel like almost a member of the family, because then I had the youngster under my wing a little bit. That was almost more pressure than having a role in the World Championship team.

Coming from my little company Autopoint Specialist Engineering in the village of Bodle Street, with a 1300cc Suzuki Swift, to taking that same driver to the World Championship and fighting at the front, I'm privileged to have had that opportunity, and to have quite a lot of responsibly in the team.

I got back into Supercar more when Kevin moved up in a satellite team [in 2016]. We fitted a different turbo on his car. It made a different noise and Mel from Oreca was worried. I told him it was just induction noise, but he was only young and he wanted to show the boss.

He fetched Kenneth, they got half way to the tent before Kenneth turned around and went back. Later Kenneth told me he had asked Mel what I had said about the noise and when Mel replied that I thought it was okay, that was when he turned around. That's really nice, but quite bloody frightening too. I feel very privileged to have been put in that position for quite a few years now, it makes you work harder I'm sure.

When we went to America the first time with Liam, we turned up at X Games [see chapter eight] with two four-by-four easy-up awnings, and three wooden boxes rammed full of what we thought we might need. Everyone else had massive American trucks and we were pretty much the laughing stock. Then we beat Marcus Gronholm, which was awesome.

It was funny though, Liam won the first rally heat against Marcus and I was having a party, celebrating and screaming down the radio. When there was a break in the radio traffic, very calmly, Kenneth said: 'Okay Liam, back to the start line, I think you have enough fuel, how are the temperatures?' Just like I'd never spoken. I didn't realise we had to do another race.

That weekend was probably the first time Kenneth opened up a bit with me. We were racing in the evenings so there was plenty of time to sit and chat. I guess that's where our relationship really started to develop properly.

Hansen on Rodemark

Graham and I speak the same language because we are quite similar in that we grew up in the sport and we have worked in a different way to a lot of the engineers and people that have come in later. Normally we are aiming at the same thing, it's not so often that we're going in different directions, although sometimes it happens.

He has a great experience in rallycross. He learned a lot from working with Martin Schanche many years ago, and a lot since then, which was also needed when we were in the factory team in 2018. Graham can really fix things when there's trouble.

The problem in a factory team when it's so big is that any solution needs to be designed, tested and be the proper thing. There's not always time in rallycross for that. If something is bent and it doesn't fit, then you need to handle that and get the car ready to run in how much time you have. Graham is a specialist at that kind of response.

He's also a great guy to be with. It doesn't matter what kind of people are around, even if it's angry and stupid people sometimes, he always fixes it. If the motivation is not in the team for some reason, or something is causing problems, he is the first person

Left: Rodemark (right) with Rickard Toftgren at Kerlabo in 2010.
Top right: With Susann Hansen in the Spotters' Tower.
Below right: Rodemark and Hansen discuss the handling of a cross-kart during the event in which they both raced at Holjes in 2019, the evening before the World RX round.

to fix and discuss it. He lifts the team and builds great team spirit.

But doesn't take any nonsense from anybody and he always says what he thinks. Even with someone like Bruno [Famin, Peugeot Sport Director] he would say: 'This is not good, we need to do this,' and then say: 'But that's only my opinion.'

I don't think Kevin would have achieved what he has so quickly without Graham. He needed someone, and if Graham hadn't been there I would have been there for him of course, but perhaps it wouldn't have been the same when the dad is there. It's always good to grow up, not to be just with mum and dad, children need to stand on their own feet.

When Timmy was doing circuit racing he was in other teams and he grew up quite well. You need to trust the people you are putting your children with and we had full trust in Graham. He became like a second dad and big brother to Kevin. He can be there, he can tell him off when there's a problem and he can be there to help him when he needs it. In racing, there's a lot of pressure, but, before Kevin was in our main team I tried not to be too much involved, I was only there if I was needed.

Romain Dartenay

Mechanic
2014 –

I worked for Peugeot Sport from 2014 as a freelance mechanic in rally, the Dakar and in rallycross. That's when I met Kenneth.

Loheac is not far away from my home so of course I knew Kenneth Hansen and it was my dream to work in motor sport with guys like him and Sebastien [Loeb].

I had my own company, but I worked for Peugeot Sport and had some other customers. I managed Kevin's car in my workshop for Peugeot [in 2017 and 2018], but it was a completely different experience in 2019. I prefer the small team because everybody needs to understand everything. Sometimes you are building differentials, sometimes you are putting up the tent, or working on the truck.

I was a bit nervous because the 2019 programme started late and we had a very short time to prepare, but when I said yes to Kenneth, I understood it would not be easy. But, we managed well. Kenneth lives in Sweden and me in France, but I called him and sent many emails every day. It was a good challenge.

Some people told me that I was stupid because it's not possible to go with two cars in the World Championship with five mechanics and two engineers, but it was that or nothing.

We had no technical problems, the cars were good and we pushed hard. The guys worked all day and sometimes all night and we had a good atmosphere. In big teams sometimes it's not easy to speak to the boss, but in this team it was very easy to say to Kenneth or Susann: 'I need this,' or 'I would like that.'

It was a dream to win the World Championship and to win with Hansen Motorsport was very nice, that was the goal.

I have some experience with rallycross, but Kenneth has more than anybody in the world.

It was fun to see him and Graham [Rodemark] race the cross-karts in Holjes and to help them. Now it's possible to say in my life I went to a race with Kenneth Hansen [as a driver]. That's very nice.

Anthony Lebrec

Mechanic
2016 –

When I was young, when I saw Kenneth drive at Essay [France] near where I lived, never did I think one day I'd work for him. It's a dream.

I first met him in Norway 2016. I was working for myself and one day Romain [Dartenay] said that he needed help for one or two races. I said yes, and I never looked back.

In the beginning I worked on Davy Jeanney's car, then Sebastien Loeb's and then Kevin's. In 2019 I moved to Timmy's car.

But 2019 was different because we were only five mechanics and all of the guys had to help each other. Kenneth wanted a chief mechanic for each car and I was chief on Timmy's, but if Romain wanted help, we went to Kevin's car, and the same the other way around. It was a great atmosphere just like a big family, we're all friends.

For sure it's easier to work with 15 people, but sometimes it's not possible to win a race with 15 people. If you have three or four guys who know rallycross, everything is possible. Together [as mechanics] we won the French Championship, European Championship. The World Championship was the last championship to win.

Timmy had a big crash in Abu Dhabi, but it was better to happen then. We just said: 'It's not finished, it's just the beginning. Push to the maximum and go.'

Top right: Romain Dartenay talks to Hansen during the 2019 season in which the Frenchman and his staff were key to Team Hansen MJP's success.
Bottom right: Lebrec hard at work beneath one of the 2019 Peugeot 208s.

2019 was the second time that Kenneth Hansen went to the FIA Prize-giving to collect the trophy for winning the World Rallycross Teams' Championship.

Throughout his driving career, Hansen was at the forefront of efforts to improve the sport in which he competed, acutely aware of the potential rallycross harboured, and the need for increased promotion and exposure.

At the end of 2012, rallycross underwent arguably its biggest ever shift, with the introduction of a commercial rights holder for the FIA European Rallycross Championship.

A year later, the FIA World Rallycross Championship was formed, with Hansen's team attracting works-backing from Peugeot Sport to take part in the new series.

With Hansen at the helm of Team Peugeot-Hansen, the squad became only the second ever outfit ever to win the World RX Teams' Championship in 2015. And in 2019, Team Hansen MJP did the double as a private effort, securing both the Drivers' and Teams' Championships.

7. WORLD CHAMPIONS

As one of the first truly professional rallycross drivers, Hansen had good reason to both want and need the sport's level of exposure to increase.

While plenty of drivers competed in rallycross as a full-time exercise, that was usually alongside other business exploits that, at least in part, facilitated their racing activities.

For Hansen, from 1990, his only focus was on running his team, 24 hours a day, 365 days a year.

For decades it was widely regarded within the sport that with the correct promotion, what in reality was a well-funded amateur discipline had the potential to be so much more.

Attempts were frequently made to increase exposure through television coverage, including sparing involvement from Formula 1 supremo Bernie Ecclestone, of which Hansen was also a part, but with the European Championship made up of individual events, each with their own organiser and promoter, making changes was a challenge.

In the first decade of the millennium British journalist Tim Whittington began to look for ways to make a change and bring the disjointed championship together. Discussion and plans within the sport came to nothing and at the end of 2010, together with Dutch colleague Henk de Winter, Whittington approached FIA directly, and subsequently introduced it to global sports, events and talent management company IMG. In 2012 IMG concluded a 20-year rights deal with the FIA.

As can be expected with a major shift in any sporting discipline, there were those in the sport vehemently against the rights of the European Rallycross Championship being sold to IMG, but Hansen and his family was well aware that if the sport was to grow, a single promoter was required.

For that reason, the Swede's team was the first to commit to the new regime, and on a bitterly cold October day at Santa Pod – the most unlikely venue for a rallycross promotional event – he stood shoulder-to-shoulder with former Hansen driver Liam Doran, IMG's Martin Anayi and title sponsor Monster Energy's Jimmy Goodrich as the new age was introduced.

The lure of a promoter immediately attracted Norway's biggest motorsport star, Petter Solberg,

having drawn a close to his World Rally career.

The new epoch brought live television by the fourth round in Finland, and it was fitting that come the end of the new era's first campaign, it was Hansen's team that won the title with Russian driver Timur Timerzyanov, who successfully defended his 2012 crown. But, while the history books show that Hansen drivers won three of the nine events that season, and Timerzyanov scooped the biggest prize, arguably the most significant result of the year for the team was at Loheac in September, despite Timerzyanov being best-placed Hansen driver in fourth.

It was in the Breton circuit's paddock that Peugeot Sport Director Bruno Famin visited teams with a view to entering the planned World Rallycross Championship.

Such was the success of the first season that IMG's plans to grow the sport into an FIA World Championship were accelerated. In December the World Motor Sport Council confirmed that the FIA World Rallycross Championship would be introduced for 2014.

Left: As a pioneering professional in rallycross, Hansen had to be a desk jockey as well as car builder and salesman.
Above: Collecting to 2015 FIA World Rallycross Teams' Championship.

Hansen signed a deal with Peugeot to run a works-backed operation, initially using Supercars developed at his Gotene workshops based on Peugeot's new 208 R5 rally chassis.

The first campaign for the project was difficult, despite Timerzyanov leading at the end of the first day of the season, but Timmy Hansen claimed the squad's first World RX win in Italy later in the year.

In 2015 the team achieved 11 podium finishes, including five victories, with drivers Timmy Hansen and Frenchman Davy Jeanney. While Hansen battled with Solberg for the Drivers' crown and eventually finished second in the points, Team Peugeot-Hansen secured the Teams' title at the penultimate round.

Without having had an opportunity to add a World Championship crown to his 14-European titles as a driver, attending the FIA Gala in Paris with wife Susann to receive the Teams' trophy is high on Hansen's list of career highlights, but the team was still missing the World Drivers' title.

Hansen Motorsport's tenure as a World Championship team in its own right was shelved for a

Above: Hansen signs autographs for fans of all ages at Lousada in Portugal.
Right: Joy at winning the Teams' Championship in South Africa 2019.

single-year in 2018 when Peugeot took the rallycross programme in house, and continued to employ all four members of the Hansen family. But when the French marque's board made the shock decision to terminate the programme, the family was left unemployed.

Hard work over the winter ensured a return to the series in 2019 as a private effort, supported by Red Bull, Total and Max Pucher's Papyrus Converse concern to run early 2018 specification works-built 208 WRXs.

While the team also competed in Pucher's new single-make Titans RX series where Kevin Hansen won the title, in World RX's most competitive year to date, Hansen's team amassed five wins (one for Kevin and four for Timmy) and the brothers were joined by Andreas Bakkerud in a three-way fight for the title at the final round in South Africa. Team Hansen MJP secured the Teams' title at the end of qualifying and Timmy Hansen led Bakkerud in the championship by just two points at the start of the final six-lap race of the season. Bakkerud took an early lead from pole sitter Hansen, but both lost ground when the Norwegian ran wide and Hansen made a move for track position.

Bakkerud finished the race in second place, but fourth for Hansen was enough for the pair to finish level on points.

An almost three-hour post-race investigation by the FIA Stewards concluded that no action would be taken over the first lap incident, and Hansen claimed the title having won four events to Bakkerud's single victory. In one of the most dramatic conclusions to an FIA World Championship in history, the coveted World Championship Drivers' crown was finally added to Hansen Motorsport's well-stocked trophy cabinet.

Shirley Gibson

**Former URDA President
1990 – 1997**

My husband Rob began racing in the European Championship in 1990, that's when I first got to know Kenneth. The United Rallycross Drivers Association (URDA) had been formed in 1986. There was a move to revive it in 1990 and in the middle of the year Kenneth and Martin Schanche asked me if I would be URDA's accountant. Then, in the winter, they asked me if I would be President of URDA. Kenneth was heavily involved with that. His input was absolutely amazing and I couldn't have done it without him.

What Kenneth wanted was for the sport to move forward in every single aspect. He was one of the forerunners in organising circuit safety, so we appointed our own circuit safety manager and he was also heavily involved in getting the television rights and convincing other drivers to help with that. Of course he was racing for himself, but he wanted so much more for the sport itself. He was pushing all the time. We even had ideas at one time about going our own way and starting our own championship, but in the end that didn't happen.

In those years Brian Kreisky from Videovision did the television production, but was more interested in using footage in his 'Havoc' crash videos than in getting rallycross onto the kind of broadcasters we wanted.

I remember a meeting in Belgium where Martin said to me; 'You're English, Bernie Ecclestone is English. Ring him up and tell him you want the broadcast rights.'

So I rang Bernie. He wanted to know who I was, what I did, so many different questions, but he gave URDA the rights, which didn't go down very well at all with the organisers. It was a bit of a battle to get our production company sorted but I went to Paris to see Eurosport and we got rallycross back on the television.

All of the drivers chipped in a little bit. For about three years, we would wait at the prize-givings and the drivers would give me the envelopes with their travel money and prize money in [at the time there was a set prescribed schedule of prize money and travel money paid in cash to finalists at the end of the event]. Kenneth and

Martin persuaded all other drivers to support the plan.

Kenneth was at the forefront saying that we needed one scrutineer to cover the whole championship, things like that made a big difference. It was Kenneth, Martin and Will Gollop who actually made all of that happen.

Like it was on track, it could still be a little fraught between Kenneth and Martin sometimes, but a lot of that was because of the language. I don't mean how Martin used language, which could be colourful, but the mannerisms and the way he wanted to approach things. 'Let's just ask them nicely.' Kenneth would say, whereas Martin was saying: 'We'll tell them!'

They were united in that they both wanted the sport to succeed and grow, but it needed a promoter, like IMG, and people like Tim Whittington and Henk de Winter to push it forward with the FIA and bring it to a company like IMG's attention.

With everything that Kenneth does, his attitude is right. He's just Mr Professional, he is Mr Rallycross I think.

Above: Hansen was one of those leading the work to improve TV coverage of rallycross. Left: Shirley Gibson led the drivers' group URDA in the 1990s.

Tim Whittington

Journalist
1984 – 2012

FIA World Rallycross Championship Coordinator
2013 –

Outside of the small group of people directly involved, Susann Hansen was the first person to know that there would be a promoter for the FIA Rallycross Championship. Kenneth would have been the first person in the paddock I told, but at the time we got approval from FIA to start talking to teams and organisers it was a few days before Holjes in 2012, and on that occasion Susann was running the team because Kenneth was in America for X Games. Susann was so excited when I explained what was happening that she immediately asked if she could call Kenneth to tell him. Of course she could!

By that time I'd been working on the idea of getting a promoter into rallycross for more than four years.

More or less since I started working in rallycross in 1984 there was a common desire for the sport to be promoted better; I can't count how many times I'd been told 'Rallycross needs a Bernie'. When times were good that desire was perhaps lower than at lean times, but it was never far below the surface.

In the first decade of the 21st century the European Rallycross Championship was a mess. The number of competitors was generally okay, but the organisational standards and promotion of events was inconsistent; effectively the championship consisted of 10 or 11 individual events with no common narrative.

The cars were becoming more expensive and drivers and teams needed more of a return. Rallycross was standing still and in motorsport terms standing still is like going backwards because everyone else and everything else is moving forward, improving and progressing quickly. I'd been talking to FIA for several months before getting IMG involved. The connection came via Steve Saint, TV producer on Speedway GP which IMG owns. He introduced me to IMG's motor sport bosses, Paul Bellamy and Rob Armstrong. We met twice at the end of 2011 and I then introduced IMG to FIA. From there things moved quickly and by July 2012 we were going public.

Kenneth had always stood out from the crowd in terms of how he presented himself and his team; his first European Championship event was my first outside the UK as a journalist and it was immediately apparent that this new boy was a little different from the rest of the paddock.

Over the years Kenneth always seemed to be a step ahead of the rest on marketing, PR and presentation. From his second year in Europe he has always had multi-national brands backing him.

Kenneth – and Susann – immediately understood the possibilities of rallycross being promoted by IMG; I don't think it's a coincidence that Timmy Hansen was suddenly racing in rallycross by the end of 2012. Kenneth was aware of what IMG had done with Speedway GP and became a good ally for us; not everyone was as open to the changes that were coming as he was, so having someone like him on our side and being openly positive was good.

Top left: Susann Hansen talks to Tim Whittington.
Bottom left: Timmy Hansen moved away from a circuit career and into rallycross after the news that IMG would promote rallycross from 2013.

Martin Anayi

World Rallycross Managing Director
2013 – 2015

I was working with the IMG team (Rob Armstrong and Paul Bellamy) that had bought FIM World Speedway, initially as their lawyer. They had very successfully transformed the sport into a major stadium series with a great TV product.

In about 2011 we started to look at opportunities to expand the IMG Motorsport team and our business operations. I was doing some client management in Formula 1 but we wanted to bring IMG in as the 'owner' of a motor sport. We were offered FIA Formula E, World Rally, and Truck Racing and were also looking at motocross but then Steve Saint brought us an idea that he said was perfect for TV and close to Speedway on four wheels – the European Rallycross Championship. He introduced us to Tim Whittington and Henk de Winter who took us through the sport and we fell in love with it.

Once we had confirmed with FIA that we wanted to invest in rallycross – which they couldn't believe – I went on a tour to meet teams, drivers and promoters. Kenneth and Susann were among the first that I met.

I remember meeting the Hansens in the week between the Belgian and Dutch races of the 2012 European Rallycross Championship season; we met the management of both tracks [Maasmechelen and Valkenswaard] in the same period but ultimately neither of them decided not to be part of what we were doing.

When I met with the Hansens and others, I realised that we needed to concentrate our efforts on convincing those that were open to the idea and with their help we entered into deals with Morgan Ostlund at Holjes, Patrick Germain at Loheac and Pat Doran at Lydden Hill; the rest fell into place thereafter. I learnt a good lesson in life there.

Kenneth and Susann gave me 100% confidence that this sport could turn the world order on its head. I smile about that meeting as they must have thought: 'Who they hell is this guy?', but they were respectful and I am grateful for their patience. I am sorry I didn't see it through for them.

It was important we brought Kenneth with us not only as the most successful driver and team but also for the future of the sport with Timmy and Kevin. In one family we had the legend, the strong female leadership and the future in Timmy and Kevin.

The first year was a blur. We had so much to do and so little time from signing the drivers, teams, event promoters, creating the RX brand, hiring an operational team, creating a TV production team, signing sponsors and doing TV deals. When the first race at Lydden started we realised we had a great opportunity, but also how much work we had to do to bring it up in terms of professionalism.

We had teams like Kenneth's well ahead of almost everyone else. We used them as the gold standard and as they improved so did everyone else in the paddock.

The transition to World Championship was demanded by our top teams so that they could bring in manufacturer support and big brands. However, in hindsight we went a year too early and should have concentrated on making our European product even better before making that step. The promoters we had didn't live up to expectations in year one of World RX but the urgency was there so we took the plunge. I think an error we made was not keeping the initial dialogue with the likes of Kenneth going to the same degree through that process as when we started in 2012.

The Hansen team's World Championship title in 2015 was really a defining moment for me, and almost full circle. Although we had to be impartial, it was very pleasing and we were all quite emotional really about that result. Kenneth's family are the past, present and future of rallycross without a shadow of a doubt.

From the left: Monster Energy's Jimmy Goodrich, IMG's Martin Anayi, Liam Doran and Kenneth Hansen at the official launch for the 2013 FIA European Rallycross Championship.

Bruno Famin

Peugeot Sport Director
2012 – 2019

I went to Loheac in 2013 to meet the rallycross world and the main teams. Of course I knew before that Kenneth was the biggest name in rallycross but right away I had a good feeling with him and Susann. For me, feeling is very important and I was very happy that we had the same view of how to handle a team. After that we made the common decision to go together.

We were very happy to win a race in the first year as Team Peugeot-Hansen then to win the team's title. It was a steep learning curve to learn about each other and the new World Championship but that's part of it and we worked like hell to fight for the championships while we were there.

It's true that Team Peugeot-Hansen was a family team. For sure we [Peugeot] were racing to make communication and business, but we did that in a very good atmosphere, which is always better for results. We were very happy to have integrated in the Hansen family, I think the team worked very well it was really like a big family

Things changed quickly in rallycross, it became much more professional and everybody had to improve, from the technical development, pure racing activities, activations, communication with marketing and our team developed and improved all together in that time.

Kenneth's experience was very important for us. The technical experience for the setup of the car, on the sporting side for the spotters and so-on. I think it's much better to have someone like him as a former driver to be team manager and manage drivers. Not all drivers would be as good as a team manager, but I think Kenneth is very good.

When we moved to operating a team ourselves [Team Peugeot Total] having Kenneth as a team manager was crucial because he is the one who knows rallycross. He knows the tracks, the officials, the drivers, all the marshals almost. And like I said he knows all about the sporting side, how the track will change when it rains for example.

Mr Kenneth Hansen was part of the Team Peugeot Total because he is Mr Rallycross.

Above: Bruno Famin and Hansen shake on the Peugeot deal for 2014.
Right: Hansen shows Jean Todt around one of the Peugeot 208 WRXs in 2019.

Jean Todt

FIA President
2009 –

Hansen is an iconic name in his category of sport and you have few names like him; he's a great talent and puts all of his passion and talent into the category. I'm very happy about that. To have talented, passionate people who put in so much effort to develop themselves, but also by developing themselves, they develop their category of the sport, so it's always a win-win situation.

It's very good that he has two sons competing and that's what is very attractive with rallycross, this kind of family minded [atmosphere]. You know, you come with your friends, you come with your family and so it's enjoyment and passion. I think it's the best combination.

In the middle of nowhere [like at Loheac, there is], so much energy for the sport and you can thank all the people, because it doesn't happen just by chance, it happens because you have passionate people who believe in it.

Davy Jeanney

**Team Peugeot-Hansen driver
2015 – 2016**

When we won the Teams' World
Championship in Italy it was
amazing and emotional. Kenneth is
so much less emotional and quieter
than Susann, but that day I knew
he was very, very happy and it was
special. Similar to when I took my
first victory [in Germany, the same
year] and Timmy was together
with me on the top of the car at
the finish. For sure winning the title
was a lot of emotion and a good
moment, especially for Kenneth.

Andrew Coley

World Rallycross television commentator
2013 –

I saw that IMG was taking over the promotion of European Rallycross for 2013, so I went to them and basically said that I really wanted to do it. I'd done some rally and circuit racing commentary before, so felt I was a good fit. The first thing we did together was the championship launch at a freezing media day at Lydden Hill, and Kenneth was there. Back then he obviously didn't know who I was but I was there to try and make sure I was fully informed when I started the job.

I asked Kenneth if I could have a couple of minutes of his time. When he speaks to someone it's deep in the eye, he's got the most piercing blue eyes and he doesn't break his stare at all, but he said yes. I was asking him all sorts of things, trying to get my head around the differences between the cars I was covering at the time in rallying and rallycross. He was so generous with his time and advice. When you come to a sport as an outsider and you go to ask a legend a load of pretty basic questions to get your knowledge up to speed, and when there's no question from them about dedicating time to those questions, that shows their quality.

One of my favourite things about Kenneth is when you go over to his team and everything, like it sometimes does in motorsport, is hitting the fan, Kenneth is just calmly wandering around the awning, gathering up the pieces and making sure it goes back together as it should. I think it's incredibly important that whoever's at the helm of the team has that innate calmness around them.

I love my parents dearly, but I don't want to move back in with them, and I'm pretty sure they don't want me living with them full time either. The Hansen family is so close, and when you're living in the same space in the paddock and under the intense amount of pressure and scrutiny that you're under in a World Championship, that there aren't more arguments, or more shouting, is a mark of how close they are.

2015 was a brilliant year for World RX. After an average start, the Hansen Peugeots suddenly came into form mid-season, starting with that incredible win for Davy Jeanney at Estering. He seemed almost unstoppable, our TV cameras caught an incredible slow-mo of him kissing the barrier at the apex of the last corner, risking everything to set fastest times.

But it was Timmy who had the amazing run of results in the latter half of the year, just as 2014 champion [Petter] Solberg was faltering. Timmy's shot at the title really finished in Italy, when his dreams ended in the wall in a messy semi-final start.

Despite that, Kenneth's team had done enough to take a deserving title in the Teams' Championship. I remember gold wigs, huge smiles, and a very big party.

While Timmy had come close to Driver's title in 15, other drivers always seemed to have faster cars in the next years.

Then, after Peugeot pulled the plug in 2018, I remember the paddock atmosphere at the last round in South Africa being really negative, with no-one clear about who would return the following year.

I saw the Hansen family at my hotel before I flew home. The boys and Susann were pretty down, their dream factory drives and potentially their careers gone. But Kenneth still had that glint in his eye and talked about working hard to try to do 'something'.

Just a year later they had done quite 'something', in what was the most nail-biting, rollercoaster season of World RX to date by taking both the Teams', and in some ways more importantly, Drivers' titles.

The Hansen name, so familiar to rallycross trophy engravers in Europe, was finally etched on the biggest trophy of them all.

Top left: World Teams' Champions in 2015.
Left: World RX commentator Andrew
Coley says Hansen's willingness to share his
knowledge is a mark of quality.

Max Pucher

Team Hansen MJP partner
2019

I've spoken with many teams over the years about a collaboration, to reduce the costs and pool resources. When Peugeot stopped, I called Kenneth and said: 'So, what's your plan for next year?'

Basically we agreed that I would bring my sponsor to run the Hansen's in Titans RX and if World RX should happen for them, we could see whether there was a way that I could support that. But originally, we didn't think that that would ever happen. When we looked at the opportunities, it looked as if neither Peugeot nor Total would support the project. It was a big surprise in the end that Kenneth managed to convince them.

Even if nothing else had happened, even if we wouldn't have been the leading team, which was obviously my expectation anyway, it's one of the best things I ever did because the Hansen family are the very best people I've ever worked with; personally, technically and in terms of human quality. I would be happy to spend the money on that even if we hadn't been leading. From the first test days for Titans RX, I was immediately part of the family. There's 120% trust in both directions, there's an incredible openness and warmth, it's just fantastic.

I knew them well, because we have been good friends since I was racing in World RX and I knew they are really nice people, but my knowledge of their quality was low. I'm so glad that I did it; I'm so happy that I was able to give them the opportunity to race in this series and I wished for nothing more, not so much for myself but for them, to become world champions.

Left: Hansen with engineer Graham Rodemark and Max Pucher.
Above: Team Hansen MJP won in its first event in Abu Dhabi in 2019.

Timmy Hansen

**Hansen Motorsport driver
2013 –**

I took Peugeot's first World Rallycross victory in Italy in 2014. Then the next year at Holjes I crossed the line first and that was really special [he later lost the win in the Stewards' room because of a clash in the final corner]. But in France, in a Peugeot at Loheac, the win in 2015 was definitely huge; one of the biggest single race achievements in my career up to that point.

It was probably quite a boring race from the outside, but in that final, I won the start and it was one of my best races because I put everything together.

We had been fast there in 2014 too but I stalled on the start line. I learned a valuable lesson there and I still refer to Loheac 2014 when I line up at the start now. It shows that experience makes you better.

It was incredible to win the Teams' Championship in 2015 as our family team with Peugeot. It was great because Kevin was racing in the Supercar Lites class, it was going very well for him and he was usually in the Spotters' Tower when I was driving.

I think at the time we maybe took it a bit too much for granted because things were going so well and I still wanted to win the Drivers' title.

We had invested all of our time into working with Peugeot and when they quit we were left with nothing. We had scaled-down our team, we had no people left and had to start again. I thought that I may have done my last rallycross.

But, hour-by-hour, day-by-day, we got closer, and then further away, and then closer, but we never lost hope. We believed that it could be done, like in a stupidly optimistic way and in the end we got there. It was incredible just to get the team together. Then came more problems, because we had to run everything with the budget that we said could be doable, which meant working a lot and combining World RX, Titans RX and Nitro RX.

Left: Italy 2014, the first World RX win for Peugeot.
Above: Loheac 2015.

We believed all the time, we were very focused on exactly what to do, and race-by-race it went well; we won Nitro and came first and second in Titans RX.

That is where we are at our best; being a small group of people with a massive heart and giving everything that we have all of the time. Being involved with a factory team, or being a factory driver, it's a different way of working; more people, a bigger process and the heart is a bit exchanged for man-power.

I guess this is the way that dad won all of his titles and I think I put in some of the best performances of my career in 2019.

Before the last World RX event in South Africa we had two more titles to get to make it the perfect year. For me it came with a lot of pressure. It's a tough situation knowing that everything would be so tight. In the quiet days when you're at home in the gap before the race, there are a thousand thoughts going through your mind of what can go wrong in different scenarios, like you're getting ready for the race by thinking about everything. It's a tough process and it takes a lot of energy.

I felt quite relieved that we were actually doing something when we went to South Africa and I think we put together a fantastic event,

both me and Kevin. I qualified on pole for the final, and was very confident that I would take the start, so it was a surprise for me that I wasn't leading. That was not according to my plan and I knew that in that situation, I wasn't champion. I needed to pass. When Andreas [Bakkerud] made a mistake in turn six, I knew what I had to do and I went on the inside.

I thought: 'Shit, it's over!' [after the contact and spin]. Then I saw that I hadn't lost as much as I was afraid I had. Timo Scheider was in front and I knew I had to be faster than him; I had to gain a full joker lap time on him and then take my joker. But before that could happen

he got a technical problem and I heard on the radio that I was in position to be champion.

Obviously the turn six incident was investigated, but the Stewards decided there would be 'no further action'. That felt great because I felt I tried to make an honest pass, and I did. I think the unfortunate part of the incident was that Andreas hit the wall lightly. He didn't lose much, but he bounced into me and made me spin. It would have been much nicer if I had just passed him, which I was on the way to do, and won the race. That would have been a better way to end the championship, but still, my name will always be on the trophy.

It was a fantastic year; more challenging, but also more rewarding, than ever. It was the best season ever of World RX, because it was 100% rallycross again. I think the big winner was the sport.

For me, rallycross is the best motor sport in the world and finally it got to show how incredible it could be. As a driver, you dream of the ultimate thing to achieve, like Johan Kristoffersson did in 2018 [when he won 11 of 12 rounds]. But you can not be more than World Champion.

Dad has so many European titles but now we have two Teams' World Championships and the

Drivers' trophy at home. It's a cool feeling to continue his legacy, and that I have won the big title too now. I'm not equal, because I have to do it 13 more times maybe, but at least I'm kind of on the way.

Left: Timmy and Kenneth Hansen, World Rallycross Championship Drivers' and Teams' Champions at the 2019 FIA Gala.
Top right: Watching the last race of 2019 with the rest of the team in the garage in Cape Town.
Centre and bottom right: Waiting outside the Stewards' room in Cape Town.
Centre pic: With event winner Niclas Gronholm and his team manager, former Hansen driver Jussi Pinomaki. It took almost three hours before the 'no further action' decision was made and Timmy Hansen was confirmed as FIA World Rallycross Champion.

Kevin Hansen

Hansen Motorsport driver
2013 –

To be up at the front in World Rallycross, having the same equipment as the others and my team mate to fight with was a bit different in 2019 to what I'd had before. It had been a long time since I was at the front regularly, and all year I think I still thought they had the upper hand, that cost me quite a lot in the long run.

I won the first round; I don't think I expected to win at all. I wanted to, for sure, I know I am fast but I didn't expect it. It was nice to win a round, but because I got it when the positions were reversed after some contact in the race, I still don't feel like I have a proper win.

I had a shot at the championship going into the final race, but because the three of us that could win it were so consistent in the end, it was out of my hands. I did the best I could and had to hope for luck, in the end I just fell a bit short and I think that symbolised the year.

It was nice to be in the fight and during the last race in South Africa, Timmy and I handled everything very well and took one session at a time, which was crucial to keep the pressure down. We had good control of the weekend until the start of the final when Timmy had a mis-shifted gear and lost the start to Andreas [Bakkerud]. From that point, we didn't have the control because we had a plan if Timmy took the start, but he didn't and everything was a bit stressful. When Timmy went to overtake Andreas, I didn't see that he'd managed it or not, there was dust everywhere, it was fully crazy! I spun too, and when the dust cleared it was not a nice feeling because I thought it was over. In the end we got it done, but it was a bit too close.

I was in the Stewards' room afterwards as a witness and felt that nothing was secure. We had won the championship fair and square in my opinion, and it was four wins to one on count back. It had been fought out on track but then it went to the Stewards. We had to wait such a long time for the decision. When we got the news, it was a very happy sensation. Still to this point it's incredible that our team won both titles when just to be on the grid was absolutely amazing.

I led half the championship, but I was happy to be third. Going to the FIA Gala you feel that you have achieved something great when you are among people like Sebastien Ogier, Fernando Alonso, Lewis Hamilton, Timmy and everyone that is there. I think

at that moment in Paris I appreciated the season even more, which is what the FIA Gala is all about.

Kenneth missed the race in Latvia because he was filming for the Mastarnas Mastare [Champion of Champions] reality TV show in Greece. I thought it was going to be more strange him not being there, but the team really came together, we tried to fill his place and I think we did that well. It was a challenging weekend for us in the end whether Kenneth had been there or not, but he followed closely from a distance and we could feel he was among us.

Now we know we can do a good job when he is not there, hopefully he feels that he doesn't have all the responsibility on his shoulders. But for sure, I prefer when he is there.

Above: Susann, Timmy and Kevin Hansen talk to Kenneth Hansen by phone during the 2019 Latvian event.
Top right: Kevin Hansen got his first World RX win in Abu Dhabi.
Bottom right: The family Hansen celebrate on the podium in Cape Town.

Kenneth Hansen

For a long time, people like me and Martin Schanche worked as a group to try and make the sport better. I often felt I was involved too much but we wanted to put pressure on the organisers to make things better.

In 1989 most of the drivers stayed away from the race in Spain and in 1992 it was the same in Austria, both times because we felt the events were not good enough. I was once fined £1000 because I did not go to the FIA Off-Road prize-giving in Poland. I'm not sure of the date, the mid 2000s. The previous year it had been in the Czech Republic and the way the drivers were treated was very bad, so I told the Andy Lasure [then President of the FIA Off-Road Commission] that I would not go to Poland unless I was guaranteed it would be better. I didn't get a reply so I didn't go. Every time these things were because we wanted to improve the sport.

Through the years, we had tried to have a teams' association and a drivers' association and tried to get things together. The organisers had an association too, but with 12 different minds, they could be common in one or two points but then there were 10 points that they didn't agree.

We understood that we had to have one boss, one company taking charge as a promoter, we knew that the sport was worth so much more and had so much more potential, we just needed to wake people up and make them understand what rallycross is.

When IMG came, it was like someone arrived that we'd been waiting a long time for. We also knew that when someone comes, it will not all be positive and good things, there would also be some negatives that we or the organisers were not so happy with, but that's how it is when you try to move things forward. We supported IMG a lot when they came, I think we were the first team that said officially: 'This is brilliant for rallycross.'

Some organisers didn't agree, so they went in a different direction, but we had been there for so long. I had even sat at prize-givings to collect prize money from the drivers because we had an agreement that all the drivers would put their prize money into a fund we used to pay for TV production. Drivers and teams were working behind the scenes to try and improve things, I think a lot of people didn't realise what we were looking for. And of course people don't like change. When electric cars come into rallycross it will be a similar.

We didn't believe it would be a World Championship as fast as it was, it's difficult to say if that was good for it to happen so early or not, but it's definitely good to have become a World Championship. IMG believed in it and took it there. Of course, some things we didn't agree with and were not happy about, but that's the nature of it.

Bruno Famin came to Loheac in 2013 and visited different teams. He said to me that Peugeot Sport believed in rallycross and that it could have a good future, so they wanted to do something. We knew that Citroen was going circuit racing, so for us it was interesting. We continued to talk and early in 2014 we agreed to work together in the World Championship.

From the first meeting with Bruno I felt that it worked, it's a personal chemistry. He was a great supporter for us, otherwise we wouldn't have worked with Peugeot. I think he still had a big passion for Le Mans, but he started to love rallycross more and more. He got the rallycross disease and if you get it, it's difficult to get rid of.

The decision to work with Peugeot in 2014 was late, but we always want to win, that's the way

we are. I think Bruno knew that it would be a learning year, but I expected us to be stronger from the beginning. We had a good test before Loheac in September, to get the car setup better, and then we won in Italy.

We hoped for more, but we didn't know how much it would mean to us until we won the Teams' Championship in 2015. That was special, but of course we really wanted to win the Drivers' Championship too.

At the end of the 2017 season we learned that Peugeot would take the programme in-house. We had two feelings; we had made something and they were taking over, but also that we had succeeded in bringing rallycross to a high level and a priority sport for our manufacturer so we were honoured to make that happen.

There was a lot of discussion about the people that could be involved, we proposed how we would like to see the team, and we were promised that Hansen would still be in the name. During the winter that changed more or less completely, and we ended up working for Peugeot. We always tried to be passionate with the people that worked there and do our best, but it felt that the knowledge me and Susann have was not always respected.

It was a very good period to learn a lot because we were a small team growing up to be a bigger team and we didn't handle everything well. Peugeot was a factory team and the rallycross part was quite small for them. There was a lot we could learn for the future that we want to do ourselves, but there are also a lot

of things that was not done well; you can be much more efficient. When it's a factory team with so many people involved, it's very different to a private team and sometimes it's not possible to operate as effectively.

Rallycross isn't Formula 1. It isn't circuit racing. Rallycross is different to everything because the conditions and grip change quite quickly. That's difficult to come to as a manufacturer. I think we were on the way to do something and we didn't succeed to go there [with Peugeot]. The sport is simple but also very, very difficult.

After every race we talked, and after the race in Germany [2018] I was to have a phone call with Bruno on Thursday. But, he called me earlier than planned on the Thursday morning. It was unusual, normally the calls were a later than

planned. I asked him how things were, and he said: 'It's not very good'. Then he explained that Peugeot had decided to stop. It felt like a bottle of cold water being poured over me, because I didn't expect it. That was a big surprise.

Bruno had got the message on Wednesday evening and he gave it to us on Thursday morning. People like Bruno who have been involved with factories in motor sport for a long time are not easily surprised, but even for Bruno it was a shock because he didn't expect it. That was the second time it happened to him after Peugeot also stopped the Le Mans programme in 2012.

The way we worked with Peugeot, over the years they pushed us to only do that, so it meant we had all our eggs in one basket. All four of us were out of work overnight. Of course, now

Previous page: Hansen has always tried to work with other drivers to improve rallycross. Here he is with Michael Jernberg, Lars Larsson and Martin Schanche.
Top left: As driver and team owner Hansen had to lead on all the team's activities.
Above: In contrast the Peugeot team of 2018 often had more than 30 personnel at each event.

I feel we should have been a little more independent and had some other business interests too.

Some people said we would always have a team in the World Championship, but it was so fragile for a long time over the winter before 2019, right to the absolute end. One wrong decision could have meant that we were not there and our lives would have been quite different.

Peugeot made us an offer to rent the cars. It was okay, but not brilliant and we managed with our three main sponsors; Total, Red Bull and MJP. Those were the three crucial points for us to be there, and all of the other partners also that helped us along the way, not only sponsors on the car.

From a business point of view, we shouldn't have been there because it was definitely not good business, but the passion was there and we know that rallycross is what Hansen is, so we had to be on the playing field.

We were one of the smallest teams to compete in a World Championship. We couldn't do it any other way because we haven't the resources. The cooperation with our mechanics, from Ragues in France, was fantastic. To have no breakdowns during the year was marvellous.

And our engineers like Graham Rodemark and Clement Laute. These people were not there for a salary, they put a part of their lives into it. That's how we have done rallycross, there have been ups and downs during all the years. Some years we didn't have good support or a lot of people, and some years it was better in terms of budget and possibilities. 2019 was really a fighting year and then in the end to take the titles, it was just like a dream.

We worked so hard for it, Kevin and Timmy understood that it was not only about their own success, it was about their brother and the team. They were racing hard all year, we didn't have team orders and they had some great fights, like in Spa and Sweden, but they gave each other space all year too.

We were fighting against other teams that played the game too in the end, but it was Timmy that could take the title.

It was such a difference to the year before. After all these years in rallycross, to be able to take the greatest titles, as World Champions, it felt so good.

Top left: Fans still seek out Hansen for an autograph even in the current era.
Bottom left: Mission accomplished! World Champions of 2019.

The razzmatazz of American motor sport may not appear to be a comfortable fit for someone as serene in nature as Kenneth Hansen.

But, while Hansen has never competed in the US as a driver, his team was among the initial wave of those to cross the Atlantic and take part in the first European-style rallycross races in North America. In only a handful of events, with a number of different drivers and cars, Hansen has achieved impressive success in the US, including a pair of X Games gold medals and two Nitro Rallycross victories.

8. AMERICA

2010 RallyCar Rallycross Championship

New Jersey Motorsports Park, Millville, New Jersey
2-3 October, 6-7 November

In the last half of 2010 'real' rallycross finally reached America with a series of four events being run at New Jersey Motorsports Park, south of Philadelphia. The first event was run at the end of August, followed by a second at the start of October and double-header weekend to form rounds three and four in early November.

At the close of the 2010 European Rallycross Championship season, the Citroen C4 that Hansen's team mate Liam Doran had raced to third overall in Europe, was packed-up and flown to America. Doran was keen to race in the RallyCar Rallycross Championship events and opted to fly his car to the US in order steal a march on those were shipping cars for the November events alone.

Having never previously competed outside Europe, despite its international success in the sport, the American experience was something new for the Gotene-based squad. Doran finished on the podium in the final of the four-round series.

Liam Doran sustained some damage during three starts in the RallyCar Rallycross Championship at New Jersey, but came away with third place in the final of the four-event series.

Kenneth Hansen

The first time we went to race in America it was an adventure, it was new for us and for rallycross. We thought we would be quite strong. With our experience, the car and team we thought it would not be difficult. But it's never easy to go to a national championship; like when I did the French Championship. On paper you should dominate, but it never goes like that.

There was also a new challenge with the logistics compared to what we were used to, but Liam arranged the flying and so on, that was a big help.

I was nervous to go there really, we didn't know where we were going, we didn't know anything about it, but we knew we were quite good at rallycross so that made the feeling a little better. But apart from that we really didn't know what to expect.

Those first races were very new, run by people who did not know the European way of rallycross, so one thing was happening, then 10 minutes later it was the opposite way. But it was fun – it's always fun to see new things and ways of doing things when you go into a different championship or new race.

Because we had done so much in Europe it was interesting to be there for the start of rallycross in America and see how they handled it. I think that was the start of a new culture for rallycross.

In those races at New Jersey there was a very different level between the cars. Of course the good ones were good but the slower guys were really slow, so there was a wide spectrum. The track was not perfect, but I think a lot of the damage we saw was

also because of the drivers. Liam was not perhaps well known for being the most gentle driver. After the first race, we arranged to go to a workshop, it was really more of storage area than a workshop. There were some NASCAR racecars there as well, and we managed to borrow some welding machines and things to repair the damage. We left the car there.

Then at the start of the second weekend we did, I said to Liam to take it a little carefully as the track was quite slippery. But on the first lap, he hit a stack of tyres and one side of the car was completely done! That was a bit emotional, we were all a little upset and not so happy but of course we fixed it and it was a really good experience to be there.

Liam Doran

Being really young, stupid and whatever I might have been back then, I was keen as anything to follow my dreams. My dream was to race in rallycross, but the dream to race in America was even stronger. The idea was to get into X Games, because we'd heard that X Games was going to have rallycross.

Back then the sport was small, budgets were small and it was very different to how it became later. Going to America was really outside Kenneth's comfort zone. I had to persuade him and then persuade him some more. He basically sent me off saying 'Normally you drive for me and I take all responsibility, but this time you're going to be taking responsibility because I'm not sure about it.' The tracks, the other drivers, the championship

organisation, all these things which were unknown. But it paid off massively for me and Kenneth soon changed his attitude.

When you look where Kenneth went after that; a couple of years later he's running Sebastien Loeb at X Games, I'd say that move to America was probably one of the first steps his team made to seeing the 'bigger picture'.

The idea of those first races was that it wasn't really crucial to go and dominate, it was to be part of it, that was the key at that point because it was all such a mess; it was all just complete luck. But to be there was the important thing; a young guy, with a strange car – nobody there had seen a Citroen before – to create a bit of spectacle. I'm not saying I wouldn't have liked to win, but we could see why we weren't winning; there were a lot of problems with the events. But I was there for the 'bigger picture'.

Liam Doran (right) on the podium with round four winner Toomas Heikkinen and champion Tanner Foust.

2011 X Games 17

Staples Center, Los Angeles, California
28-31 July

Following Hansen's first transatlantic adventure, half way through the 2011 European Rallycross season the team returned to the States, to compete in X Games at the Staples Centre in Los Angeles. Dropping conveniently into the European season's summer break, Hansen ran the same Citroen C4 it was fielding for British driver Liam Doran in Europe. With support from Monster Energy, the squad took part in both the head-to-head rally car racing, and more conventional rallycross events.

In the rally car final, Doran took on double-World Rally Champion Marcus Gronholm, and beat the Finn to claim the gold medal. The following rallycross final didn't go so well for the Hansen driver, despite being fastest through qualifying and making the best launch at the start, Doran was pushed off at the first corner by Ford driver Tanner Foust, and finished eighth.

Having beaten everyone to the rally car gold, Liam Doran's X Games rout was halted by this push from Tanner Foust at the start of the rallycross final.

Kenneth Hansen

We went back to America the next year for X Games with Liam. That was a little different because it was in the middle of the European Championship season, so it was more complicated with the logistics and I was afraid that it would affect the second part of the season in Europe.

It was new for us again, and when I do something I want to be quite under control. We are often a little careful – sometimes too careful, so it was good that Liam pushed us to go there to explore new things – we learnt a lot.

The event was more different than it was in New Jersey, but it was better organised.

We did the rally and the rallycross events. We won the rally final against Marcus [Gronholm] but the rallycross was more difficult because on the front row of the final it was three Fords and one Citroen. The Citroen didn't reach the first corner. I think we were not allowed to be first there.

I didn't think about it at the time, but when you look back at what you have done with drivers it feels good because it feels like you have given them the opportunity to have a memory for life. Susann and I are not running the team just to be there. If we are there we want to win. That could be our problem sometimes, we work a little too much from the heart, but on the other hand, if you should be there in rallycross after all these years you need to have fun and you need to enjoy it. I enjoyed that weekend at X Games and I know that the result at X Games was very big for Liam's career.

Liam Doran

My first European Championship win in Finland was the second most important of my career. The X Games win was the most important, for both me and Kenneth, I'd say. I'd only just signed the contract with Monster Energy, then here I am a few weeks-in winning the biggest prize at the time, a gold medal at X Games, live on ESPN in the US. It had massive, massive value.

That probably paid for me to be around for the next five years, it was that valuable.

Without that I would have never come as far as I have and I strongly believe, and Kenneth

would probably agree, that that was the first really big publicity event he was involved with as well. It was his car and it put his name in front of a lot of people outside of rallycross in Europe.

It opened a lot of doors. The next year he ran Sebastien Loeb at X Games, then built a relationship up with him and a manufacturer then they later went on to work together on a factory level.

The first year in America was just to break the ice and be involved, in the second year we started having to perform. I had a terrible year in the European Championship that season, but it didn't really matter because that one win cemented everything.

I beat Marcus Gronholm, who would have been one of my idols

growing up, he was one of the top names in motor sport, not just in rally and rallycross. I was a bit arrogant about it, but back then I was a little bit different from how I am now. We'd done so much and taken so many risks to get there, but then for it to have happened that easily on the day, it felt mad. But it did and I made that a little bit too obvious.

On the second day, in the rallycross event we were fastest and were almost guaranteed to win. Then there was the four or five car Ford team, almost looking, well, I guess embarrassed. Getting shown up by this random car from Europe that no-one had ever heard of before, running out of a little tent. Half the paddock drove for the same Ford team [Olsbergs

MSE] and we were causing them a massive problem. All the American bosses from Ford were watching, and at the same time Citroen didn't even know we had gone there. I'm not going to accuse anyone, but they may or may not have set out some tactics, 'You must get him out the way – he cannot beat all of us!'

Doran and Hansen returned to America and brought home gold from the X Games.

2012 X Games 18

Staples Center, Los Angeles, California
28 June – 1 July

Hansen returned to X Games in 2012 to run a Citroen DS3 Supercar in the rallycross event for the most successful rally driver of all time, Sebastien Loeb.

Instigated by Red Bull as an opportunity for two of the brand's highest-profile athletes, Travis Pastrana and Loeb to compete head-to-head, the project was run as an official Citroen Racing programme. The car was called the DS3 XL (for X Games and Loeb) and was billed as being developed by Citroen in France, based on a Hansen Motorsport Supercar.

The reality was that the car was actually the DS3 which Timur Timerzyanov had raced in the early part of the 2012 European Championship season, using a two-litre Oreca-built engine. And while then eight-time WRC champion Loeb took the seat for the American race, a new DS3 was constructed in Gotene for Timerzyanov to continue his European campaign.

Hansen's team travelled to Citroen Sport's Versailles base to work with the marque's engineers and tested first with Philippe Bugalski and then Loeb at the Dreux circuit near Paris, before flying the consignment to Los Angeles for X Games 18.

Hansen oversaw the running of the car and the sporting arm of the operation, meaning he missed the Swedish round of the European Championship at Holjes – which ran on the same weekend – for which wife Susann took charge.

While the X Games event was marred by serious accidents for Finnish drivers Marcus Gronholm and Toomas Heikkinen, and despite X Games being Loeb's rallycross debut, the Frenchman dominated to take the gold medal ahead of American drivers Ken Block and Brian Deegan.

Kenneth Hansen

It was during one of the first practices there in LA, I was Sebastien's spotter. I didn't know how he was feeling in the car and I saw he had got a puncture so I got on the radio and told him. 'I know,' he replied and I thought: 'Okay, this guy has full control.'

He won the first heat against Tanner [Foust], I think he was almost one second quicker per lap, so I said to Sebastien after the finish, to try and help him understand the competition 'You don't need to push so much, it's enough to win the race. It's nothing to do with the time, if you win, it's good enough.'

'I didn't push,' he replied. That's when I knew that if everything went okay we would be fine, and when I really understood why this guy is one of the greatest drivers of all time.

X Games was the first time we had links with Red Bull, who together with Citroen wanted us to do the project. It was different for us, but we didn't feel like it was too much. Perhaps we should have felt the pressure more, but we did it as we wanted to, like normal and it was fun to work with Sebastien because even though we had both been with Citroen for many years, it was the first time we did anything together.

We had one test day with Philippe Bugalski in France. Sadly he had an accident at home later that year and passed away. His feeling was brilliant, very professional and the perfect test driver. The day after we were with Sebastien and we needed to learn a little together. He is a very good driver, but sometimes rallycross can be a little different, so I needed to advise him on some small things.

It felt strange to do that to, at that time, an eight-time World Champion, but we worked on things like the starts and we felt quite comfortable for when we went to the US. Of course when you fly cars and with all the customs and freight rules you feel a little nervous that everything is working, but that side was fine.

It was a bad race because Marcus and Toomas had big crashes. We were very afraid after Marcus had his accident, he hit a concrete post that was sticking out of a wall very hard and we didn't know how he was. We needed to do the timed qualification for the race but because we didn't know how he was, we didn't know whether to continue or not. In the end we had some discussions and we decided together to go for the timed qualification and then see how things were.

We found out Marcus would be okay, so we could do the complete event. In the end it was lucky we did the timed qualification.

Sebastien Loeb

I think I'd seen Kenneth before but I don't remember exactly where or when, probably with Citroen. Except for that, the first time I really met him and we did things together was X Games.

I tested in Dreux and he helped me a lot because he has a lot of experience in rallycross and I didn't know anything about it, so it was very good to have him to teach and coach me. I discovered him to be someone who is a very, I would say a normal guy, very friendly and very passionate about rallycross, for sure. He never really gets upset, so it's always really good to work with him.

I didn't know what to expect. For sure when I take the start of a race, I always want to do my best and try to win if I can, but I had no idea what I would be able to do there.

I quickly realised that the start would be crucial. It went very well though and we won, so that was a great result.

The Loeb/Hansen partnership was immediately successful and took an X Games gold medal.

2018 Nitro Rallycross

**Utah Motorsports Campus, Utah
23-24 September**

Created by American extreme sports star Travis
Pastrana to be part of his Nitro World Games, the first
Nitro Rallycross event, backed by Red Bull, was held at
Utah Motorsports Campus in September 2018.

From his and Peugeot Sport's links with energy drink
giant Red Bull, Hansen travelled to the circuit while the
rallycross layout was under construction to impart his
expertise, and returned with the Team Peugeot Total
squad for the event, running oldest son Timmy in an
early 2018 specification Peugeot 208 WRX.

The new event included banked gravel corners and
an enormous 90-foot [27.5 metre] gap-jump, new
challenges for the team which ultimately won the final.

*Just another day at the office: Hansen
returned to America with Team Peugeot Total
and oldest son Timmy for the Nitro event and
won again.*

Kenneth Hansen

I went to Utah for a while before the race to look at the track and try and advise the guys there with my experience, what they wanted to do was totally different to the kind of rallycross tracks we have in Europe.

They built the track and when we went there for the race it was better than expected.

In the US it's more than just a race, it's about the show and Travis wanted to do something different, to wake rallycross up again and make it a little new.

We calculated that with all the jumps the car would be flying seven times a lap if you took all of them; the option to use the jumps or not created something different.

We knew it would not be perfect, it would probably be dusty and there would be difficulties with the track markers and things, but it was about trying something new.

We couldn't do all the big jumps, but we had the speed, then in the end we needed to do the big gap jump if we were to win, and we needed some success after a long dry period without winning in the family.

Timmy said after practice, when he landed the car badly, that he didn't feel comfortable, because he had a young family, which of course I understood so I straight away said then we wouldn't do the gap jump.

But after qualifying, we understood that we could not win the race if we did not jump. We listened to what the other teams said was a good speed to take it, then in the evening we managed to make a rev limiter – we had a fantastic engineer who found a way into the ECU to make it work. You had to be in the right gear, then press a button on the way to the jump. Then, in the air, you released the rev limiter and pulled one gear up, to make the acceleration lift the front of the car, because our car wanted to nose-dive.

In the corner before the jump you couldn't get too sideways because then it could be difficult to achieve the right speed, but you didn't want to be on the rev limiter too early either because then you lost too much time.

The next morning Timmy did the gap jump, and 21 more times after that I think.

It was fantastic to win that event, like I said we had been a long time without being on the top step of the podium. Together as a team we made the limiter so we could do the jump and that meant we were able to win. And Timmy drove brilliantly.

I like the different way they do things in America and you learn something new every time you go there. I don't think I would like to live there, but to go there, do something different, learn from it and to win, that was a pleasure.

*Team work enabled Hansen to take the gap
jump and win at Nitro Rallycross.*

Timmy Hansen

I hadn't raced in America before, that was my first time and the American way is very different from the European way. There it is much more about the show, about entertaining the fans and I must say I really liked working in that way. I understand that I'm quite careful as a person, but when I went there I wanted to embrace the culture and just went with it all.

It was fun answering the questions in a more American way, being more open. American people are very positive, at least that was the impression I got – they are not afraid about talking very positively about things, and they are not afraid about hyping things up, I really like that.

The interview questions were very different, but I embraced what it is like and adapted. Maybe we Europeans have a bit to learn from them about that side.

I got the information about Nitro Rallycross from Red Bull when they were working on the concept, and I thought it sounded absolutely amazing, almost too crazy to be actually doable, especially when I saw the drawings of the track

But I love a challenge, and I love trying new things. Peugeot wanted to go and I was happy that it was me who got the opportunity to drive.

The circuit was probably the best I've driven in any category, at any time. I've driven on most of the best European racing circuits from when I was in Formula cars, I've done all of the good rallycross tracks, I've played video games of different places, but I've never seen anything like that.

It felt a bit like when you drive on that rainbow circuit on Super Mario, but it was real. It was crazy, completely unrealistic, but it was such a great feeling to drive there.

What made it great was, okay there was the big jump, but there were also a lot of small jumps that added to the racing. The best thing though was the banked gravel corners. Driving on gravel is awesome, everybody knows it's really slippery, but the result when you add a banked corner is that you could throw the car in like on gravel but there was more grip than you'd ever have on tarmac. It was such a cool driving style to be super aggressive.

Honestly, the big jump? Scary! Absolutely the most scary thing that I have ever done in a racecar. Travis [Pastrana] went first and showed it was possible, and in practice I was really the first one saying 'Yeah, let's go'. The first time was good, but a bit too short. Dad said on the radio that I needed to jump a little more. On my second jump I jumped too far, and the car really wanted to rotate forward. I wasn't absolutely flat on the throttle through the air, so that made it dive on the nose and damaged the front really badly.

We were just a small crew there and we didn't have enough spares to have another crash like that. There were alternative routes so we decided focus on the smaller jump and take the racing from there.

But the track was developed during the race and the big jump was much faster in the end, we stuck to our plan through the heats and went directly to the semi-finals, but we realised we would not be able to win if we didn't take the big gap jump.

We changed the car and I did the jump in morning practice the next day, and I made it, I overcame the fears. That was the big story for us during the weekend, if we hadn't done that we wouldn't have won the race.

There were a lot of close battles and because of all the different lines that you could choose it really allowed us to stay close to one another.

Of course, winning was fantastic. It was great for the boys, they had worked hard repairing the damage after the jump incident, we were a small team but everybody put their heart into the project and we won. It's always fantastic to cross the finish line with no-one ahead of you.

Mattias [Ekstrom] and I had a big fight in the final, like we did in the heats. I was second after the start then I chased him and used the joker to pass him and win. Then on the podium he didn't want to shake my hand, I have no idea why.

2019 Nitro Rallycross

Utah Motorsports Campus, Utah
16-17 August

Hansen's team, by now running as a privateer effort again, rather than working for Peugeot, returned to the Nitro World Games Rallycross event with two cars for the 2019 event. Held in August between the Canadian and French World Rallycross rounds, the team achieved a double podium.

The event used an unconventional race format, with early qualifying sessions awarding the first places for the final, before subsequent qualifiers determined the remainder of the grid. Hansen's youngest son Kevin was one of the first to qualify, netting a front-row start for the final.

Then, despite not completing a single lap on the day of the final before lining up on the grid for the main event, he took the lead before the first corner and stormed to victory. Timmy Hansen, meanwhile, also qualified but dropped to last after the start, before battling his way back to third. The Hansen MJP pair were joined on the podium by fellow Swede and Subaru Motorsports USA driver, Patrik Sandell.

Kenneth Hansen

The first challenge was quite a big one, that was the logistics to go to Nitro with the cars we were racing in the World Championship; to deal with the customs going from Canada to the US, then to fly them home after.

We were also a little worried about crashes, because of the very limited time, but it worked out quite well.

The challenge on the track was quite different compared to the year before, there were quite a lot of changes, but the big jump had better angles.

To have one car directly qualify for the final was a big thing. There was less stress because of that, but it was also difficult because Kevin didn't have any warm-up or anything before the final. We asked for it, but the organiser said:

'They are so good that they have qualified directly, so they don't need a warm-up.' It's a different way to look at it.

In the final there were six cars and all of them could win, but Kevin took control, he was very determined. He didn't make any mistakes, he was a little safe on the last lap so it was tight at the end, but there was one corner where it was very easy to get overtaken, so you needed to give away a little time to be safe.

For the final we needed to use the joker, which was a tunnel under the track that we didn't use the year before, then we had to use the table top jump and the big jump at least one time each. As a spotter, that was a big challenge too, but we took the jokers early so we were able to push over the

big jump [the fastest route], that made quite a difference.

Timmy struggled a little at the start, but after that he was flying on the circuit, absolutely fastest and ended up in third place.

It was a fantastic event overall and for us. We performed so well that Travis [Pastrana, event founder] said they would never invite any more Swedes!

First and third in the 2019 Nitro Rallycross, the Hansen brothers were joined on the podium by compatriot Patrik Sandell.

Kevin Hansen

After being there with Timmy the year before, I understood the spirit of the track and how to drive it, but when I got out myself it was so different to what I expected.

First we had a jump practice, that was a bit scary because it was completely new for me. I knew I would get over, but it was the sequence of holding the rev-limiter button, pulling a gear in the air and landing.

In the end the big jump was the easy one. The actual lap, was so different because somehow you have to nail that track in a different way to the tracks we normally go to.

With the banked corners and the jumps everywhere, you have to work the track so much more, like you went up one level. That was really difficult, but a lot of fun. I think it was the most fun I've had in any car.

In practice I wasn't fast, but for the one-shot qualifying I was a bit lucky and because I had been slow in practice, I had good track conditions. Then I had a bad first head-to-head race, again because of the track conditions, but I was good in the last one, not just because of the conditions being better.

I went straight into the final, and then had nothing to do for 24 hours. It was good that Timmy was driving to get into the final so I could focus on him and understand as much as I could.

But, not having driven a single lap before the final was a new challenge as well.

In a final you have to be perfect, but we were well prepared and I didn't even do a practice start, I just rolled up to the grid. I nailed the start and then did the best six laps of my career, so I think I earned that result.

I was so happy because I pushed like an idiot for six laps and I knew I had to make it perfect to take the win. It was the first time really that I was nervous about whether I would be at the level I know I can be after not driving all day. I've never pushed that hard and I've never done such good laps.

Only Cabot Bigham and I hadn't raced at the track before, I was the youngest in the field and it was amazing to win what was in my opinion the biggest single race of the year.

Our team has always done well in America. They're one-off events and we know we need to perform. It's high pressure, but somehow it's low pressure too. We are a small team in the World Championship but even smaller for NRX, but there is so much spirit that we knew we could do well.

The track is at such high altitude that when I celebrated with the team afterwards, I almost passed out. I couldn't get my breath back. I was exhausted, but it was so cool.

Timmy Hansen

Nitro had really blown my mind with how racing could be when I went there in 2018. Driving on that track was unreal. As unreal as it looks. Just trying to survive it and do that huge jump, and to have won it meant that I'd spent all year looking forward to going back there.

The track conditions weren't on my side this time really. I was fastest in practice and then I got to go last in qualifying. I fought my way through to the final and lined up on the second row. But I had a bad launch, the car just bogged down, and I was at the back. I also had an engine issue through the final, but I just thought: 'Okay, now I'm going to risk it all.'

On a track like that the room for the driver to make the difference is massive, so I went all-in on everything and it worked. At one point, Kenneth came on the radio and said 'It's good, you're catching like hell!'

He was a big part of why that race went so well, on the radio, because he is so fully committed. He really helped me to find all that speed, to get all the time that I needed. That event is 100% America. There are these big American flags when you arrive and that never stops; the biggest jumps, the biggest FMX [Freestyle Motocross] quarter pipe, the biggest everything. Everywhere it's about putting craziest first and you really feel that. It's about putting on a great show, people want to be amazed.

Another trip to America and more trophies, Hansen's small team won again in Nitro Rallycross.

Hansen and his Volvo Amazon in 1986, the year of his first Swedish Championship win.

Hansen's strike rate in a career of over three decades is extraordinary.

But while the Swede would become the most successful rallycross driver in the history of the sport, and set records that are unlikely ever to be beaten with a combination of sensational speed, incredible consistency and a measured approach, he didn't always have things his own way.

Gotene's man wasn't always the fastest, title-fights often went down to last round deciders and in his earliest days in rallycross just finishing events was a challenge.

This chapter details Hansen's rallycross career year-by-year.

9. 30 YEARS

1983

Having begun the transition from karting to cars with folkrace outings in 1982, Hansen travelled to Dalarna, Central Sweden in early 1983 to meet a rallycross driver disgruntled with the sport and wanting a way out. There Hansen exchanged his standard Volvo P1800 for a Volvo Amazon rallycross machine, the first step in an adventure that would lead to him becoming the most successful driver in rallycross history.

But his early races were clouded by technical issues, especially surrounding the fuelling and compression ratio of the car's B20-based 2.4-litre engine.

Third in the B final at Hyllinge, a round of the West District Swedish Rallycross Championship was Hansen's first rallycross finish and the highlight of the year, a result he still remembers as feeling: 'Like winning the World Championship.' Little did he know then what the future would bring. A further third in the B final at Tomelilla followed later in that first season.

1984

With grids of over 40 cars, even the West District Swedish Rallycross Championship was a competitive affair in the mid 1980s and while better results came for Hansen in 1984, victory, or even a podium finish was a way off yet, although he did finish second in a Car Speedway event at Sturup.

Race-by-race, Hansen learnt an increasing amount about his equipment, and continually refined the Amazon, although he admits that sometimes a combination of enthusiasm coupled with desperation to succeed meant mistakes were made and backward steps were taken as often as steps forward.

Focusing on getting as much of the car's mass over the rear-axle as possible – critical for start line traction – Hansen also implemented a home-made rear wing to give his rivals a false impression that the Amazon was aerodynamically advanced, when the likelihood is that the large rear spoiler was more for show than function.

1985

Just qualifying for many events in the early stages of Hansen's rallycross career was a challenge. Those competitors outside the top three (automatic qualifying positions) had to qualify for each round of the Swedish Cup, which then became the Swedish Championship in 1985. With over 100 drivers vying just to get onto the grid for the main events, competitors would sometimes travel in excess of 1000 kilometres to take part in qualifying races, often with as little running as two sets of two laps on track, before loading up and heading home.

A staggering degree of commitment required to take part in a national series, that may well have seen off the weaker minded racers, or those who lost the enthusiasm to continually find the budget to repeatedly travel across the country for little track time.

It was in 1985 though that Hansen overcame the reliability issues that had dogged his rallycross career so far, and karting exploits before that, to score his first ever rallycross victory at his home circuit, Kinnekulle, in Gotene on July 25. The victory came at the penultimate round of the West District series, and was followed by a podium finish in the final round at Norrkoping. In the Swedish Championship, Hansen only once made it into the A final, in the eighth and final round at Jonkoping, where he finished sixth.

1986

The first round of the Swedish Rallycross Championship took place at Tomelilla. Having qualified for the A final, Hansen ran fourth on the opening lap of the race and overtook the three cars ahead to claim victory, and lead the championship for the first time.

Success in the West District series followed, but Hansen wouldn't win another round of the Swedish Championship that year and in fact struggled to get on the podium. However, he entered the final round at Haninge as part of a four-way scrap for the title.

Trying to gain an edge on their rivals, and unbeknown to each other, three of the drivers in that title fight, including Hansen, implemented different systems for rudimentary pre-race tyre warming for that final round, a concept previously unheard of in Swedish national rallycross events. Second in the A final was enough for Hansen to lift his first rallycross crown in his last year with the Volvo Amazon. As part of Hansen's busiest season until that point, he also took part in five Swedish Hillclimb events, claiming two wins and only once finishing off the podium.

1987

Interviewed live on Swedish television following his maiden domestic crown at the end of 1986, Hansen was asked 'What's next?' Without thinking, he responded that after winning at home, the next step should be to go into Europe, although well aware that he didn't have the machinery or funds to do so.

Without Hansen's knowledge, a friend advertised the title-winning Amazon in a newspaper, partially in jest, but the car sold, and for a good price too.

At that time employed by a Volvo dealership in Skovde, a fortnight after his Swedish success the firm's marketing manager came to Hansen pleased with the regional coverage his title had returned and said: 'You want to drive the European Championship. We've bought a car for you. Lars Nystrom's Group A Volvo (240 Turbo). If you want it, pick it up and you can drive in the European Championship.'

Hansen describes that moment as like 'Winning a million Euros'. Arguably, it was the most important moment of his entire career.

Armed with a freshly converted bus, the 26-year-old embarked on an international adventure.

A solid seventh at the opening round in May at Melk (Austria) was followed by his first podium in round three at the ultra-fast Hameenlinna circuit in Finland. A second rostrum appearance at Arendonk (Belgium) came in the summer, before the Swede finished second to Trevor Reeves at Lydden Hill (Great Britain) and completed the campaign fifth in the standings.

1988

Having focused solely on European competition in 1987, Hansen embarked on a duel campaign in 1988 racing in both the European and Swedish series.

In Europe, Hansen made the A final seven times and finished on the podium in Loheac (France), Maasmechelen (Belgium) and Lydden Hill (Great Britain) to end the year sixth in the points, but at home things went much better. Second in the opening round at Haninge, Hansen won his first event in over a year at Tomelilla in June and by the end of the campaign at Sturup, he was in contention for the title. In extreme wet conditions Hansen made extra cuts in the Volvo's tyres, benefited from increased traction and beat reigning European Champion Per-Ove Davidsson to the title, the first time Hansen had taken on and beaten a top-level driver to both a race victory, and championship crown.

1989

With the 240 coming to the end of its competitive life it was time for Hansen to change machinery. After coming close to buying a Volkswagen Golf, that more suited his wallet, Hansen financed his next move with a bank loan and sourced a version of the car that had become the leading force in the category, a Ford Sierra RS500 Cosworth, from England.

Without the kind of spares package he had been used to in previous seasons, due to the costs attached to the desirable RS500 components, Hansen ran the '89 season on a tight budget, much of which was blown in the first half of the year when the rear differential failed and needed replacing. But, the step up in machinery also brought a step up in results, and Hansen immediately entered the winners' circle, in Melk (Austria) just two years after his European debut at the circuit.

He also won at Luneville in France, and visited the podium a further five times on his way to his first European crown.

That success was achieved despite being disqualified from the Norwegian round at Lyngas for using the wrong fuel after confusion by his team between the different fuels used in the Swedish and European championships [see chapter two]. The mistake, for which Hansen holds up his hands, earned the Swede 'Car Doping' headlines in Norway, something that would stay with him for years to come.

Back home, Hansen won all but one round of the Swedish series to secure another national title.

1990

Hansen's first European title defence started poorly; fourth at Fuglau (Austria) in round one, and stuck in the B final in round two, his home event at Tomelilla.

But, Hansen claimed his first win of the campaign in round three at Hameenlinna (Finland), the scene of his maiden international podium in 1987, and subsequently qualified for the A final at the remaining seven rounds, winning in Ireland, the Netherlands and Norway, and capping off his run to a second straight title with another podium at Lydden Hill (Great Britain).

For the second season in succession, Hansen won four of the five Swedish Championship events with a worst result of third at Skelleftea, and claimed another domestic crown. The season also brought victory in a one-off appearance at the Crosskart GP at Kinnekulle.

1991

For 1991 a circuit racing RS500 was acquired and converted to rallycross trim. The European season began at Lousada (Portugal) with victory over Norwegian Eivind Opland, before a pair of second places in Austria and Finland were followed by a string of six further victories, more often than not ahead of Bjorn Skogstad. This was, arguably, Hansen's most dominant period in the Group A category. Winning a third straight title, the third successive year of beating Norwegian Skogstad to the top spot. The European trail concluded at Estering (Germany), where Hansen finished sixth, as Skogstad claimed victory, but by then it mattered little.

By his own high standards, Hansen's 1991 campaign in the Swedish Championship began slowly, missing the A final in Jonkoping and Arvika, but three wins followed to secure another crown.

1992

For 1992, Hansen elected to ditch the converted circuit racing RS500 in favour of a new car built in-house, the first car that his small team had built from scratch.

But, it was Hansen's chief Group A rival Bjorn Skogstad who took first blood in the swansong year of the category, with victory at Lydden Hill (Great Britain) in the season opener. By the fourth round of the year, and a victorious first visit to Suonenjoki (Finland), it was the Swede who had moved into the points lead.

The best seven scores in the 11-round series decided the title. At the end of the year Hansen and Skogstad had three wins apiece, and a string of second places. Separated by two points in the final reckoning, it was down to a tie-break and Hansen's second place to Skogstad's third from Lousada (Portugal) early in the campaign gave Hansen a fourth straight title, the last before a raft of rule changes for top-flight rallycross.

For 1993, the second-level in international competition would switch from Group A to Group N (Production-based) rules, while the top class would finally get rid of the Group B cars in favour of machines based on Group A rules.

In his homeland, Hansen simply dominated the national championship, winning every round to take his sixth crown, while he also won a one-off 'Champions Race' at Holjes (Sweden) and netted the Finnish Rallycross Championship title too, for winning a single event at Pieksamaki in July.

After holding talks with several manufacturers, Hansen entered into deeper discussions with Citroen Sweden about a step up in category for 1993. Those talks resulted in a visit to Citroen Sport in France, where Hansen secured sponsorship of a works engine and arm's-length support, a similar arrangement to that held by Frenchman Jean-Luc Pailler. The ultimatum from Citroen Sport boss Guy Frequelin was clear: one of the pair had to win the title.

So, Hansen's Gotene workshop produced its most sophisticated car to that point, a four-wheel drive Citroen ZX to the new regulations.

On the eve of the first round at Fuglau (Austria), Martin Schanche all but condemned the new machine's steering arrangement. Then, when Hansen lost a wheel in practice, Schanche's thoughts looked like they may have been true. But things improved thereafter and, come the final, Hansen describes the feeling of lining up next to, then chasing Schanche in the race as: 'Like a dream.' That feeling was escalated when Hansen pressured the then five-time European Champion into a mistake and it was the Swede that claimed victory, ahead of Pailler in a Citroen one-two.

A second victory came at Holjes (Sweden) in a year where Hansen was never out of the A final. Further wins at Valkenswaard (Netherlands) and Lyngas (Norway) meant he entered the final round at Estering (Germany) battling for the title. A puncture in the last race of the year meant it was Pailler that secured Citroen's crown. In Sweden, Hansen achieved four podiums from four starts, including victory at Alvsbyn and claimed his seventh national title.

Armed with an updated version of the ZX, Hansen began 1994 with victory at Melk (Austria).

Having run fellow rallycross driver, partner and later wife Susann Bergvall in the title-winning RS500 in Swedish events in 1993 Kenneth Hansen Motorsport concluded that it would be better for Susann to drive the same marque of car as Hansen, and as such a Citroen AX was acquired for use in the 1400 Cup.

At the second round of the European season at Lousada (Portugal) the couple scored a dream result, Hansen winning the Division 2 (Supercar) final and Bergvall claiming the honours in the 1400 Cup.

Through the 11-round European campaign, Hansen was only once off the podium and scored five wins, including beating Martin Schanche at Lyngas (Norway) in the penultimate round; a titanic duel that has gone down in rallycross folklore [see chapter two].

By the final round at Estering (Germany), second place to Pailler mattered little as Hansen claimed his maiden top-category European title, while a German win for Bergvall meant she won the 1400 Cup title.

Hansen also won all but one round of the Swedish Championship to secure yet another crown, and found time to win standalone 'Champions' races in both Sweden and Norway, win a Swedish Hillclimb event at Ratten and claim his first British Rallycross Grand Prix win at Brands Hatch (Great Britain) in December.

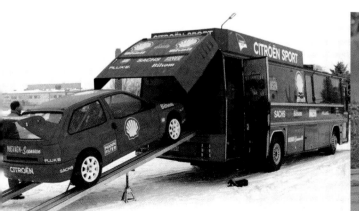

1995

It's a mark of Hansen's hit rate that 1995 can be considered one of his more barren seasons, despite starting the European campaign with a trio of podiums in the opening three rounds, followed by three straight wins, at Arvika (Sweden), Brands Hatch (Great Britain) and Mondello Park (Ireland). Even though he visited the podium in nine of the 12 rounds, Martin Schanche's tally of six wins, including five straight victories in the second half of the campaign, meant it was the Norwegian that scooped the crown. Hansen finished second overall, the same position he held at the conclusion of the Swedish series, with two wins to his credit, finishing second to Michael Jernberg. By winning the British round of the European Championship Hansen also secured his second successive British Rallycross Grand Prix title. He finished third in the Swedish Champions race at Strangnas and took part in a hillclimb at Ratten, where he also finished second.

Partner Susann Bergvall was twice on the podium in the 1400 Cup and ended the year fifth in the standings before hanging up her helmet to focus on the pair's young family, first son Timmy having been born in 1992, and running the team.

1996

Only once off the podium through the 11-event European Championship, Hansen retook the title in 1996 with a further evolution of the Citroen ZX, by then in its fourth term. Hansen's worst result of the season came at the second round with sixth at Lousada (Portugal) after being black flagged for contact with Will Gollop. On home ground at Kinnekulle, Hansen was beaten by Citroen counterpart Jean-Luc Pailler, much to the Frenchman's delight.

A quartet of second place finishes and a trio of wins, including the season finale at Estering (Germany) secured Hansen the crown by a margin of 10 points ahead of Norwegian Ludvig Hunsbedt. The Gotene man finished second in the Swedish series, this time to Per Eklund, and concluded the year by winning his third British Rallycross Grand Prix at Brands Hatch (Great Britain).

1997

The fifth and final year for Hansen with the ZX returned just one victory. His only top-step appearance of the European Championship season came at Maasmechelen (Belgium), while the other winners' spoils were achieved just over the border in a non-championship Euro Rallycross Masters event at Valkenswaard (Netherlands) a week later in August.

Hansen visited the European Championship podium on a further four occasions, each time in second position, and ended the campaign as runner-up to Ludvig Hunsbedt.

Events in Sweden were divided between the new Shell Helix Cup and the usual national championship but Hansen didn't prosper in either. By the end of the season attention in the Swede's Gotene workshop had already turned to a new development for 1998.

1998

An amazing trend for Hansen Motorsport machines, especially through Hansen's own driving career, was the win rate for new cars. A good example of that is 1998, where the new Citroen Xsara, a car Hansen says has been described to him many times as: 'The most beautiful rallycross car ever', claimed victory in the European season-opener at Melk (Austria).

It wasn't all plain sailing at round one though. The new car's engine expired on the first day, before Hansen fought back to qualify on pole for the A final. Beaten into the lead by Per Eklund, Hansen only won the race thanks to a last-lap pass.

Hansen would only stand on the top of the podium three times through the year, with additional victories at Maasmechelen (Belgium), where he beat pole man Martin Schanche, and at Lyngas (Norway).

His worst result of the campaign came at Arvika (Sweden) where, having won the B final to qualify for the main event, Hansen was black flagged for contact with Eklund's Saab and classified sixth.

But, come the penultimate round at Estering (Germany), second to Schanche was enough to secure the Swede's record seventh European crown. A win-less season in the Swedish series ended with fourth in the points, while Hansen finished second to Michael Jernberg in an invitational race in the centre of Gothenburg in August [see chapter two].

1999

Hansen's second year with the Xsara got off to a relatively slow start, although he did claim victory from the back of the grid at round three, in Portugal.

Battling in the pack for much of the campaign, the Swede delivered a strong performance at Maasmechelen (Belgium) in the second half of the year to keep his title hopes alive, but only just, as points leader Per Eklund finished second. Third, behind the veteran driver, at the next round in the Netherlands all but ended Hansen's title aspirations, which concluded abruptly when he was involved in an A final accident involving Eklund, Ludvig Hunsbedt and Michael Jernberg in Norway.

As Eklund claimed the laurels, Hansen's hopes of an eighth European crown ended on top of a barrier, which just about summed up his season. However, he ended the campaign by dominating the final round in Germany, where nephew Magnus Hansen secured the Division Two title in a Group N Xsara.

At home in Sweden, Hansen won three of the five rounds to claim another domestic crown.

2000

Having campaigned a French machine since graduating to the sport's highest level in 1993 (as he would continue to do for the rest of his career), events in France played a pivotal role in Hansen's 2000 season.

He opened his European title challenge with a win at Essay (France) in June, before dominating his home round at Holjes two events later. A further win in the Netherlands, in part thanks to pole sitter Martin Schanche withdrawing before the final due to engine issues with his Opel Astra, meant that second place to Schanche at the next round in Norway put Hansen within touching distance of another crown.

Hansen was runner-up to Jean-Luc Pailler in Poland, where Per Eklund was excluded for using illegal tyres, following a protest by Hansen's team [see chapter one]. All of which gave Hansen an unbeatable lead in the series before he put the icing on the cake at the season finale in Germany with another victory.

It was in 2000 that Hansen also dipped his toe in the water of the highly competitive French Championship, and won on his debut at Luneville.

In the Swedish Championship though, the best Hansen could manage was a pair of second places and he finished third in the points.

2001

Not content with assaults on the European and Swedish Rallycross Championships, Hansen also embarked on a programme in the French Championship in 2001.

Two cars Citroen Xsaras were used to complete this ambitious task; in June Hansen raced to third at Arvika in the Swedish series, before flying to France where he finished third at Luneville the following day and in July he placed second in the Jarbo hillclimb on Saturday and third in Kerlabo on Sunday. Winning events in both national series through the year, Hansen eventually placed third in Sweden, and second in France. The Swede's European campaign began with a trio of victories, starting at the opening round in Loheac (France), in front of 30,000 spectators. Hansen's win only came after swapping tyre brands [see chapter two] but by the eighth round in Norway, Hansen had one finger on the biggest prize.

The Citroen driver made it directly into the A final and won on track to mathematically claim his ninth European crown. But a failed protest by rival Ludvig Hunsbedt for an overtaking move by Hansen in the final was later overturned by the NBF (Norwegian ASN), which stripped Hansen of the win.

The following round in Poland rubbed salt into the wound when Hansen was black flagged in the final for contact with Per Eklund. In the season finale at the Estering (Germany) Hansen finished second to Eklund, but crucially ahead of Hunsbedt to claim the title outright. His points margin was later made more comfortable when he regained the Norwegian win after winning an appeal to the FIA.

2002

Arguably Hansen's greatest season. The Swede's European campaign started with a brace of commanding victories in Portugal and France before finishing second in Austria to Per Eklund.

Hansen was fastest in the first two qualifiers so often in 2002 that he regularly sat out the third with pole for the A final already in the bag. After Austria the Swede bounced back with a further two victories in the Czech Republic and at home in Sweden to end the first half of the year at the top of the points chart.

A further top-step appearance at round eight in Norway all but secured the title.

The week prior to the ninth round of the European series in Poland, Hansen completed a full-house of Swedish Championship victories in the finale at his home circuit, Kinnekulle, to secure his tenth national crown, then followed up by sealing his tenth European title by qualifying for the finals at Slomczyn.

With the points pressure off, Hansen then stormed to his sixth European win of the season for good measure. Such was his form in 2002 that the season-finale in Germany was the only points scoring event of the year at which Hansen didn't appear on the podium.

2003

Victory over former Citroen counterpart Jean-Luc Pailler (who had switched to Peugeot in 2000) in the season-opener at Lousada (Portugal) gave Hansen an early points lead. The pair drew level after the second round on Pailler's home turf, at Essay (France).

Hansen secured his second win of the campaign at Greinbach (Austria) in round three, Pailler was sixth and thereafter his title hopes faded. Hansen won round five at Holjes (Sweden) to finish the first half of the campaign on top. After the summer break a further three wins at Maasmechelen (Belgium), Valkenswaard (Netherlands) and the season closing German round at Estering gave Hansen a comfortable margin over nearest points challenger Per Eklund. His 11th European title.

In the Swedish series a pair of wins coupled with a brace of fourth place finishes was only good enough for the runner-up spot.

2004

Another new Citroen Xsara was created in Hansen Motorsport's Gotene workshops for 2004, and Hansen's title defence began with a podium in the season-opener at Lousada (Portugal), where Morten Bermingrud (in an ex-Hansen Xsara) won a race that was restarted after contact in the first start.

Hansen also finished behind Bermingrud in round three at Sosnova (Czech Republic) but victory at Melk (Austria) moved Hansen into the points lead.

Another win followed at the next round in Norway, but the Lyngas event was even more special for the Swedish team. 2004 was the first time it had run a second driver at this level. Driving Hansen's 2003 Xsara, Stig-Olov Walfridson contested the Swedish Championship and a pair of European events at Lyngas and Holjes (Sweden). In Norway, while Hansen won, Walfridson was promoted to second in the final when Tommy Rustad was disqualified.

Another win came at Maasmechelen (Belgium) in August and a week later, third place at Valkenswaard (Netherlands) secured Hansen's 12th crown.

He also won the season finale at Estering (Germany), but only after being black flagged in the final of the penultimate round for contact with Per Eklund.

In the Swedish series, Hansen finished fourth, with one victory to his credit, while Walfridson was seventh at the end of the year.

2005

Hansen's campaign for a 13th European title could easily have taken a hit in the first corner of the opening round at Essay, where the Citroen man was involved in contact that punctured the right-rear tyre of his Citroen Xsara [see chapter two]. But Hansen delivered a performance worthy of his champion status by fending off pressure from Sverre Isachsen to claim victory.

He won the following two events too, at Lousada (Portugal) and Greinbach (Austria) but wouldn't visit the top step of the rostrum again in Europe that year. Retirement from the B final at Sosnova (Czech Republic) was Hansen's worst result, while he finished sixth in Holjes (Sweden) after making contact with title-rival Michael Jernberg in a fight for the win.

A trio of third places in the second half of the campaign took the title battle to the final round, where Hansen finished second and Jernberg crashed out, handing the Citroen driver the crown.

It was also during 2005 that Hansen climbed to the top of the all-time points chart, surpassing Martin Schanche's 2957 total to pocket another record.

In Sweden, Hansen contested three rounds, won at Arvika and finished third in the standings. At the end of the year he came second to Irishman Christopher Evans in the season-closing Rallycross Superprix at Croft (Great Britain).

2006

A year prior to Citroen's official World Rally team introducing the new C4 onto the world's rally stages, Hansen Motorsport developed a rallycross version of the new French hatchback for its 2006 campaign.

And, just as with the Xsara and ZX before it, the car was immediately on the ultimate pace. Hansen attributes his squad's new car success to a methodical, conservative approach, choosing to carry over as many elements as possible from the predecessor into a new creation to ensure performance and reliability, before working on optimising the complete package. Clearly, it was a recipe for success.

Hansen won the 2006 season-opener with the new car at Lousada (Portugal) ahead of compatriot Lars Larsson, who would turn out to be Hansen's chief opponent. It was Larsson who won the second round at Mayenne (France), but Hansen ended the first half of the year on top, thanks to a string of podiums, including a titanic battle with Sverre Isachsen at Holjes (Sweden) where Hansen finished second. He also claimed victory at Greinbach (Austria), carving his way through the A final field to claim the spoils.

But, while Larsson notched up a pair of victories in the second half of the year, the best Hansen could manage was a second place finish to Michael Jernberg at Momarken (Norway) and at Estering (Germany), so Larsson claimed the crown. Hansen finished second, and was third in the Swedish Championship. He concluded the year with a victory in the Rallycross Superprix at Croft (Great Britain).

2007

Hansen Motorsport produced a second-evolution Citroen C4 for 2007, and while the Swede wouldn't win a round in the first half of the campaign, by employing the kind of consistency that had carried him to his record-breaking successes, he netted a string of podiums in the opening three rounds and was top of the order at the half way point of the season.

The second half of the year began in disaster. In torrential rain at Momarken (Norway), while battling for third in the A final, Hansen attempted to pass Lars Larsson's Skoda Fabia over the circuit's jump. The cars touched wheels and Hansen's C4 was sent into a heavy roll. Hansen was unhurt, but the same couldn't be said for the car, which was all-but destroyed. Hansen Motorsport's small team cancelled family holidays, and while Hansen admits to being apprehensive about climbing back into the repaired car [see chapter two], he finished fourth in the next round at Maasmechelen (Belgium).

A week later at Valkenswaard, he qualified on pole for the A final and crossed the finish line first to claim an emotional win and retake the points lead.

With second to Larsson in the penultimate round at Slomczyn (Poland) Hansen led the standings into the finale at Sosnova (Czech Republic). But, an engine failure in practice, crashes after contact in the first two qualifiers and a puncture in the third left him 18th and out of the finals for the first time since 1989.

Victory at home track Kinnekulle was the highlight of a selected Swedish Championship programme, while Hansen also claimed another Rallycross Superprix victory at Croft.

2008

The third season with the C4 started by getting pipped to the post in round one at Lousada (Portugal) by Ludvig Hunsbedt, but it didn't take long for Hansen to notch up a victory in 2008.

Having breezed to success at Nyirad (Hungary), the Swede didn't make it beyond the B final at Greinbach (Austria), but that would be one of only three occasions in the 11-round schedule that he wouldn't stand on the podium.

At Holjes, double World Rally Champion Marcus Gronholm made the first of three 2008 appearances and, come the last lap of the final, the Finn and Hansen met at the joker merge. It was Gronholm who claimed the win, Hansen more concerned about championship points than a risky fight for the victory.

A run of podiums ended in the penultimate round at Slomczyn (Poland) but fourth, ahead of closest challenger Hunsbedt was enough for Hansen to secure his 14th, and final, European crown.

In 2007 Hansen supplied a Citroen C4 to the Prime Minister of Tatarstan, Rustam Minnikhanov. The relationship continued into 2008 and Hansen was invited to take part in the annual President's Cup race near Kazan. Driving one of two Minnikhanov-owned C4s built in Gotene, Hansen claimed the win.

2009

For the first time in over a decade, FIA championship rallycross returned to Great Britain. The opening round of the European season took place at Lydden Hill, the venue at which the sport had been created by television producer Robert Reed in February 1967. It was fitting therefore that the sport's most successful driver, Kenneth Hansen, claimed victory. It would be his final top-flight success.

Although Finnish driver Jussi Pinomaki was run under a different banner, Hansen Motorsport fielded both his and Hansen's Citroen C4s for the European season. It also ran a third car for former Indy 500 winner Kenny Brack in the Swedish round at Holjes.

While Pinomaki joined Hansen in the majority of A finals in the first half of the season, including beating the Swede to a podium place at Nyirad (Hungary), his year was marred by a huge accident at Melk (Austria) [see chapter five]. It was also at Melk where Hansen scored his second podium of the campaign, but he would only make the rostrum on two further occasions, at Maasmechelen (Belgium) and Slomczyn (Poland). He concluded the year third in the standings behind Sverre Isachsen and Michael Jernberg. Incredibly, the result was Hansen's worst overall finish in the series in over 20 years.

The Swede was also again invited to the President's Cup event in Tatarstan. where he claimed victory.

2010

By now Hansen Motorsport was no stranger to running multiple cars in European Championship events, but 2010 was the first time the squad officially fielded a two-car effort under the same banner, with British driver Liam Doran joining the team for what would be Hansen's final full season at the wheel.

Hansen finished third in the season opener at Montalegre (Portugal), then scored a double podium for the squad by finishing second at Lydden Hill (Great Britain) with Doran third. He finished the first half of the campaign with rostrum appearances at Nyirad (Hungary) and Holjes (Sweden).

Hansen was denied victory at Kouvola (Finland) when he was hit by Sverre Isachsen while leading the A final, the Citroen slowed by the resulting puncture. The team won, however, as Isachsen stopped just short of the finish line and Doran claimed his first win [see chapters one and five].

The A final had to be restarted at Estering (Germany) after the first attempt at running the race had ended with a number of cars, including both Hansen machines, involved in a first corner incident. Hansen would eventually finish second, and ended the year with a pair of third place finishes at Slomczyn (Poland) and Sosnova (Czech Republic).

While Doran won again in Poland, Hansen's consistency meant it was the Swede that took the runner-up position in the points. Doran was third while Isachsen won the title. Taking a break from the European tour in August, Hansen also found time to compete in the President's Cup for the third year running, and again claimed victory.

2011

With his Hansen Motorsport concern having signed Liam Doran and Timur Timerzyanov for the 2011 European Championship, Hansen ended his full-time driving career by choice, while still in a position to challenge for titles.

He elected to instead focus on running the team, helping its young drivers and on the development of the new Citroen DS3, which brought the switch to a transversely-mounted engine.

Hansen tested the new car on Wednesday June 29 at the Lidkoping circuit near the team's Gotene base, ahead of the Swedish European Championship round at Holjes.

The car made its first public appearance at the Holjes press day less than 24 hours later, and Hansen returned to competition in the new car that weekend.

Maintaining the trend for new machinery produced in Gotene being successful from the outset, Hansen qualified for the B final and won the race to progress to the A final, in which he avoided drama, made a last corner overtake on Sverre Isachsen and finished second to Tanner Foust.

It was a similar story in the season finale in the Czech Republic, as Hansen used his wealth of experience to avoid trouble and again finish second, this time to Sverre Isachsen, and ahead of Foust. The Czech event, Hansen's 249th European Championship start remains his most recent, and possibly final, top class appearance as a driver.

2012

Using pressure from his local motor club, Gotene MK, to appear at his home event as a convenient excuse to climb aboard one of his team's Citroen DS3s – and wanting to get a feel for how the latest-specification cars performed so he could better help the squad's drivers, Hansen made a one-off return for the single-round Swedish Championship for Supercar at Kinnekulle in September.

Racing the car that Timur Timerzyanov drove to the European title that year; the first Supercar crown for the team with a driver other than its founder, Hansen was second quickest in Q1, qualified fourth for the final and finished third to join winner Peter Hedstrom and old rival Stig-Olov Walfridson on the podium.

To the end of 2019 that event remains Hansen's final competitive outing in a Supercar. As the years tick by it seems increasingly unlikely that Hansen will return for a serious effort, but in his own words, 'I'm not finished, just taking a break.'

Should he not race a Supercar again, it's fitting that in his final three outings, in Europe the previous year and also at the circuit closest to his home in 2012, he was each time on the podium.

2019

After a rallycross hiatus of almost seven years, punctuated by occasional test outings in his team's Supercars and a guest appearance in the Peugeot 208 Cup 10 hours of Magny-Cours circuit race in France (sharing a car with sons Timmy and Kevin in July 2017) Hansen returned to competitive action for a one-off guest appearance on the eve of the Swedish World Rallycross Championship round at Holjes; technically his 31st year of rallycross competition.

With his sons having set up the Yellow Squad by Hansen team to develop young drivers in the entry-level Cross Car category earlier in 2019, the team fielded a trio of machines in the Cross Car Star Challenge at Holjes.

While Team Hansen MJP World RX engineer Graham Rodemark and regular Yellow Squad driver Julius Ljungdahl raced Speedcar machines in the event, Hansen drove Yellow Squad's new FIA compliant TN5; a machine built by World Rally Championship star Thierry Neuville's Life Live company.

With an entry list that included old rivals Marcus Gronholm, Sverre Isachsen, Stig-Olov Walfridson and others, Hansen finished fifth in semi-final one and was classified ninth overall, before reverting to team boss mode for the weekend's World RX event, in which Kevin Hansen took the championship points lead by finishing second.

The man and his cars

Just as the liveries on Hansen's Citroens often only had subtle year-on-year differences, his own appearance has changed surprisingly little during his time in rallycross. He has weathered the trials and tribulations of entering the sport, competing at the highest level and running his own team over four decades.

Volvo. Ford. Citroen. Few drivers have competed in their chosen motor sport discipline for so long with such a small variety of machinery. And Hansen only raced Citroens for his 20 years in rallycross' top class. His three decades at the wheel and the cars he raced are illustrated here.

1983 Amazon B20

1984 Amazon B20

1985 Amazon B20

1986 Amazon B20

1987 Volvo 240 Turbo

1988 Volvo 240 Turbo

1989 Ford Sierra RS500 Cosworth

1990 Ford Sierra RS500 Cosworth

1991 Ford Sierra RS500 Cosworth

1992 Ford Sierra RS500 Cosworth

1993 Citroen ZX

1994 Citroen ZX

1995 Citroen ZX

1996 Citroen ZX

1997 Citroen ZX

1998 Citroen Xsara

1999 Citroen Xsara

2000 Citroen Xsara

2001 Citroen Xsara

2002 Citroen Xsara

2003 Citroen Xsara

2004 Citroen Xsara

2005 Citroen Xsara

2006 Citroen C4

2007 Citroen C4

2008 Citroen C4

2009 Citroen C4

2010 Citroen C4

2011 Citroen DS3

2012 Citroen DS3

The raw statistics of Hansen's incredible career are noted below. But, the next 14 pages document every retirement, podium, victory and success achieved by the Swede and his team.

10. RESULTS

1983 ....Result

Kenneth Hansen – Amazon B20

Tomelilla Trophy
SWE ....Tomelilla .... DNF

Swedish Rallycross Cup
SWE ....Norrkoping.. DNF
SWE ....Borlange .... DNF
SWE ....Haninge .... DNF
SWE ....Jonkoping...DNQ

West District Swedish Rallycross Championship
SWE ....Knutstorp..8
SWE ....Kinnekulle 11
SWE ....Tomelilla 8

1984 ....Result

Kenneth Hansen – Amazon B20

Swedish Rallycross Cup
SWE ....Tomelilla 8
SWE ....Jonkoping..40
SWE ....Bergby 12
SWE ....Vingaker...40
SWE ....Borlange .... DNF
SWE ....Hedemora 12

West District Swedish Rallycross Championship
SWE ....Kinnekulle 6
SWE ....Norrkoping... 11
SWE ....Sturup...30
SWE ....Holjes .... DNF
SWE ....Jonkoping... 11
SWE ....Knutstorp..12

Car Speedway
SWE ....Gotland 10
SWE ....Sturup...2

Falkopings MK Invitational Race
SWE ....Kinnekulle 2

Finnskoga International Race
SWE ....Holjes... DNF

1985 ....Result

Kenneth Hansen – Amazon B20

Swedish Rallycross Championship
SWE ....Knutstorp... 11
SWE ....Norrkoping...15
SWE ....Borlange .... DNF
SWE ....Umea 12
SWE ....Alvsbyn 26
SWE ....Haninge 31
SWE ....Hedemora 34
SWE ....Jonkoping...6

West District Swedish Rallycross Championship
SWE ....Sturup...43
SWE ....Jonkoping...4
SWE ....Kinnekulle 1
SWE ....Norrkoping..3
SWE ....Tomelilla 7

Car Speedway
SWE ....Goteborg..7

Swedish Hillclimb Championship
SWE ....Norrkoping..8

1986 ....Result

Kenneth Hansen – Amazon B20
Swedish Rallycross Championship – Champion
SWE ....Tomelilla 1
SWE ....Bergby.. 22
SWE ....Vannas 4
SWE ....Borlange 5
SWE ....Haninge 2

West District Swedish Rallycross Championship
SWE ....Sturup.. 2
SWE ....Kinnekulle 2
SWE ....Holjes.. 1
SWE ....Norrkoping... 2
SWE ....Tomelilla 4
SWE ....Jonkoping.. 6

Car Speedway
SWE ....Goteborg... 9
SWE ....Linkoping 4

Swedish Hillclimb Championship
SWE ....Goteborg... 1
SWE ....Uddevalla.. 1
SWE ....Bastad.. 2
SWE ....Roforsloppet 18
SWE ....Norrkoping... 2

Falkopings MK Anniversary Race
SWE ....Kinnekulle 1

Finnskoga International Race
SWE ....Holjes.. 11

1987 ....Result

Kenneth Hansen – Volvo 240 Turbo
Euro RX – fifth
AUT ....Melk 7
SWE ....Tomelilla 14
FIN ....Hameenlinna 3
ESP..........Sils-Girona 7
FRA ....Torcy-Le Creusot..................................DNQ
IRL...........Mondello Park... 7
BEL..........Arendonk 3
NLD.......Valkenswaard 5
NOR ......Lyngas 7
GBR ....Lydden Hill 2
DEU........Estering... 3

1988 ....Result

Kenneth Hansen – Volvo 240 Turbo
Euro RX – sixth
ESP..........Sils-Girona 9
AUT ....Horn-Fuglau 6
SWE ....Knutstorp... 7
FIN ....Hameenlinna 6
IRL...........Mondello Park... 11
FRA ....Loheac.. 3
BEL..........Maasmechelen... 3
NLD.......Valkenswaard 15
NOR ......Lyngas 6
GBR ....Lydden Hill 3
DEU........Estering... 4

Swedish Rallycross Championship – Champion
SWE ....Haninge 2
SWE ....Tomelilla 1
SWE ....Alvsbyn... 2
SWE ....Bergby.. 1
SWE ....Sturup... 1

From 1987 until 1992 Hansen raced in the FIA European Rallycross Championship in a class for two-wheel drive Group A touring cars referred to as 'Division One'.

In 1993 Hansen moved to what is regarded as the top class of the FIA European Rallycross Championship. Based on Group A, but permitted far greater modification including turbocharged engines and conversion to four-wheel drive, from 1993 until the end of 1996 this was referred to as 'Division Two' The FIA changed the class numbering for 1997 when this category became known as 'Division One'. The cars were widely referred to as 'Supercars' and for 2011 the FIA again changed the designation and officially name the class Supercar.

The 2011 move to descriptive names also meant that the class for 1600cc front-wheel drive Group A cars, changed from being known as 'Division One-A' to 'Super1600'.

1989 .... Result

Kenneth Hansen – Ford Sierra RS500 Cosworth

Euro RX – Champion

AUT ....Melk I
SWE ....Haninge 2
FIN ....Hameenlinna 17
IRL ....Mondello Park 2
FRA ....Luneville I
BEL ....Ingelmunster 2
NLD ....Valkenswaard 2
NOR ......Lyngas .... DSQ
GBR ....Lydden Hill 3
DEU ....Estering 6

Swedish Rallycross Championship – Champion

SWE ....Tomelilla 2
SWE ....Kinnekulle I
SWE ....Alvsbyn I
SWE ....Borlange I
SWE ....Bergby I

FIA Inter-Nations Cup for Rallycross

BEL ....Maasmechelen 2
(Hansen is a member of the six-driver Swedish team
which finishes second in this nation-on-nation event)

1990 .... Result

Kenneth Hansen – Ford Sierra RS500 Cosworth

Euro RX – Champion

AUT ....Horn-Fuglau 4
SWE ....Tomelilla 10
FIN ....Hameenlinna I
IRL ....Mondello Park I
FRA ....Paris-Trappes 6
BEL ....Arendonk 6
NLD ....Valkenswaard I
NOR ......Lyngas I
DEU ....Estering 4
GBR ....Lydden Hill 3

Swedish Rallycross Championship – Champion

SWE ....Kinnekulle I
SWE ....Holjes I
SWE ....Jokkmokk I
SWE ....Skelleftea 3
SWE ....Haninge I

Swedish Hillclimb Championship

SWE ....Ljusdal 3

Crosskart GP / HVA 500cc

SWE ....Kinnekulle I

FIA Inter-Nations Cup for Rallycross

GBR ....Croft 3
(Hansen is a member of the six-driver Swedish team
which finishes third in this nation-on-nation event)

Kenneth Hansen Motorsport
Susann Bergvall – Volvo 240
Swedish Ladies Rallycross Championship – fifth

SWE ....Kinnekulle 4
SWE ....Holjes 8
SWE ....Jokkmokk 4
SWE ....Skelleftea 7
SWE ....Haninge 4

1991 .... Result

Kenneth Hansen – Ford Sierra RS500 Cosworth

Euro RX – Champion

PRT ....Lousada I
AUT ....Melk 2
FIN ....Hameenlinna 2
FRA ....Nantes-Savenay I
IRL ....Mondello Park I
SWE ....Holjes I
BEL ....Maasmechelen I
NLD ....Valkenswaard I
NOR ......Lyngas I
GBR ....Lydden Hill 2
DEU ....Estering 6

Swedish Rallycross Championship – Champion

SWE ....Jonkoping 8
SWE ....Arvika 7
SWE ....Haninge I
SWE ....Pitea I
SWE ....Kinnekulle I

Norwegian Masters

NOR ....Tynset Motorsenter 2

Momarkedet

NOR ....Momarken Bilbane I

Kenneth Hansen Motorsport
Susann Bergvall – Volvo 240
Swedish Ladies Rallycross Championship – second

SWE ....Jonkoping 6
SWE ....Arvika I
SWE ....Haninge 3
SWE ....Pitea 7
SWE ....Kinnekulle 2

1992 ....Result
Kenneth Hansen – Ford Sierra RS500 Cosworth
Euro RX – Champion
GBR ....Lydden Hill 2
PRT ....Lousada 2
FIN..........Suonenjoki I
SWE ....Kinnekulle 3
FRA ....Bergerac-Faux 4
IRL...........Mondello Park.. I
BEL..........Ingelmunster 2
NLD........Valkenswaard 2
NOR ....Lyngas I
DEU ....Estering... 3

Swedish Rallycross Championship – Champion
SWE ....Haninge I
SWE ....Vannas I
SWE ....Alvsbyn I
SWE ....Hedemora I
SWE ....Tomelilla I

Champions Race
SWE ....Holjes.. I

Evening Race
SWE ....Strangnas 5

Finnish Rallycross Championship – Champion
FIN..........Pieksamaki I

Kenneth Hansen Motorsport
Susann Bergvall – Volvo 240
Swedish Ladies Rallycross Championship – fourth
SWE ....Vannas 2
SWE ....Alvsbyn 3
SWE ....Hedemora 7
SWE ....Tomelilla 2

1993 ....Result
Kenneth Hansen – Citroen ZX
Euro RX – second
AUT ....Horn-Fuglau I
PRT ....Lousada 2
FRA ....Loheac 6
IRL...........Mondello Park.. 4
SWE ....Holjes.. I
FIN..........Hameenlinna 6
BEL..........Arendonk... 2
NLD........Valkenswaard I
NOR ....Lyngas I
DEU ....Estering... 6

Swedish Rallycross Championship – Champion
SWE ....Tomelilla 2
SWE ....Jokkmokk.. 3
SWE ....Alvsbyn I
SWE ....Kinnekulle 2

FIA Inter-Nations Cup for Rallycross
DEU ....Nurburgring.. I
(Hansen is a member of the six-driver Swedish team
which wins this nation-on-nation event)

Kenneth Hansen Motorsport
Susann Bergvall – Ford Sierra RS500 Cosworth
Swedish Rallycross Championship Division One – sixth
SWE ....Tomelilla 3
SWE ....Jokkmokk.. 7
SWE ....Alvsbyn 6
SWE ....Kinnekulle 9

1994 ....Result
Kenneth Hansen – Citroen ZX
Euro RX – Champion
AUT ....Melk I
PRT ....Lousada I
FRA ....Essay 4
IRL...........Mondello Park.. 2
GBR ....Croft... 2
SWE ....Alvsbyn I
FIN..........Hameenlinna 2
BEL..........Maasmechelen... I
NLD........Valkenswaard 3
NOR ....Lyngas I
DEU ....Estering... 2

Swedish Rallycross Championship – Champion
SWE ....Tomelilla I
SWE ....Kinnekulle I
SWE ....Holjes.. I
SWE ....Arvika 2

Norwegian Champions Race
NOR ....Dokka... 2

Swedish Champions Race
SWE ....Strangnas I

British Rallycross Grand Prix
GBR ....Brands Hatch I

Swedish Hillclimb Championship
SWE ....Ratten... I

Kenneth Hansen Motorsport
Susann Bergvall – Citroen AX Sport
ERA 1400 Cup – Champion
AUT ....Melk I0
PRT ....Lousada I
FRA ....Essay 3
IRL...........Mondello Park.. 2
GBR ....Croft... 9
SWE ....Alvsbyn 8
FIN..........Hameenlinna 6
BEL..........Maasmechelen... I2
NLD........Valkenswaard 8
NOR ....Lyngas I
DEU ....Estering... I

Swedish Cup – Champion
SWE ....Tomelilla 5
SWE ....Arvika I
SWE ....Kinnekulle I
SWE ....Holjes.. 2

1995 .... Result

Kenneth Hansen – Citroen ZX
Euro RX – second
AUT ....Horn-Fuglau 3
PRT ....Lousada 2
FRA ....Faleyras 3
SWE ....Arvika 1
GBR ....Brands Hatch 1
IRL..........Mondello Park 1
BEL.........Ingelmunster 2
NLD........Valkenswaard 2
NOR ......Lyngas 5
FIN..........Hameenlinna 4
CZE ....Sosnova 6
DEU.......Estering 1

Swedish Rallycross Championship – second
SWE ....Tomelilla 3
SWE ....Holjes 1
SWE ....Alvsbyn 3
SWE ....Hedemora 1
SWE ....Kinnekulle 4

British Rallycross Grand Prix (Euro RX event)
GBR ....Brands Hatch 1

Swedish Champions Race
SWE ....Strangnas 3

Swedish Hillclimb Championship
SWE ....Ratten 2

Kenneth Hansen Motorsport
Susann Bergvall – Citroen AX Sport
Euro RX 1400 Cup – fifth
AUT ....Horn-Fuglau .... DNQ
PRT ....Lousada 7
FRA ....Faleyras... DNQ
SWE ....Arvika 2
GBR ....Brands Hatch 5
IRL..........Mondello Park 2
BEL.........Ingelmunster 14
NLD........Valkenswaard .... DNQ
NOR ......Lyngas 7
FIN..........Hameenlinna 4
CZE ....Sosnova... DNQ
DEU.......Estering.. 11

Swedish Rallycross Championship Div. Three – second
SWE ....Tomelilla 2
SWE ....Holjes 4
SWE ....Alvsbyn 2
SWE ....Hedemora 2
SWE ....Kinnekulle 7

1996 .... Result

Kenneth Hansen – Citroen ZX
Euro RX – Champion
AUT ....Melk 3
PRT ....Lousada 6
FRA ....Mayenne 2
SWE ....Kinnekulle 2
IRL..........Mondello Park 3
GBR ....Lydden Hill 1
BEL.........Maasmechelen 1
NLD.......Valkenswaard 2
NOR ......Lyngas 2
CZE ....Sosnova 2
DEU ....Estering 1

Swedish Rallycross Championship – second
SWE ....Tomelilla 5
SWE ....Holjes 6
SWE ....Alvsbyn 1
SWE ....Strangnas 1
SWE ....Arvika 2

British Rallycross Grand Prix (Euro RX event)
GBR ....Lydden Hill 1

1997 .... Result

Kenneth Hansen – Citroen ZX
Euro RX – second
AUT ....Horn-Fuglau 4
FRA ....Luneville 4
PRT ....Lousada 2
GBR ....Pembrey 4
SWE ....Holjes 2
FIN..........Hameenlinna 2
BEL..........Maasmechelen 1
NOR ......Lyngas 2
CZE ....Sosnova.. 5
DEU.......Estering... 6

Swedish Rallycross Championship – eighth
SWE ....Alvsbyn 2
SWE ....Kinnekulle 4

Shell Helix Cup – fourth
SWE ....Kinnekulle 3
SWE ....Arvika 6
SWE ....Holjes 6

Euro Rallycross Masters
NLD........Valkenswaard 1

1998 .... Result

Kenneth Hansen – Citroen Xsara
Euro RX – Champion
AUT ....Melk I
PRT ....Lousada 2
FRA ....Essay 5
SWE ....Arvika 6
GBR ....Pembrey 2
FIN ....Hameenlinna 2
BEL ....Maasmechelen I
NOR ....Lyngas I
DEU ....Estering 2
CZE ....Sosnova 2

Swedish Rallycross Championship – fourth
SWE ....Tomelilla 2
SWE ....Holjes 4
SWE ....Pitea 5
SWE ....Alvsbyn 5
SWE ....Kinnekulle 2

Invitational race
SWE ....Goteborg, Heden 2

1999 .... Result

Kenneth Hansen – Citroen Xsara
Euro RX – second
CZE ....Sedlcany 4
FRA ....Faleyras 2
PRT ....Lousada I
SWE ....Holjes 10
FIN ....Hameenlinna 5
BEL ....Maasmechelen I
NLD ....Valkenswaard 3
NOR ....Lyngas 6
DEU ....Estering I

Swedish Rallycross Championship – Champion
SWE ....Tomelilla 4
SWE ....Hyllinge I
SWE ....Strangnas I
SWE ....Haninge I
SWE ....Kinnekulle 2

2000 .... Result

Kenneth Hansen – Citroen Xsara
Euro RX – Champion
PRT ....Lousada 6
FRA ....Essay I
CZE ....Sosnova 2
SWE ....Holjes I
BEL ....Maasmechelen 6
NLD ....Valkenswaard I
NOR ....Lyngas 2
POL ....Slomczyn 2
DEU ....Estering I

Swedish Rallycross Championship – third
SWE ....Tomelilla 2
SWE ....Strangnas 6
SWE ....Arvika 6
SWE ....Kinnekulle 2

French Rallycross Championship – 11th
FRA ....Luneville I
FRA ....Abbeville 2
FRA ....Dreux 3

2001 .... Result
Kenneth Hansen – Citroen Xsara
Euro RX – Champion
FRA ....Loheac... I
PRT ....Lousada... I
AUT ....Melk.. I
CZE ....Sosnova... 5
SWE ....Holjes.. I
BEL.........Maasmechelen...................................... 3
NLD.......Valkenswaard.. 4
NOR ......Lyngas... I
POL........Slomczyn...12
DEU........Estering... 2

French Rallycross Championship – second
FRA ....Essay.. 2
FRA ....Faleyras... 2
FRA ....Luneville... 3
FRA ....Bergerac-Faux...................................... I
FRA ....Lavare... I
FRA ....Kerlabo... 3

Swedish Rallycross Championship – third
SWE ....Strangnas... 6
SWE ....Arvika.. 3
NOR.......Flisa.. I
SWE ....Kinnekulle.. 4

Swedish Hillclimb Championship
SWE ....Jarbo... 2
NOR.......Lillehammer.. 2

2002 .... Result
Kenneth Hansen – Citroen Xsara
Euro RX – Champion
PRT ....Lousada... I
FRA ....Faleyras... I
AUT ....Greinbach... 2
CZE ....Sosnova... I
SWE ....Holjes.. I
BEL.........Maasmechelen...................................... 3
NLD.......Valkenswaard.. 2
NOR ......Lyngas... I
POL........Slomczyn.. I
DEU........Estering... 5

Swedish Rallycross Championship – Champion
SWE ....Arvika.. I
SWE ....Kalix.. I
SWE ....Jarbo (Hillclimb) I
SWE ....Kinnekulle.. I

British Rallycross Grand Prix
GBR ....Croft.. 8

2003 .... Result
Kenneth Hansen – Citroen Xsara
Euro RX – Champion
PRT ....Lousada... I
FRA ....Essay.. 2
AUT ....Greinbach... I
CZE ....Sedlcany.. 6
SWE ....Holjes.. I
BEL.........Maasmechelen...................................... I
NLD.......Valkenswaard.. I
NOR ......Lyngas... 2
POL........Slomczyn.. 8
DEU........Estering... I

Swedish Rallycross Championship – second
SWE ....Tomelilla.. 4
SWE ....Kalix.. I
SWE ....Strangnas... 4
SWE ....Kinnekulle.. I

2004 .... Result
Kenneth Hansen – Citroen Xsara
Euro RX – Champion
PRT ....Lousada 3
FRA ....Essay 6
CZE ....Sosnova 2
AUT ....Melk 1
NOR ....Lyngas 1
SWE ....Holjes 2
BEL..........Maasmechelen 1
NLD.........Valkenswaard 3
POL.........Slomczyn 6
DEU........Estering.. 1

Swedish Rallycross Championship – fourth
SWE ....Tomelilla .... DNQ
SWE ....Kalix 5
SWE ....Strangnas 1
SWE ....Kinnekulle 4

Kenneth Hansen Motorsport
Stig-Olov Walfridson Citroen Xsara T16
Euro RX – 13th
NOR ....Lyngas 2
SWE ....Holjes 8

Swedish Rallycross Championship – seventh
SWE ....Tomelilla 3
SWE ....Kalix 6
SWE ....Strangnas 11
SWE ....Kinnekulle 7

2005 .... Result
Kenneth Hansen – Citroen Xsara
Euro RX – Champion
FRA ....Essay 1
PRT ....Lousada 1
AUT ....Greinbach 1
CZE ....Sosnova 10
NOR ....Momarken 2
SWE ....Holjes 6
BEL..........Maasmechelen 3
NLD.........Valkenswaard 3
POL.........Slomczyn 3
DEU........Estering.. 2

Swedish Rallycross Championship – third
SWE ....Arvika 1
SWE ....Kalix 3
SWE ....Kinnekulle 2

Rallycross Superprix
GBR ....Croft... 2

2006 .... Result
Kenneth Hansen – Citroen C4
Euro RX – second
PRT ....Lousada 1
FRA ....Mayenne 3
CZE ....Sosnova 3
AUT ....Greinbach 1
SWE ....Holjes 2
HUN ....Nyirad 5
BEL..........Maasmechelen 4
NLD.........Valkenswaard 6
NOR ....Momarken 2
POL.........Slomczyn 6
DEU........Estering.. 7

Swedish Rallycross Championship – third
SWE ....Arvika 3
SWE ....Holjes 2
NOR ....Momarken 2
SWE ....Kinnekulle 4

Rallycross Superprix
GBR ....Croft... 1

2007 .... Result

Kenneth Hansen – Citroen C4
Euro RX – second
PRT ....Montalegre 3
FRA ....Essay 2
HUN.......Nyirad 2
AUT ....Greinbach.. 7
SWE ....Holjes 4
NOR ......Momarken... 5
BEL..........Maasmechelen... 4
NLD.......Valkenswaard 1
POL.........Slomczyn 2
CZE ....Sosnova 18

Swedish Rallycross Championship – fifth
SWE ....Holjes 4
NOR ......Momarken... 5
SWE ....Kinnekulle 1

Rallycross Superprix
GBR ....Croft... 1

Hansen Motorsport
Rustam Minnikhanov – Citroen C4
Euro RX – 21st
PRT ....Montalegre 13
FRA ....Essay .... DNQ
HUN.......Nyirad 15
AUT ....Greinbach.. DNQ
SWE ....Holjes .... DNQ
NOR ......Momarken... DNQ
BEL..........Maasmechelen..................................... DNQ
NLD.......Valkenswaard .... DNQ
POL.........Slomczyn 15
CZE ....Sosnova 11

2008 .... Result

Kenneth Hansen – Citroen C4
Euro RX – Champion
PRT ....Lousada 2
FRA ....Kerlabo 3
HUN.......Nyirad 1
AUT ....Greinbach.. 8
NOR ......Momarken... 2
SWE ....Holjes 2
BEL..........Maasmechelen... 3
NLD.......Valkenswaard 2
CZE ....Sosnova 1
POL.........Slomczyn 4
DEU........Estering.. 7

President's Cup
RUS.........Kazan... 1

Hansen Motorsport
Rustam Minnikhanov – Citroen C4
Euro RX – 31st
PRT ....Lousada .... DNQ
FRA ....Kerlabo .... DNQ
AUT ....Greinbach... 15
SWE ....Holjes .... DNQ
BEL..........Maasmechelen..................................... DNQ
NLD.......Valkenswaard .... DNQ
CZE ....Sosnova .... DNQ
DEU........Estering.. 15

Johan Larsson – Citroen Saxo
Euro RX Divison One-A – 17th
DEU........Estering.. 4

continued
Kenneth Hansen Racing
Linus Ohlsson – Citroen C2
Junior Touring Car Championship – 14th
SWE ....Knutstorp R1 19
SWE ....Knutstorp R2 12
SWE ....Sturup R1 16
SWE ....Sturup R2 .... 22 (DNF)
SWE ....Karlskoga R1 11
SWE ....Karlskoga R2 9
SWE ....Goteborg R1 7
SWE ....Goteborg R2 .... 20 (DNF)
SWE ....Sturup R1 12
SWE ....Sturup R2 14
SWE ....Falkenberg R1 14
SWE ....Falkenberg R2 10
SWE ....Knutstorp R1 .... 21 (DNF)
SWE ....Knutstorp R2 12
NOR ......Valerbanen R1 7
NOR ......Valerbanen R2 3
SWE ....Mantorp Park R1 8
SWE ....Mantorp Park R2.......................... 24 (DNF)

Eric Larsson (Faren) – Citroen C2
Junior Touring Car Championship – 17th
SWE ....Knutstorp R1 14
SWE ....Knutstorp R2 10
SWE ....Sturup R1 13
SWE ....Sturup R2 12
SWE ....Karlskoga R1 14
SWE ....Karlskoga R2 8
SWE ....Goteborg R1 13
SWE ....Goteborg R2 14
SWE ....Sturup R1 13
SWE ....Sturup R2 15
SWE ....Falkenberg R1 9
SWE ....Falkenberg R2 .... 17 (DNF)
SWE ....Knutstorp R1 17
SWE ....Knutstorp R2 14
NOR ......Valerbanen R1 .... 23 (DNF)
NOR ......Valerbanen R2 15
SWE ....Mantorp Park R1 .... 23 (DNF)
SWE ....Mantorp Park R2.......................... 25 (DNF)

2009 ....Result

Kenneth Hansen – Citroen C4
Euro RX   third
GBR ....Lydden Hill 1
PRT ....Montalegre 5
FRA ....Essay 5
HUN.......Nyirad 4
AUT ....Melk 2
SWE ....Holjes 5
BEL..........Maasmechelen 3
DEU........Estering.. 11
POL.........Slomczyn 3
CZE ....Sosnova... 11

Swedish Rallycross Championship – eighth
SWE ....Holjes 2

President's Cup
RUS........Kazan.. 1

Hansen Motorsport
Jussi Pinomaki – Citroen C4
Euro RX – ninth
GBR ....Lydden Hill 4
PRT ....Montalegre 9
FRA ....Essay 4
HUN.......Nyirad 3
AUT ....Melk .... DNQ
SWE ....Holjes 16
BEL..........Maasmechelen 9
DEU........Estering... DNQ
POL.........Slomczyn 9
CZE ....Sosnova... 19

Rustam Minnikhanov – Citroen C4
Euro RX – unclassified
FRA ....Essay .... DNQ
HUN.......Nyirad .... DNQ
AUT ....Melk .... DNQ
BEL..........Maasmechelen .... DNQ
DEU........Estering... DNQ
CZE ....Sosnova.. DNQ

Kenny Brack – Citroen C4
Euro RX – 27th
SWE ....Holjes 10

Swedish Rallycross Championship – 11th
SWE ....Holjes 4

Evan Hvaal – Citroen C4
Euro RX – 32nd
POL.........Slomczyn 13
CZE ....Sosnova.. DNQ

continued
Johan Larsson – Citroen Saxo
Euro RX Divison One-A – fifth
GBR ....Lydden Hill 7
PRT ....Montalegre 8
FRA ....Essay 5
HUN.......Nyirad 5
AUT ....Melk .... DNQ
SWE ....Holjes 5
BEL..........Maasmechelen 9
DEU........Estering.. 2
POL.........Slomczyn 5
CZE ....Sosnova... 7

Swedish Rallycross Championship – Champion
SWE ....Kinnekulle 1

Kenneth Hansen Racing
Eric Larsson (Faren) – Citroen C2
Junior Touring Car Championship – 15th
SWE ....Mantorp Park R1 12
SWE ....Mantorp Park R2 13
SWE ....Karlskoga R1 6
SWE ....Karlskoga R2 12
SWE ....Goteborg R1 .... 20 (DNF)
SWE ....Goteborg R2 .... 19 (DNF)
SWE ....Falkenberg R1 13
SWE ....Falkenberg R2 10

Linus Ohlsson – Citroen C2
Junior Touring Car Championship – Champion
SWE ....Mantorp Park R1 .... 16 (DNF)
SWE ....Mantorp Park R2 8
SWE ....Karlskoga R1 9
SWE ....Karlskoga R2 10
SWE ....Goteborg R1 1
SWE ....Goteborg R2 1
SWE ....Knutstorp R1 2
SWE ....Knutstorp R2 10
SWE ....Falkenberg R1 2
SWE ....Falkenberg R2 6
SWE ....Karlskoga R1 7
SWE ....Karlskoga R2 8
SWE ....Knutstorp R1 2
SWE ....Knutstorp R2 3
SWE ....Mantorp Park R1 3
SWE ....Mantorp Park R2 3

2010 ....Result

Kenneth Hansen – Citroen C4
Euro RX – second
PRT ....Montalegre 3
FRA ....Kerlabo 6
GBR ....Lydden Hill 2
HUN.......Nyirad 3
SWE ....Holjes 2
FIN.....   .Kouvola 4
BEL..........Maasmechelen 7
DEU........Estering.. 2
POL.........Slomczyn 3
CZE ....Sosnova... 3

President's Cup
RUS........Kazan.. 1

Kenneth Hansen Racing
Liam Doran – Citroen C4
Euro RX – third
PRT ....Montalegre 4
FRA ....Kerlabo 3
GBR ....Lydden Hill 3
HUN.......Nyirad 7
SWE ....Holjes 7
FIN..........Kouvola 1
BEL..........Maasmechelen 2
DEU........Estering.. 6
POL.........Slomczyn 1
CZE ....Sosnova... 6

British Rallycross Championship – unclassified
GBR ....Lydden Hill 1

RallyCar US Rallycross Championship – fourth
USA........New Jersey 3
USA........New Jersey 8
USA........New Jersey 3

Johan Larsson – Citroen C2
Euro RX Divison One-A – sixth
PRT ....Montalegre 12
FRA ....Kerlabo 15
GBR ....Lydden Hill 7
HUN.......Nyirad 3
SWE ....Holjes 6
FIN..........Kouvola 7
BEL..........Maasmechelen 2
DEU........Estering.. 11
POL.........Slomczyn 6
CZE ....Sosnova... 5

Swedish Rallycross Championship – second
SWE ....Holjes 1
FIN..........Kouvola 1

Mats Lysen – Citroen C4 T16
Norwegian Rallycross Championship
NOR.......Lyngas 5

Eric Larsson (Faren) – Citroen C2
Norwegian Rallycross Championship Division One-A
NOR.......Lyngas 3

2011 .... Result

Namus Hansen Motorsport
Timur Timerzyanov – Citroen C4
Euro RX – third

GBR	Lydden Hill	5
PRT	Montalegre	3
FRA	Essay	5
NOR	Hell	3
SWE	Holjes	15
BEL	Maasmechelen	1
NLD	Valkenswaard	11
AUT	Greinbach	2
POL	Slomczyn	7
CZE	Sosnova	4

Doran Motorsport
Liam Doran – Citroen C4
Euro RX – seventh

GBR	Lydden Hill	4
PRT	Montalegre	5
FRA	Essay	3
NOR	Hell	9
SWE	Holjes	10
BEL	Maasmechelen	3
NLD	Valkenswaard	15
AUT	Greinbach	9
POL	Slomczyn	11
CZE	Sosnova	11

British Rallycross Championship – unclassified
GBR ....Lydden Hill 8

X Games 17
USA.........Los Angeles – Rally 1
USA.........Los Angeles – Rallycross.............. 8

Hansen Motorsport
Johan Larsson – Citroen C2
Euro RX Super1600 – 4th

GBR	Lydden Hill	10
PRT	Montalegre	4
FRA	Essay	14
NOR	Hell	6
SWE	Holjes	4
BEL	Maasmechelen	8
NLD	Valkenswaard	9
AUT	Greinbach	7
POL	Slomczyn	4
CZE	Sosnova	7

Kenneth Hansen – Citroen DS3
Euro RX – 15th

SWE	Holjes	2
CZE	Sosnova	2

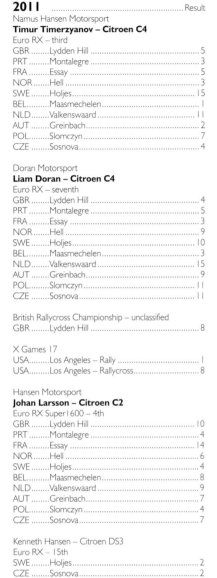

2012 .... Result

Namus Hansen Motorsport
Timur Timerzyanov – Citroen DS3
Euro RX – Champion

FRA	Dreux	4
AUT	Greinbach	1
HUN	Nyirad	1
NOR	Hell	3
SWE	Holjes	1
BEL	Maasmechelen	1
NLD	Valkenswaard	1
FIN	Kouvola	1
DEU	Estering	14

Citroen Hansen Motorsport
Alexander Hvaal – Citroen C4
Euro RX – seventh

GBR	Lydden Hill	DNQ
FRA	Dreux	2
AUT	Greinbach	2
HUN	Nyirad	4
NOR	Hell	6
SWE	Holjes	3
BEL	Maasmechelen	19
NLD	Valkenswaard	8
DEU	Estering	DNQ

Timmy Hansen – Citroen DS3
Euro RX – 24th
FIN ....Kouvola 5

Eric Faren – Citroen C2
Euro RX Super1600 – seventh

GBR	Lydden Hill	12
FRA	Dreux	33
AUT	Greinbach	10
HUN	Nyirad	4
NOR	Hell	10
SWE	Holjes	4
BEL	Maasmechelen	17
NLD	Valkenswaard	13
FIN	Kouvola	4
DEU	Estering	12

Swedish Rallycross Championship
SWE ....Kinnekulle 1

continued
Hansen Junior Team
Ada-Marie Hvaal – JRX 'Citroen DS3'
JRX Cup – third

SWE	Holjes	2
BEL	Maasmechelen	4
NLD	Valkenswaard	2

Kevin Hansen – JRX 'Citroen DS3'
JRX Cup – Champion

SWE	Holjes	1
BEL	Maasmechelen	2
NLD	Valkenswaard	3
SWE	Kinnekulle	1
FIN	Kouvola	1
DEU	Estering	1

Hansen Motorsport
Johan Larsson – Citroen DS3
Swedish Rallycross Championship
SWE ....Kinnekulle 5

Sebastian Loeb – Citroen DS3
X Games (GRC – 17th)
USA.........Los Angeles.............................. 1

Kenneth Hansen – Citroen DS3
Swedish Rallycross Championship
SWE ....Kinnekulle 3

2013 .... Result

Namus Hansen Motorsport
TImur Timerzyanov – Citroen DS3
Euro RX – Champion
GBR ....Lydden Hill 5
PRT ....Montalegre 6
HUN.......Nyirad 2
FIN..........Kouvola 2
NOR.......Hell 2
SWE ....Holjes 11
FRA ....Loheac 4
AUT ....Greinbach... 2
DEU........Estering... 4

Citroen Hansen Motorsport
Timmy Hansen – Citroen DS3
Euro RX – third
GBR ....Lydden Hill 3
PRT ....Montalegre 11
HUN.......Nyirad 1
FIN..........Kouvola 3
NOR.......Hell 9
SWE ....Holjes 3
FRA ....Loheac 8
AUT ....Greinbach... 10
DEU........Estering... 13

Alexander Hvaal – Citroen DS3
Euro RX – sixth
GBR ....Lydden Hill 8
PRT ....Montalegre 4
HUN.......Nyirad 6
FIN..........Kouvola 12
NOR.......Hell 4
SWE ....Holjes 7
FRA ....Loheac 10
AUT ....Greinbach... 1
DEU........Estering... 1

Eric Faren – Citroen C2
Euro RX Super1600 – fourth
GBR ....Lydden Hill 3
PRT ....Montalegre 2
HUN.......Nyirad 7
FIN..........Kouvola 3
NOR.......Hell 5
SWE ....Holjes 4
FRA ....Loheac 5
AUT ....Greinbach... 5
DEU........Estering... 5

continued
Hansen Junior Team
Kevin Hansen – JRX 'Citroen DS3'
JRX Cup – Champion
HUN.......Nyirad 3
FIN..........Kouvola 3
NOR.......Hell 2
SWE ....Holjes 1
AUT ....Greinbach... 1
DEU........Estering... 1

Swedish JRX Championship
SWE ....Kinnekulle.. 1

2014 .... Result

Team Peugeot-Hansen
World RX Teams' Championship............................... 3

Timmy Hansen – Peugeot 208
World RX – fourth
PRT ....Montalegre 8
GBR ....Lydden Hill 7
NOR.......Hell 6
FIN..........Kouvola 9
SWE ....Holjes 11
BEL.........Mettet 2
CAN.......Trois-Rivieres 7
FRA ....Loheac 3
DEU........Estering... 6
ITA ....Franciacorta 1
TUR ....Istanbul Park... 2
ARG ....San Luis 4

Timur Timerzyanov – Peugeot 208
World RX – seventh
PRT ....Montalegre 7
GBR ....Lydden Hill 29
NOR.......Hell 4
FIN..........Kouvola 11
SWE ....Holjes 7
BEL.........Mettet 7
CAN.......Trois-Rivieres 3
FRA ....Loheac 6
DEU........Estering... 7
ITA ....Franciacorta 4
TUR ....Istanbul Park... 8
ARG ....San Luis 8

Hansen Junior Team
Kevin Hansen – Supercar Lites
RX Lites Cup – second
FIN..........Kouvola 1
SWE ....Holjes 2
ITA ....Franciacorta 3
TUR ....Istanbul Park... 2

GRC Supercar Lites – ninth
USA.........Los Angeles... 3
USA.........Los Angeles... 6

RallyX Nordic Supercar Lites – Champion
SWE ....Knutstorp.. 2
SWE ....Arvika 1
SWE ....Strangnas 2
SWE ....Knutstorp.. 1
SWE ....Solvalla.. 3

2015 .... Result

Team Peugeot-Hansen
World RX Teams' Championship................................ 1

Timmy Hansen – Peugeot 208
World RX – second
PRT ....Montalegre 3
DEU........Hockenheim 3
BEL.........Mettet 8
GBR ....Lydden Hill 8
DEU........Estering... 3
SWE ....Holjes.. 2
CAN........Trois-Rivieres 7
NOR.......Hell 1
FRA ....Loheac.. 1
ESP ....Catalunya-Barcelona 3
TUR ....Istanbul Park.. 1
ITA ....Franciacorta 7
ARG ....Rosario 6

Davy Jeanney – Peugeot 208
World RX – fifth
PRT ....Montalegre 5
DEU........Hockenheim 10
BEL.........Mettet 9
GBR ....Lydden Hill 11
DEU........Estering... 1
SWE ....Holjes.. 12
CAN........Trois-Rivieres 1
NOR.......Hell 2
FRA ....Loheac.. 11
ESP ....Catalunya-Barcelona 4
TUR ....Istanbul Park.. 5
ITA ....Franciacorta 10
ARG ....Rosario 8

Andrew Jordan – Peugeot 208
World RX – 24th
GBR ....Lydden Hill 7

Hansen Talent Development
Eric Faren – Peugeot 208
World RX – 26th
SWE ....Holjes.. 10

RallyX Nordic – second
SWE ....Skovde 4
SWE ....Strangnas 6
SWE ....Kalix... 2
SWE ....Arvika 2
SWE ....Solvalla.. 1

Janis Baumanis – Peugeot 208
World RX – 40th
GBR ....Lydden Hill 20
TUR ....Istanbul Park.. 17

Euro RX – 14th
NOR.......Hell 3

Tamas Pal Kiss – Peugeot 208
Euro RX – 18th
ITA ....Franciacorta 6

continued
Fredrik Salsten – Peugeot 208
Euro RX – 20th
ESP ....Catalunya-Barcelona 7

Hansen Junior Team
Kevin Hansen – Supercar Lites
RX Lites Cup – Champion
PRT ....Montalegre 2
GBR ....Lydden Hill 1
SWE ....Holjes.. 2
NOR.......Hell 2
ESP ....Catalunya-Barcelona 2
TUR ....Istanbul Park.. 2
ITA ....Franciacorta 2

RallyX Nordic Supercar Lites – second
SWE ....Skovde 6
SWE ....Strangnas 7
SWE ....Kalix... 1
SWE ....Arvika 4
SWE ....Solvalla.. 7

2016 .... Result

Team Peugeot-Hansen
World RX Teams' Championship................................ 2

Sebastien Loeb – Peugeot 208
World RX – fifth
PRT ....Montalegre 5
DEU........Hockenheim 10
BEL.........Mettet 2
GBR ....Lydden Hill 10
NOR.......Hell 5
SWE ....Holjes.. 2
CAN........Trois-Rivieres 9
FRA ....Loheac.. 3
ESP ....Catalunya-Barcelona 8
LVA.........Riga 1
DEU........Estering... 8
ARG ....Rosario 8

Timmy Hansen – Peugeot 208
World RX – sixth
PRT ....Montalegre 9
DEU........Hockenheim 18
BEL.........Mettet 7
GBR ....Lydden Hill 3
NOR.......Hell 2
SWE ....Holjes.. 3
CAN........Trois-Rivieres 1
FRA ....Loheac.. 8
ESP ....Catalunya-Barcelona 2
LVA.........Riga 3
DEU........Estering... 11
ARG ....Rosario 13

Peugeot-Hansen Academy
Davy Jeanney – Peugeot 208
World RX – 12th
PRT ....Montalegre 11
DEU........Hockenheim 9
BEL.........Mettet 11
GBR ....Lydden Hill 13
NOR.......Hell 11
SWE ....Holjes.. 12
FRA ....Loheac.. 9
ESP ....Catalunya-Barcelona 12
LVA.........Riga 10
DEU........Estering... 10

Kevin Hansen – Peugeot 208
World RX – 15th
PRT ....Montalegre 13
DEU........Hockenheim 19
GBR ....Lydden Hill 4
FRA ....Loheac.. 11
DEU........Estering... 4

Euro RX – Champion
BEL.........Mettet 1
NOR.......Hell 1
SWE ....Holjes.. 1
ESP ....Catalunya-Barcelona 1
LVA.........Riga 2

HTD Salsten Racing
Fredrik Salsten – Peugeot 208
Euro RX – sixth
BEL.........Mettet 13
NOR.......Hell 6
SWE ....Holjes.. 2
ESP ....Catalunya-Barcelona 6
LVA.........Riga 8

2017 .... Result
Team Peugeot-Hansen
World RX Teams' Championship.................................. 2

Sebastien Loeb – Peugeot 208
World RX – fourth
ESP..........Catalunya-Barcelona 14
PRT ....Montalegre 2
DEU.........Hockenheim 5
BEL..........Mettet 7
GBR ....Lydden Hill 4
NOR.........Hell 3
SWE ....Holjes 3
CAN..........Trois-Rivieres 3
FRA ....Loheac 2
LVA..........Riga 3
DEU..........Estering.. 11
ZAF ....Killarney 10

Timmy Hansen – Peugeot 208
World RX – fifth
ESP..........Catalunya-Barcelona 5
PRT ....Montalegre 4
DEU.........Hockenheim 3
BEL..........Mettet 2
GBR ....Lydden Hill 6
NOR.........Hell 5
SWE ....Holjes 4
CAN..........Trois-Rivieres 6
FRA ....Loheac 6
LVA..........Riga 9
DEU..........Estering.. 2
ZAF ....Killarney 2

Kevin Hansen – Peugeot 208
World RX – eighth
ESP..........Catalunya-Barcelona 11
PRT ....Montalegre 8
DEU.........Hockenheim 8
BEL..........Mettet 21
GBR ....Lydden Hill 13
NOR.........Hell 9
SWE ....Holjes 13
CAN..........Trois-Rivieres 10
FRA ....Loheac 8
LVA..........Riga 10
DEU..........Estering.. 6
ZAF ....Killarney 6

2018 .... Result
Team Peugeot Total
World RX Teams' Championship.................................. 3

Sebastien Loeb – Peugeot 208
World RX – fourth
ESP..........Catalunya-Barcelona 2
PRT ....Montalegre 2
BEL..........Mettet 1
GBR ....Silverstone 3
NOR.........Hell 8
SWE ....Holjes 9
CAN..........Trois-Rivieres 3
FRA ....Loheac 6
LVA..........Riga 3
USA..........Circuit Of The Americas............................ 4
DEU..........Estering.. 8
ZAF ....Killarney 3

Timmy Hansen – Peugeot 208
World RX – sixth
ESP..........Catalunya-Barcelona 7
PRT ....Montalegre 4
BEL..........Mettet 3
GBR ....Silverstone 8
NOR.........Hell 5
SWE ....Holjes 4
CAN..........Trois-Rivieres 2
FRA ....Loheac 5
LVA..........Riga 5
USA..........Circuit Of The Americas............................ 6
DEU..........Estering.. 7
ZAF ....Killarney 6

Nitro Rallycross – Champion
USA..........Utah Motorsports Park............................. 1

Kevin Hansen – Peugeot 208
World RX – eighth
ESP..........Catalunya-Barcelona 13
PRT ....Montalegre 8
BEL..........Mettet 9
GBR ....Silverstone 6
NOR.........Hell 4
SWE ....Holjes 5
CAN..........Trois-Rivieres 9
FRA ....Loheac 7
LVA..........Riga 6
USA..........Circuit Of The Americas............................ 7
DEU..........Estering.. 6
ZAF ....Killarney 4

2019 .... Result
Team Hansen MJP
World RX Teams' Championship.................................. 1

Timmy Hansen – Peugeot 208
World RX – Champion
UAE.........Yas Marina 11
ESP..........Catalunya-Barcelona 1
BEL..........Spa 4
GBR ....Silverstone 1
NOR.........Hell 6
SWE ....Holjes 6
CAN..........Trois-Rivieres 13
FRA ....Loheac 1
LVA..........Riga 1
ZAF ....Killarney 4

Nitro World Games Rallycross – third
USA..........Utah Motorsports Campus......................... 3

Team Hansen – Pantera RX6
Titans RX Europe – second
FRA ....Essay 7
FRA ....Essay 1
GBR ....Lydden Hill 2
GBR ....Lydden Hill 2
POR ....Montalegre 3
POR ....Montalegre 1
AUS.........Fuglau 5
AUS.........Fuglau 1
HUN.......Nyirad 1
HUN.......Nyirad 2
GER........Estering.. 4
GER........Estering.. 5

Kevin Hansen – Peugeot 208
World RX – third
UAE.........Yas Marina 1
ESP..........Catalunya-Barcelona 2
BEL..........Spa 8
GBR ....Silverstone 7
NOR.........Hell 2
SWE ....Holjes 2
CAN..........Trois-Rivieres 6
FRA ....Loheac 3
LVA..........Riga 4
ZAF ....Killarney 5

Nitro World Games Rallycross – Champion
USA..........Utah Motorsports Campus......................... 1

Team Hansen – Pantera RX6
Titans RX Europe – Champion
FRA ....Essay 2
FRA ....Essay 2
GBR ....Lydden Hill 3
GBR ....Lydden Hill 1
POR ....Montalegre 1
POR ....Montalegre 2
AUS.........Fuglau 2
AUS.........Fuglau 3
HUN.......Nyirad 3
HUN.......Nyirad 1
GER........Estering.. 2
GER........Estering.. 1

Yellow Squad by Hansen
Kenneth Hansen – TN5 XC
Crosscar Star Challenge
SWE ....Holjes.. 9